SHOOTING THE ACTOR

In addition to his distinguished career in the theatre, Simon Callow has appeared in the films *Amadeus*, *A Room with a View* and *Four Weddings and a Funeral*. He is also the author of *Charles Laughton: A Difficult Actor*, *Being an Actor* and *Orson Welles: The Road to Xanadu*.

ALSO BY SIMON CALLOW

Simon Callow

SHOOTING THE ACTOR

WITH INTERVENTIONS FROM
Dušan Makavejev

𝒱

VINTAGE

Published by Vintage 2004

8 10 9

Copyright © Simon Callow and Dušan Makavejev 1990, 2003

Simon Callow has asserted his right under the Copyright,
Designs and Patents Act, 1988 to be identified as the author
of this work

This edition first published in Great Britain in 2004 by
Vintage

Vintage
Random House, 20 Vauxhall Bridge Road,
London SW1V 2SA

Random House Australia (Pty) Limited
20 Alfred Street, Milsons Point, Sydney
New South Wales 2061, Australia

Random House New Zealand Limited
18 Poland Road, Glenfield,
Auckland 10, New Zealand

Random House (Pty) Limited
Isle of Houghton, Corner of Boundary Road & Carse O'Gowrie,
Houghton 2198, South Africa

The Random House Group Limited Reg. No. 954009
www.randomhouse.co.uk/vintage

A CIP catalogue record for this book
is available from the British Library

ISBN 9780099471974

Penguin Random House is committed to a sustainable future for
our business, our readers and our planet. This book is made from
Forest Stewardship Council® certified paper.

Printed and bound in Great Britain by Clays Ltd, Elcograf S.p.A.

FOR MATT JONES

CONTENTS

INTRODUCTION TO
THE 2003 EDITION

In 1990, my friend and first publisher Nick Hern, who had commissioned *Shooting the Actor* and was about to publish it, had the worst year of his life. The head of the company with which he had merged his independent outfit succumbed to a form of dementia and started to throw out his colleagues—literally, onto the street, with their filing cabinets and the rest of their office furniture. Accordingly, when the book appeared, it did so without much help from Nick or the parent organisation. It had a few reviews in obscure publications, and those few reviews were savagely dismissive. A year or two later, Nick relocated his organisation to Random House, where he met Frances Coady, publisher of Vintage Books UK. She read the book enthusiastically, and republished it under her imprint, when it was re-reviewed with some favour. I was very happy about this; I had always liked the book, manic-depressive though it sometimes is, as much because of Dušan Makavejev's somewhat dyspeptic contributions as for my own. I believed, and still believe, that it offers an accurate account of what it's like for an actor to be involved in a movie. This particular movie was not a happy one for me, but, *pace* Tolstoy, all movies, happy or unhappy, are happy or unhappy in the same way.

The book has remained in print in Britain to the present day, but when Frances, now head of Picador, suggested publishing the book in America, I seized the opportunity to write a little about some of the other films in which I have appeared, which happens to include some very successful ones. In fact, the book now constitutes a sort of autobiography in film, just as *Being an Actor* is an autobiography in theatre. The original text of

Shooting the Actor—the main body of the book, needless to say—will be found in its chronological place, that is, after *A Room with a View* and before *Mr. & Mrs. Bridge*. At the end, by way of conclusion, I have added a section called *What It's Like*, which (as in *Being an Actor*) reverses the telescope, focussing on the general rather than my particular experience of acting in film.

If I have omitted a film (and a list of all my films is attached as a sort of index) it is not because it's unremarkable in any way, but because I don't believe it adds anything to what I've learned about acting in movies over the last twenty years of being involved in them. And I haven't written at all about the film I directed in 1990, *The Ballad of the Sad Café*. That's another book altogether.

First Sighting

My life in film has been a completely unexpected bonus. I never expected nor particularly desired to work in movies, nor until quite late in my career did anybody seem to think that the movies were crying out for me. I had very little notion of what the process of making a film might be like, despite exposure to movies about movies like Truffaut's *La Nuit Américaine*, which I took to be as true to life as the film *42nd Street* was to putting on a musical in the theatre—that is to say, total fantasy. When, during the late seventies, I was working regularly in television, film was regarded as a completely different activity, film actors a separate breed. The process of making television was not dissimilar to making theatre: there were extensive rehearsals followed by a very brief filming period, in which scenes were mostly shot in sequence.

It was my great friend, the literary agent Peggy Ramsay, who, believing that I should fill this gap in my education, arranged for me and my partner Aziz to visit the set of *Quartet*, a Merchant Ivory film being shot in Paris in 1980. It was an astonishing experience, and I had to offer my silent apologies to Truffaut: it was *La Nuit Américaine* all over again. The location was the legendary nightclub *Le Bœuf Sur le Toit*, and the place was swarming with gorgeously clothed people milling about under bright lights. Despite the twenties setting, it was impossible to tell where the film stopped and life began: there were waiters who seemed to be real, silent and weary actors (I caught sight of Maggie Smith in an exquisite beaded *cloche*, decoratively slumped in a corner) while highly animated other people screamed and rushed around. Make-up was being applied, costumes were being adjusted, microphones were being replaced. I had been told to find the producer Ismail Merchant, and this presented no difficulties: there he unmistakeably was, this immensely handsome, wildly energetic figure in a Nehru jacket and long flowing cotton pants, doling out bowls of curry to the cast and the crew on whom he bestowed seraphic smiles, punctuating this courtly activity with screamed instructions to various functionaries who were clearly failing in their duties. One of these, to whom the most savage outbursts were directed, was a taller, grey-haired man of fastidious demeanour who was calmly rearranging forks at a table in the centre of the restaurant. One phrase of Ismail's repeatedly aimed at this man rose above all the hubbub: 'Shoot, Jim, shoot!!' This was evidently James Ivory, the director, who continued arranging forks. When he was good and ready, he murmured something to an assistant and suddenly the cry 'Shooting!' echoed round the four points of the compass like a Monteverdi motet: 'Shooting!!! Shooting!! Shooting! *Shooting*.' A deep silence fell, a little wave of tension ran through the building, and a great crane with a camera and a cameraman perilously attached to it proceeded to make its way down the room like some elegant dinosaur. Then suddenly the cry: 'Cut!!!' along with its Monteverdian echo: 'We've cut!! We've cut! *We've cut*.' Again and again and again this was repeated until the problem—whether mechanical or interpretative; it was impossible to tell—was resolved.

It was mightily impressive, but I didn't quite know whether I liked it. It seemed ungraspable. How would one make one's contribution? Alan Bates wandered by. We had been introduced at the National by John Dexter. He said, with a little roll of his eyes, 'Filming!' I said that I'd never done any. 'Oh,' he said, 'that won't last long, will it?' After that, I suppose I started to nurture at the very least some curiosity about exploring the new medium. I saw Jim and Ismail again in London with their friend Felicity Kendal, with whom I was still acting in *Amadeus*, and all the conversation was about the roles that I might play for them. Nothing happened because I was acting on stage more or less continuously. I left the National shortly afterwards and did three plays in swift succession. When I was playing in J. P. Donleavy's *The Beastly Beatitudes of Balthasar B* at the Duke of York's Theatre, in the autumn of 1981, Jim and Ismail formally asked me to act in their film *Heat and Dust*, and for a while it seemed that it might happen, but the play—which was doing rather shakily at the box office— kept getting reprieved and finally they had to cast someone else. This was a setback, not only for my movie career, but also for my mother's. Ismail had phoned me one day when it seemed more rather than less likely that I might be able to do it and said, "How is your mother?" He had never met her, but I reassured him about the state of her health. "Would she like to come to India to be in a film? I need some very elegant older ladies to visit the harem." I assured him that I would enquire, though I never did. If I'd never acted in a film, I was damned if she was going to. Sorry, mamma.

• • • • • • • • • • • • • • • • • •

Debut

In general, my brief exposure to film-making formed in me an impression (which I cannot say has ever entirely left me) of a madhouse run by the inmates. My first encounter with the medium as a participant provided more evidence for this intuition. It came about most unexpectedly. Milos Forman had been at the very first theatrical preview of *Amadeus* at the National Theatre. We learnt this from Peter Hall at a note session. Forman, it seemed, had loved the play, and remarked that Austria in the 1780s was just like Hollywood in the 1930s. Emperor Joseph II bought up all the available talent so no one else could have it, but then he didn't know what to do with it. A good thought: Milos's approval of the show was encouraging and just what we needed on that first preview. What we didn't know was that Milos had decided there and then that *Amadeus* was to be his next film. He and Peter Shaffer shared an agent, the legendary Robbie Lantz, who was at the same performance, and immediately put the wheels in motion. Meanwhile, it was clear that the play was already the most extraordinary success, even without the reviews. When they came, most of them were ecstatic, and some were violently critical; the subsequent controversy ensured that it would be impossible to get a ticket for the show for the foreseeable future. We, the actors, knew nothing about Forman's deal. Of course we knew that a film would be made, but what kind of a film? Starring whom? In London there had been a steady procession of megastars in the stalls, hovering hungrily around like legacy hunters at a sickbed. Dustin Hoffman, Robert Redford, Robert de Niro all passed through. Any or all of them seemed likely candidates. Any of them, but none of us. Even Paul Scofield, at the very height of his fame and genius in the role of Salieri, wryly remarked that he doubted whether he was in the running.

When, eventually, Milos Forman's name was announced to direct the film, that broadened the field. Forman was known to favour unknowns. Now a new question entered our minds: were we sufficiently unknown? It was pleasant to read in *Screen International* that Forman had cast Ian McKellen and me in the roles that we'd played on stage, Ian in the New York production which had just opened, me in London. However, neither he nor I nor our respective agents had been informed of this excellent arrangement, which seemed extremely careless, to say the least. A call to the producer, Saul Zaentz, established that no casting had occurred, but there was every possibility that one would be playing the role. In the fullness of time, one would be informed. Rumours started. Every week, it seemed, a new cast was announced. Hottest tip for Mozart was Dudley Moore. Why not, one wondered, revive the *Arthur* team, and cast John Gielgud as Salieri with Liza Minelli as Constanze? Further calls to the producer met with increasingly ominous vagueness. Shaffer was ensconced with Forman, wrestling with the screenplay. One day I bumped into him. Casting, he told me, was the last of their concerns. They weren't even thinking about it till the script was right, which, as far as he could see, would be never. "What's Forman like?" I asked. Peter replied with a long, feeling look, such as men use to tell of terrible wartime experiences of which it would be best not to speak. 'It's coming along,' he'd say through tightened jaw.

Then one day towards the end of 1982, more than a year since I'd left the National Theatre, a friend told me he'd been asked to screen test for the part of Mozart. I began to hear of more and more actors who'd been asked to screen test for the role. I became mildly bitter. Only mildly because everything one had heard or experienced of movies taught one that their makers believe themselves to be Nietzschean figures beyond the codes of ordinary human decency; it had been announced, moreover, that there was an absolute in-derdiction on any actor appearing in the film in a role that he or she had played on stage. It was a surprise, then, to get a call from the producer saying that Mr Forman would like to meet me. 'Meet me?' I said. 'He wants to screen test every other actor in London, but he wants to *meet* me. Well, I'm sure I'd love to *meet* Mr Forman. I'm sure he's a very interesting man." And, in this captious spirit, I made off for the Connaught Hotel. When I got to Forman's suite my worst fears were confirmed. The room seemed to contain every actor under the age of thirty who had had a good review in the last ten years. We stared at one another balefully. Then Richard Griffiths (who had appeared in Milos's film *Ragtime*) arrived—surely not to play Mozart, one thought. We got chatting. After a few minutes, the door flew open and everyone's idea of a Hollywood director strode in, chewing a very large cigar and bellowing in a richly inflected Slavic accent. He flung his arms round some of Richard Griffiths.

When he was released from the bear-like embrace, Richard introduced me. Forman sprang back. '*Ah! You* are Simon Callows. I wanted to look at you. Come in, come in,' and ushered Richard and me into another room, which also contained the snowy-bearded, perfectly rotund figure of Saul Zaentz, the producer, looking like a recently retired Santa Claus from Macy's. They were full of a recent phone call they had received from Columbia pictures, who had offered to capitalise the whole movie, 'if in the title role you will use a great star which we in the studio have under contract.' 'Great,' Milos had said. 'Who is your star?' A brief pause. 'Walter Matthau.' A stunned silence, after which Milos had spluttered, 'But Mozart was thirty when he died.' "You know that, Milos, and we know that, but *does the American public know that*?" So Hollywood really behaved the way it was supposed to. After this story, we made small talk for a minute or two, but this is not Milos's forte, and his eyes began to wander. The trickle of anecdotes ran dry. He suddenly said to me, 'I want to tell you something. I have seen ten Mozarts, and you are by far the best. Everyone else was either great at being an asshole or great at being a genius. You are the only one who combined the two. Yes, a really fantastic performance. Brilliant. No, really, great.' He tailed off, deep in thought, before erupting with more praise. 'Fantastic performance, amazing, incredible. I wonder,' he mused, his brows furrowed, '*what* could you play in our film?' He then started to scrutinise the cast list. Up and down the list his eyes went, but nothing seemed to suggest itself to him. 'What?' he asked me. 'I really can't imagine,' I replied. 'What kind of actor are you looking for to play Mozart?' 'A little one,' he said, 'like a *bird*'—he became a bird for a startling moment—'and also a brilliant actor. Tell me,' he looked at me accusingly, 'where will I find such an actor?' 'I—I don't know,' I apologised. He grunted, looking again up and down the cast list. 'Well, we must think of something for you to do. I shall think about it.'

Two days later, I was lunching at the Tate Gallery when the waitress came to my table and said, 'You're to phone a Mr Forman at the Connaught Hotel.' To my great surprise, the telephone was answered by Mr Forman himself. 'I was a fool,' the bass-baritone growl admitted. 'Of course I shall test you for Mozart.' Accordingly, a day or two later I found myself in a studio being directed for the first time by Milos. Among the other actors testing were Judy Davies, Paul Rogers, Jeremy Irons. Milos was incisive, concentrated, sparing of words. Naturalness of expression was what he wanted, he said. 'Be netcheral.' He demonstrated what he wanted by acting out the emotion in question in a style that would not have surprised the audience at a Kabuki play but which was quite alarming at close quarters. 'Mozart is happy,' he would say, showing what the word meant by organising his lips into a grin that extended to the corner of his eyes, which were

8

themselves gleaming with maniacal delight. 'You see? Netcheral.'

We filmed a couple of scenes. I heard nothing. One day, it was discovered that the part of Mozart had indeed been cast, but there was interest in my playing something else in the film 'Schumacher?' asked my agent. 'Schickelbart?' 'Schikaneder,' I prompted. 'Yes, yes, *Schikaneder*. Who on earth is he? Was he in the play?' As it happens, though he did not appear in the play, I knew all about the wonderfully ripe Schikaneder, librettist of *The Magic Flute*, first Papageno, leading actor-manager of his day, and the first man to play Hamlet in German. He had ended up in a lunatic asylum having provided the Viennese public with increasingly surreal and incoherent entertainments, a kind of Marx Brothers mayhem *avant la lettre*. But his role in the film was slender. More important, could I bear to watch some unknown Yank—I was sure that no Briton was going to be cast as Mozart—becoming world-famous in *my* part? Anyway nothing apparently came of it; I heard nothing. Until, suddenly, there was massive urgency. 'They do want you for Schillerkrantz, darling, and you have to go to Abbey Road Studios on Friday to record a couple of arias and a duet with the Academy of St Martin-in-the-Fields under Neville Marriner.' 'But I've not agreed to play the part. And there's *singing*. I daren't even sing in my bath, let alone in front of Neville bloody Marriner. Just tell them thank you very much, but no thanks.' Which she did.

The effect was most gratifying. When I reached home, four messages had been left on my answering machine—one from Peter Shaffer, one from Saul Zaentz, and two from Milos Forman. I called them all, the latter first, at home in Los Angeles, and again was amazed to get straight through to the man himself. 'I'm very happy you're doing the movie,' he said. 'I understand there's some problem with the singing, don't worry, don't worry, if necessary we'll dub it. Of course, it would be *nice* if you could really sing, but don't worry.' 'Oh, OK,' I said, 'fine.' Apparently everything was settled. Not so. He sounded suddenly anxious. 'We'd better meet again to make sure we feel the same way about the part. Then we can go ahead.' Back to the dear old Connaught the following week. The door was opened by Milos himself, all alone, again strangely bereft of lieutenants. 'Schikaneder!' he cried as I stood there in front of him, and I saw his point. I had turned up wearing my usual winter outfit: a sweeping black fedora, an ankle-length black overcoat, and a bright red carnation in my buttonhole. I was the music-hall idea of an actor-manager. We sat down and read a couple of scenes. Any attempt at characterization was stamped on. 'No, no, simple, simple. Be netcheral!' I felt I had a lot to contribute in terms of the psyche of the actor-manager. Milos was having none of it. 'It's you! I want you. I wish I could change the name of the character to Simon Callows.'

Nevertheless, he cast me. 'Very good, very good. Perfect. Only one problem: can you ride whores?' 'Good God,' I thought, 'he's auditioning my sexuality.' 'Whores?' I said weakly. 'Yes, whores, whores, clip-clop . . .' 'Oh, *horse*, yes, yes, of course, I mean, no, but I can learn easily.' 'Very good. See you next week. And remember—*no acting*.' Things were looking up. The latest version of the script contained a much-augmented role for Schikaneder, and I finally discovered that Mozart was to be Tom Hulce, whom I'd met in New York two years before—delightful, funny, and very good, a veteran both of Peter Shaffer (he took over the part of Alan Strang in the Broadway production of *Equus*) and of John Dexter, who directed it. We re-met for two seconds at Abbey Road before being summarily plunged into Mozart's musical world. We began, as usual with Milos, *in media res*. There was a scene in the screenplay which took place in Schikaneder's country cabin with Mozart, Schikaneder and three of his actresses standing round the piano improvising tunes from *The Magic Flute*, drunk and debauched. This could only be a nightmare to perform cold, so of course that's what we started with. Milos gave a vivid impression of how he imagined the scene: wild, sexy, anarchic, with raspberries and belches blown and belched, Schikaneder thumping the keyboard, Mozart giggling insanely, and the girls being very naughty—all within the framework of tunes being played, tossed around, transformed, stood on their head. 'OK?' said Milos, and went, taking Shaffer with him.

Eventually we did manage to concoct something which satisfied him. Of its nature, though, it was almost impossible to repeat; and sustaining that level of crazy ebullience for a sound recording is a desperate task. 'I have an idea,' said Shaffer, and disappeared, returning a minute later with two bottles of champagne. So it came about that the rather surprised walls of Studio One, Abbey Road, where some of the great classical recordings of the century had been made, witnessed a performance of certain tunes of the divine Wolfgang Amadeus by a gaggle of drunken actors shrieking and farting and hitting a priceless keyboard while Simon Preston, Master of the Musicke at Westminster Abbey, who was also involved in the musical preparation, looked benignly on. My aria was another matter. Papageno's numbers are not complex, but my musical ear is so slow that I would have needed at least a month to feel comfortable with them. 'Perhaps I could be dubbed?' I said to Milos. 'It's a shame, and I'm very sorry, but if I don't have to worry about the singing it'll be better for my acting.' 'Acting?' Milos's eyes narrowed. 'Acting? There will be *no acting* in my film.' 'But, Milos,' I said, 'Schikaneder's on a stage, in a theatre, acting.' A dark and terrible pause. 'Yes. OK.' Another pause. 'But this will be the *only* acting in my film!!' Having reluctantly conceded this point, he nevertheless thought that I should persist with trying to sing the numbers, so I did, with deep foreboding, which was, as it turned out, entirely warranted.

First in order of recording was Figaro's '*Non piu andrai*,' which you will recall starts with a useful little note on the cellos bearing no relation whatever to the sung note which follows. Three, four times I attempted the note, three, four times the Academy of St Martin-in-the-Fields under Neville Marriner ground to a halt. Neville had perhaps been a little unnerved by having earlier that day attempted to conduct one of Mozart's German Dances to the satisfaction of Twyla Tharp, who was choreographing the film. This satisfaction not being forthcoming, Neville, ever gallant, suggested to her that perhaps she might like to conduct it herself, whereupon without hesitation she seized the baton from him and did so. 'Better,' she said, approvingly. Anyway, on my fifth attempt at the first note of '*Non piu andrai*,' Neville cried,

'It's quite all right, Mr Callow, I had the same trouble with Birgit Nilsson only last week in Stockholm.' Gallant, indeed. He then very sensibly proposed that the orchestra should record the accompaniment and he and I would lay down the vocal track later in more relaxed circumstances. He next turned his attention to trying to make the men of the renowned Ambrosian singers sound like fifteen Czechoslovakian dwarves in the *Don Giovanni* parody which the screenplay had Schikaneder staging in his theatre. 'In the pot/We have got/A soprano/And when you make a soprano stew/Any old, any old, any old soprano will do.' The Ambrosian men were understandably tentative, but Neville had a solution. 'May I suggest that you put your coats over your heads, gentlemen?' They attempted this. Not quite right. 'Perhaps if you got onto your knees?' Still not right. 'Could you turn your backs to the microphone?' Still not entirely satisfactory. Then Neville had an inspiration. Kenny Baker, R2D2 from *Star Wars*, who was playing one of my acting troupe, was with us in the studio and Neville asked him, 'without embarrassment on anyone's part,' to demonstrate the appropriate sounds to the singers, which he did briskly and with impeccable authenticity. The men of the Ambrosian took note, and, on their knees, their coats over their heads, and with their backs to the microphone, they gave the spirited rendition of the piece which today adorns the soundtrack. Remarkably convincing it was, I must say. Kenny certainly gave it his blessing.

A week later, Neville and I had our relaxed session together, alone in the studio with only Erik Smith, the recording producer with the session, as company. I sat opposite Neville, both of us wearing headphones as, bobbing and swaying, cigar clamped grimly between his teeth, he threw his arms in my general direction in an expressive but somewhat indistinct manner, which did nothing to improve my sense of rhythm. My sense of pitch was beyond salvation, which is perhaps what led Smith to suggest that I should simply *act* the number, rather than attempt to sing it. This I did, and, d'you know, when I heard it played back I thought it was really rather good. 'It's sort of *Sprechstimme*, isn'it?' I said, pleased with myself. 'Yes,' said Neville, gloomily, 'it is.'

'Perhaps,' I continued vivaciously, 'I could do *Pierrot Lunaire*.' 'I thought you were,' said Neville. A week later, the admirable Brian Kay, late of the King's Singers, was in the studio to record the arias under my direction: potentially a humiliating but in fact an exhilarating experience, with me encouraging him to give the performance I would have done had I been able.

A month later, with this nightmare behind me, I found myself in Prague one Sunday to rehearse all my scenes in the film; I was acting in a play called *Romantic Comedy* in London with Pauline Collins at the time. Meg Tilley, who was playing Constanze, and Tom had just tottered off their planes, having been on them for sixteen hours. The set was already built, and the moment we all arrived, Milos plunged in. I had suddenly realised that he expected us to have memorised the scenes, which I did in a frenzied few minutes in my dressing room, adding to the generally febrile atmosphere. Milos said nothing about the scenes or the characters, simply giving us our physical movements. 'Action,' he said, and we were off. Within seconds, he would be on his feet, protesting. 'No, no, no, no. Simple. Please. Not like this'—a not entirely complimentary impersonation of one's physical and vocal attributes ensued—'like this'—a cartoon of the desired performance was now indicated, with many a grimace and grunt. On and on the onslaught went for the whole day. I staggered back to London, thinking it would surely be different when the cameras were there.

I was wrong. It was the same, only more so. 'Don't worry,' I said to Tom, 'we are graduates of the John Dexter school of acting,' a reference to the legendary martinet of a theatre director with whom we had both worked and whom we both, in some odd way, loved. 'Nothing this man says can harm us.' I was wrong about that, too. 'No, no, no, no, *no*!' he would cry, time and again. It was as if he couldn't believe the perversity of what we were presenting to him. How could we not be playing the scene the way he had envisaged it? Faced with the offensive performance, his technique was to attempt to destroy it by brute force. As far as one could judge, it was nothing personal: simply that this piece of wrong acting had to be expunged from the world.

With mad energy Milos would assault it, raining insults, parodistic impersonations, reproaches upon its head, until, inevitably, it succumbed. It was like being in the trenches. Most of time I simply felt shell-shocked. I was anyway struggling with my relation to the camera. I was at a loss as to where to pitch my performance—definitely not into the lens, I knew that, but then where? How? For what audience? I would try to be bigger, then smaller, then somewhere in between, all the while highly conscious of the figure of Milos just behind the camera, unconsciously twisting his features into the emotion he hoped would be passing across mine. Joy, grief, surprise, anger succeeded each other on his face with lunatic exaggeration. It was very peculiar. As related in my *Manifesto* diary, there was a problem, too, with the accent; officially we were speaking Transatlantic (a tongue known to no one in life except disc jockeys) but, after a take, Peter Shaffer and Milos would anxiously descend on me, Milos crying, 'Too English!' Shaffer murmuring, 'Too American, dear.' I had no idea who or what I was, as a character, as an actor or as a human being.

Basically, netcheralness was the goal; but Milos's definition of what was 'netcheral' was quite arbitrary. What it amounted to was that the way Milos saw it was netcheral—any other way, not. Moreover, 'Remember that I have a camera here and this light is here so it would help me very much if you will keep your head low here and turn only 30 degrees this way.' Netcheral was clearly a relative term, and one that swiftly became irksome. I found an antidote. During the hours of piano practice I happily endured under the tutelage of a young virtuoso who, after winning international prizes, had been banned by the authorities from playing, I remembered that in Germany the note B natural is called H. Thus whenever Milos would cry, 'Be natural!' I would murmur, 'H.' This was oddly consoling. Over supper at night, Milos further expounded his theories of film technique. 'Stage actors are wonderful, big, generous. But they can't use film, always *acting*, always *doing something*. On film, you must *be*. And you must *be yourself*, I cast you to be you. Otherwise I cast someone else.' There was a brief pause. 'But, Milos,' said a slightly uneasy Murray Abraham, playing Salieri, 'if you cast everyone to be themselves, well, Salieri's a very nasty man.' Milos stared at him for a long time. 'Murray,' he said, 'you think too much.' I was certainly endeavouring to play Schikaneder as a variant of myself, my actor-self, at any rate, with a few touches of the young Orson Welles thrown in. By now I knew so much about Schikaneder that I was straining to add ever more fascinating details to the character, most of which were irrelevant to the film and would probably have been confusing. One day, Lindsay Anderson, who had come to visit us on the set, asked me who I was playing. I told him at great length about Schikaneder, becoming passionate in my enthusiasm. 'But the film should be about Schikaneder,' he said, 'not bloody Mozart.'

Inevitably, I found myself watching the actor actually playing bloody Mozart rather closely. As reported, when I discovered that Tom had been cast in the role, I was very relaxed about it. There was a curious moment, however, during that one day of rehearsal in Prague. Tom had been whisked into the make-up chair on arrival, and when he walked shyly out onto the set, I had the heart-stopping experience of apparently seeing myself walking towards me: he was wearing my wig, my coat, my shoes, the costume I had worn for the two years' run at the National. He even seemed to have my face, long, like mine, and full-mouthed. In the wig he was indistinguishable from me: this was the image that had stared back at me in the mirror night after night at the National Theatre just before I went on stage. It was an uncanny moment from which I recovered soon enough, more or less, and was always willing and eager to discuss anything with Tom. In the event, we rarely talked about the man or indeed the script, which is probably just as well from both sides. Apart from anything else, it was clear that we had very different approaches to acting. Tom, like every American actor with whom I have worked, was primarily interested in truthfully representing his character's emotional life, whereas what had interested me, above all, was his mind. Inspired by Peter Hall's demand during rehearsals for the play that I had to convince him at all times that I had written *The Marriage of Figaro*, I had tried to allow Mozart's thought-processes to take me over; in particular, I had sought to give a sense of his musical brain at work. I have no idea whether I succeeded in this or not, but the result was certainly very different from Tom's conception. Apart from anything else, Tom brought a natural sweetness of disposition, a tenderness and a delicacy to the role which I could never match. Tom's Wolfie was an over-exuberant child; mine suffered from Tourette's syndrome. His death was deeply affecting and beautifully observed from a medical point of view; mine was deliberately grotesque, almost expressionist. The screenplay, anyway, was a very different entity from the play, which was possessed of a wild, distorted energy, an E.T.A. Hoffman-like exaggeration, lit by candles and filled with monstrous shadows; the Mozart of the play was, after all, the reminiscence of a dying and frightened man, and everything the audience saw was seen through that man's eyes. Even the music was distorted by Salieri's memory. The screenplay, by contrast, was a sort of realistic double portrait of Mozart and Salieri and the age in which they lived. The film's Mozart was less a creature of Salieri's deceiving imagination, more a real man, which moved millions of movie-goers, though I remained loyal to the play's more extreme vision.

As I say, Tom and I scarcely discussed such matters. For the most part, we tried to find as many different ways as possible of forgetting the unremitting tensions of the film when we weren't actually making it; and Prague, in the Communist decadence of 1982, its hidden city flowing darkly like an underground stream underneath the sometimes glittering, sometimes crumbling metropolis above, offered many delights, cultural, carnal, but not often culinary. After a while, thanks to our American dollars, we gained access to the restaurants reserved for the party elite, and like most of the citizens, we availed ourselves fully of the universally active black market. In the beautifully lit Old Town, there was a curfew from which we were, or presumed ourselves to be, exempt. Peter Shaffer and I would meander around it, half expecting a carriage to draw up and Mozart himself to leap out of it. It was, of course, a city that Mozart knew well. You can still see the adjacent hotels in which he and his librettist for *Don Giovanni*, Lorenzo da Ponte, stayed; da Ponte would toss the new pages of text across to Mozart

16

to set in time for *Giovanni*'s premiere, which took place in the very theatre where we were filming the opera sequences. We went to the theatre and the opera and to concerts for the equivalent of a couple of bucks, and wandered round the free galleries and palaces, unaccountably restored with gold leaf while the rest of the city crumbled. Beth Berridge, who had replaced Meg Tilley as Costanze Mozart when the latter tore a ligament in her foot before a frame had been shot, joined us in our frolics, as did all the many actors who came and went. I was merely a visitor to the set, if a frequent one; Tom and Beth were residents. Over the next six months, I took fifty-seven planes in and out of Czechoslovakia, staying just outside of town at the Panorama Hotel (the panorama being much like a building site in Luton); during that time I enjoyed a tender liaison with a tall and sweetly smiling young man with haunted eyes who had appeared dressed in blue satin on the set of Schikaneder's theatre, as a member of his audience. He disclosed that he was training to be an architect but really, he told me, he was a poet. And really, he was. He spoke little English, but what he did speak was memorable. 'sat'nic inwention,' he would say of the cigarettes we smoked; and as we held each other at night he would sigh, 'We are such poor souls, poor souls.' His name was Med: Mr Honey. Such are the romances of location filming, haunting, emotional and ardent with the urgency of inevitable brevity, though one of the actresses actually came home with a Czech husband. The marriage lasted a month. It is all a necessary relief from the unrelenting business of making the film which, like the warfare it so closely resembles, is an activity whose sole purpose is winning.

It took every ounce of Milos's formidable will power to whip into action the Barandov Studios, where we shot; the reek of urine was overwhelming and in the toilets, instead of lavatory paper there was a pile of old scripts. A breakfast of lager was served every morning, and it continued to be drunk till the end of the day. The core crew was American, but all the rest were Czech, and the culture gap was sharply marked, sometimes leading to confrontation. On one extraordinary occasion, we had been filming away from Prague, in the famous Palace of Kromeríz in Gottwaldov.

The scene was set in the exquiste grotto which Archbishop Colloredo of Salzburg had built for himself; it was a fancy dress party and the tables were laden with food the like of which the local extras had not seen for many a year, at the centre of which was a great glazed hog's head complete with apple in mouth. Predictably, during the takes, the food (except for the hog's head) would disappear as completely as if locusts had swept through the room. Terrible threats were uttered, and, finally, shooting late into the night, we finished the scene to everyone's satisfaction. The director of photography, Mirek Ondriček, Milos's long-time collaborator and sparring partner, a man of unintentionally fearsome demeanour since an accident which had left him with impaired vision and speech but undiminished energy, ordered the crew to set the lights for the following day. The American crew resented this deeply (it was two o'clock in the morning) but they did it. They had a little revenge plotted, though, and when they returned to the hotel, they managed to get into Ondricek's bedroom while he was still drinking in the bar downstairs, and placed the hog's head in his bed. An hour later, Ondricek retired. His roar of horror could be heard throughout the hotel, as well as his demands for justice against his tormentors. I don't know quite how things resolved themselves—I was off the following day—but it was a primitive occasion, something from Aeschylus, with overtones of *The Godfather*.

Milos was the absolute centre of operations, exerting his massive concentration on the whole huge team. Having issued his instructions, he would withdraw to his room to sleep. The shot would be set up without him, then he would emerge and the scene would proceed. If the shot was good 'Very good, very good, very good,' he would say, and withdraw back to his room to sleep while the next shot was set up. If *not*, he would descend like the cavalry to root out imperfection, whether technical or thespian. It was generally thespian. Sarcasm was his principal weapon in the war against inadequacy. 'Not bad, not bad. In your speech there were two or three lines where you sounded *almost* like a human being. This is very good, I like this.' His preferred method of demonstration would sometimes conflict with what he was saying. 'You come into the room, you open the door, you say *HELLO*!!!!, lightly, like that.' Praise was implied rather than stated, but, when it came, the sun certainly shone. One day, after rushes, he said to me, 'What we shot with you yesterday was wonderful, strong, true, netcheral,' then added, quite without malice, almost as if to himself, 'I wasn't sure it would be, but it was.' The scene he was speaking about had been achieved only by dint of violent explosions and uncomprehending abuse, not really at me, but at the inexplicably wrong things I was doing, things I had no way of knowing about, because he hadn't explained them to me. Why should he? he must have thought. They were so *obvious*. To the distinguished British actor Roy Dotrice, playing the role of Mozart's father, he cried, 'No, no, Roy, you are *acting*. Acting, acting, acting. Again, please.' Roy attempted to oblige. 'No, no, Roy. Now you are acting *not-acting*.' 'You don't miss much, Mr Forman, do you?' said Roy. 'Mismatch?' demanded Milos. 'What mismatch?' Language was sometimes a problem. Once, just as Milos was passing by, one of the crew asked me about the smoked salmon he had asked me to bring back with me from London. 'Smoked Simon?' asked Milos, with narrowed eyes.

Even while I was gleefully doing impersonations of the man and collecting Milos stories, I was aware out of the corner of my immature eyes that he was in a most peculiar and in many ways intolerable position. The power of the dollar had secured for the producers a surly co-operation from the Czech authorities, but Forman, having some years ago committed the unpardonable crime of voluntarily absenting himself from the People's Republic, was treated by them at all times with malicious intransigence. He was followed everywhere by so-called secret but in fact entirely overt police; his documents were constantly challenged; and, finally, when the crew and some of the cast went to Vienna for a few days' shooting, Milos was prevented from travelling on the same plane, forced to trail behind them a few planes later. Wherever he went in Prague, he was greeted with joyful cries; he would be invited into the kitchen of any restaurant in which we all met and food unknown to the average diner was magically produced for him to test and approve. The crew treated him with adoration, but at every other turn, he was baulked and thwarted. He was doubly hamstrung by his need to cause no trouble either for the film or his sons, who still lived in Prague. Inside his massive energy and ebullience was a sort of loneliness, the loneliness, no doubt, of the little Jewish orphan he had been in wartime Prague, but also of the man without a nation, without a language.

When I had walked on the film set and seen the dynamic at work—observed the way the labour was organised and identified the centres of command—I had thought 'There's only one job here,' but even then, young and arrogant as I was, I had sensed that the director was waging an almost unwinnable battle to assert himself over the swarming ungovernable material, human, mechanical and natural, with which he is working and that his responsibility, which is total, is out of proportion to his pleasure in the work. Of course, having made a film can be a source of deep satisfaction; but the actual making of it is as often as not nothing but arduous. By the end of the film, I no longer coveted Milos's job. In fact, I felt a kind of compassion for the man, although I allowed myself the indulgence of writing a piece for *The Guardian* called 'Acting Netcheral,' which I and everyone else thought very amusing at the time, but whose unfeeling impertinence now makes me blush. It appeared on the day of the British premiere. Milos took it in unexpectedly good part. He came up to me at the pre-premiere party with an expression of mock menace on his face. 'I read your article in the Gwarrrrdian,' he said. 'I was very happy to get it. Yes. I had run out of toilet paper.' But he stayed and chatted and he took me with him to the cinema in his limousine. I told him that I was translating and directing a play by his friend Milan Kundera. Would he come and see it? I asked. 'Of course,' he grunted, 'and I will review it for the Gwarrrrrrrdian.'

Amadeus was from the start an overwhelming success. It was my first film premiere as a participant and it was a peculiarly glittering one. Leicester Square was filled with roaring crowds, and Princess Diana, on one of her first outings as Prince Charles's new bride, made her way nervously down the line. 'Oh, I like you,' she said to me, with relief. 'You make me laugh.' Then to Tom, who was standing next to me, she said, 'You were marvellous. Where on earth did they find you?' 'Oh, I was just sort of hanging around in Hollywood,' he said. 'Really,' she replied, fascinated. The watchmaker Raymond Weil had created a special Amadeus line of watches, one of which was given to everyone whose name appeared on the poster. By an alphabetic quirk, mine was the first on it (after Tom, Beth and Murray, that is, who were on a line of their own). I basked distantly in all the acclaim and all the prizes; I happened to be in Los Angeles during the Academy Awards ceremony at which the film was showered with Oscars. I had not, of course, been invited, and watched it, like everyone else, on television with friends; I felt quite unconnected with it. I suppose at some unacknowledged level I had never really resigned myself to not playing Mozart. Had I done so, my subsequent life might have been entirely different. Or not. In the world of film, nothing is certain. Neither Tom nor Murray found a permanent niche at the top of it; Peter Shaffer never made another film. I met him for supper the day after the Oscar ceremony. He told me that he had gone out for a walk that morning, and when he came back, on quietly entering his suite he had caught a glimpse of the maid on her knees in front of his Oscar, rapt, stroking its head. Of course, celebrity is the American religion, and the Academy Award ceremony is its high mass. I myself, being agnostic, feel somewhat unnerved by the whole thing.

Merchant and Ivory and Jhabvala

Amadeus was a long time in coming out after shooting had finished; by the time it appeared, in 1984, I was shooting my next film, which was so radically different in every way that I felt as if I working not merely on a different film but in a different medium, and on another planet. As described above, I had made the acquaintance of James Ivory and Ismail Merchant in 1980, and they had declared themselves determined to make my film career take off. Such declarations are made from time to time by various people, and are best taken as a sort of *politesse*, like enquiries after one's health and good wishes for the future. But these chaps really seemed to mean it. Finally I had an exuberant call from Ismail. The adjective is entirely redundant—all calls from Ismail are exuberant, even when, as he so often is, he is cross with you: he is somehow as exhilarated by anger as by joy. He told me that they had finally found a film for me, that it was wonderful part, the most wonderful part in the film, and that if I didn't want to play the part, there was scarcely any point in making the film at all. It was an adaptation of *A Room with a View*, the screenplay was in the post, and he would be expecting a call from me the moment I had read it. I knew the novel reasonably well and was deeply touched that Ismail and Jim had had the acuity and imagination to see that I would be able to play the part of George, the book's romantic hero, forthright, passionate, sexy. I would need to lose a little weight, certainly, but that was easily done; otherwise, I was thrilled that somebody else existed on the globe who saw me as, in my dreams, I saw myself.

Some qualm nagged away at me, and I put in a somewhat studiedly casual call to my agent to check whether the part was indeed that of George. 'No, not George, darling,' she said, 'it's . . . um . . . Beebe. The Reverend Beebe.' A vicar! A bloody vicar, sexless, rational, pleasant. A bad moment: Beebe is described as being 50-ish, portly, mutton-chop-whiskered. 'Say no,' I said tersely, 'just say no.' After brief resistance, she agreed to do so. Shortly afterwards the phone rang. Ismail was raving. 'We will not do the film! It is a *wonderful* part. The most important part in the film. Only you can play it.' I listened to this barrage in silence. Then came the dulcet tones. 'Please. For us. You are now part of the family. You must be part of the film, too.' Amazingly, I continued to resist. He was now hurt, definitely hurt, very subdued, all exuberance fled. In deep sorrow, he put the phone down. A few days later, there was an invitation to have supper in his exquisitely furnished apartment near Hyde Park. All smiles, the zealous attentive host. Suddenly, when everybody is gathered—some in sarees, some in suits, all elegant and most of them famous—Ismail claps his hands. 'Wonderful news. Simon has agreed to play the part of Reverend Beebe for us in *A Room with a View*.' 'No, he hasn't,' I laughed, but by now it was just a formality. In effect I had given up, and over supper, one of those sumptuous curries which are Ismail's speciality, I gave in. I later remarked that the phrase 'to curry favour' might have been invented for Ismail; he knows that the way to an actor's art is through his stomach. Jim by now was weighing in, saying that of course I bore no physical resemblance whatever to the clergyman as described by Forster. I would convey the spirit of the man, the tenderness and wit and intelligence of the man, in a way that some actor accustomed to playing nothing but portly vicars would be unable to achieve. The mists of my own arrogance were also beginning to dissolve, dispersed by excellent wine: what on earth was I thinking of? I was turning down a very good part in a fine screenplay from a great novel; Jim was directing; I would be acting with Maggie Smith, Denholm Elliot, Judi Dench and sundry young beauties of both sexes; we would be shooting in Florence and Kent. Was I mad? And I suddenly thought, this is absurd, of course I'll play the part. And I never mentioned my fantasies about George.

By now I was much in love with the part of Arthur Beebe, perceptive, compassionate, perhaps a little repressed, conscious that the life of the senses and the emotions which he had forsworn was central to so much of human life. I knew many clergymen of a similar persuasion, quietly preoccupied with the question of good and evil, modestly determined to influence human affairs in favour of the former. Though my scenes were all fairly low key, I thought I could see a way of infusing them with a particular quality of benevolence which might really contribute something to the film. I went off on holiday to Greece with my young lover, and there, enchanted by Crete and in the grip of *amour fou*, I managed to fall off my motor-bike. As the bike went up in the air, in the face, for all I knew, of instant death, my only thought, which came to me with brilliant clarity, was: 'What about *A Room with a View*?' I was picked up by a couple of chaps in a lorry filled with olives and taken to the hospital; shortly afterwards I appeared back in London with sixteen stitches over my right eye and a shiner that a heavyweight champion would be proud of. I presented myself to Jim, like a dog that knows that it will be whipped. He recoiled, but said, 'We'll send you to our doctor and see what he says.' *Mirabile dictu*, this wise physician proclaimed himself confident that I would be ready to be shot by the first day of filming in two weeks' time; and lo! so it came to pass. (Technically speaking, it was on the theologically correct third day that my career resurrected: that first day in Florence it rained so hard that we couldn't shoot; the same thing the next day. On the third day, the sun burst forth, and my scabs fell off, to the unconfined delight of the make-up department, whose efforts to conceal them had only made me look like an early reject of Dr Frankenstein's.)

What followed was the subject of one of my first published pieces of journalism, and I reproduce it here because its 35-year-old author knew better than I do what it was like to be discovering the ins and outs of filming, and, indeed, of Florence.

24

To Beebe or Not to Beebe

Last May in Florence broke all records for rain. The sky was black, the grass was wet. For two days we could do nothing. On the third day a glint of sunlight made shooting possible, though not perfect. Eventually we had to shoot what we could regardless (Time Is Money). If the light is good, it's surprising how much rain you can have without it showing on the film. Mud is a different matter, however, and the first day's shooting chiefly concentrated on the progress of two carriages through the Fiesole countryside. Denholm Elliott, Judi Dench and I shared a carriage and our horse, Giacomo, had a regrettable tendency to fall down from time to time. There was, moreover, the matter of the falling tree.

This marvel of mechanical engineering was designed to smash across our path, frightening the ladies and giving the men a chance to take command of the situation. It had to fall late enough to look menacing but early enough to avoid the horses. Every time it fell wrongly, we had to ascend the little hill again, walking through the mud to give the horses a break, clutching our skirts or gaiters. So there we are in our carriage, chattering away, and finally the tree is right. A good take at last. But we need another to be safe. Suddenly Maggie Smith, seconded by Judi Dench, protests. The Florence Fire Brigade has been in the bushes, simulating a sudden downpour that's needed for the scene. The water has been bearing down on the horses' heads. They've been shying away in fear. For the last take, then, the water, is, as they say, cheated to fall yards ahead of them. The effect is almost identical.

All this has taken over eight hours to shoot—we were on location at seven—and will result in under a minute of film. A brilliant minute, as it happens. About 10 minutes out of those eight hours was spent in front of the cameras. And so it goes for every day. Encamped in our villa at Fiesole, which is playing the role of Forster's Pensione Bertolini in the film, we are squeezed into our costumes, and gummed into our hair pieces and our blemishes are painted out by the make-up artists. My motorcycling scar is a much loved challenge. After five minutes' assiduous application, it's invisible. Then, like souls in hell, we wait to be called. Unending supplies of coffee and biscuits and sandwiches appear at regular in-

25

tervals and then lunch and tea and eventually supper. The Edwardian costumes have a way of making everyone look cross or at the very least severe; upright, in corsets and waistcoats, we sit in the wings. Reading is difficult, writing impossible. All you can do is talk, smoke and eat. The talk becomes more and more abstract. Starting with theatrical anecdotes, by the end of a shoot you're on to Zen Buddhism and the meaning of life. The most intimate and terrible secrets have been vouchsafed and friendships have been born, flowered, declined and died. As in Bunuel's Exterminating Angel or Chekhov's plays, we are stranded together, cut off from the world, pawns of a capricious and inscrutable destiny ruled by an unholy Trinity: the director, the weather, the cameraman.

Life becomes real again when you work. Best of all is unremitting hard work, a 13-hour slog. Not only is it good to be at it, but you feel your existence is justified. You're part of things, and of course, from a solipsistic angle, you become the focus of the whole enterprise. No one on the set looks more worried than Jim. It is as if we were filming a documentary on Hiroshima instead of an Edwardian comedy. He shouts 'Cut.' 'Was that all right for you?' he asks the cameraman. 'I was a little worried about the shadow on X's face, but if it didn't worry you, it doesn't worry me.' 'How about the acting?' one of us asks. 'It was all right.' 'All right?' I demand. 'By which I mean sublime, of course,' says Jim. On the stage, you project. In film, it's different: instead of offering yourself, you admit the camera into your aura. This is a little like being X-rayed. More like dreaming. At the end of a long session, you can feel absolutely transparent, as if the camera had passed through your veins and organs. Very exhilarating. Denholm Elliott puts it another way. 'I mean,' he does the look he describes as his angry caterpillar look. 'It's only dressing for mummy and daddy, after all.' But he's swallowed the camera lock, stock and barrel, if anyone has.

At the far corner of the set, concentrating harder than anyone, is Ismail. He's willing the scene to be good, for reasons both financial and artistic; but he's also wondering whether he can't have another party soon. His therapy is culinary. The fatigue, fraughtness and fragility of filming has one remedy; food. He will commandeer any unlikely space to throw a party. Up to a point, this is because cooking is therapeutic for him; but also it's a very personal and charming hand-holding with all of us. And such is the excellence of his cooking that everybody's good nature is restored. The phrase 'to curry favour' might have been invented for Ismail.

Louche dives are a necessary diversion from film acting. Somewhere to blow out steam, fall down, jump about. The work is concentrated and not usually very sustained. It is, in fact, not unlike very bad sex; it's all over in 30 seconds, and it's an hour before you can do it again. So some sort of antidote is called for. In the case of Florence, and for the few hardy spirits who could brave it, it was a club magnificently called Chez Rudy à GoGo, a transvestite discotheque much frequented by gay German dwarfs and immensely tall, five o'clock-shadowed, bulging-calved Italian men in natty little off-the-shoulder numbers. The feeling of the place was of a tepid tribute to Weimar Berlin; but it was a relief from Edward Morgan Forster and the dog collar. Very friendly, everyone was, with no pressure of any kind. Julian Sands and I would weave a drunken path back to the Excelsior through the moonlit statues and arcades of Florence, after which I would retire to translate a few pages of a French play. This was another lifeline to sanity; something to show for one's time.

It's as well to have done something else by the end of filming. Judi Dench does embroidery, very beautifully. It was, I suppose, tactless of me to enquire if the reason it was called petit point was because there's so little point to it; tactless and wrong. She was making first night presents for her next show. We transferred to Kent after a month in Tuscany, and were plagued by the wettest summer that county had ever known. These climatic vagaries apart, the film continued on the even keel Jim and Ismail skilfully maintain; but the atmosphere is quite different when you're within 20 minutes of London; it becomes more like an ordinary job. But there was a spectacular finale; the scene in the 'Sacred Lake,' in which Mr Beebe and the two young men of the story, George and Lucy's brother, take an impulsive dip, only to be surprised by the ladies. By now it was July. A pool had been dug and at the very least lukewarm water was promised. At the very most, as it happened. For three days we stood disconsolately around, the lads flexing their pectorals, I morbidly gazing at my Michelin man contours, waiting at a moment's notice and with the promise of the tiniest sunbeam to plunge into the arctic waters of Sevenoaks.

Water, one way and another, had dominated our lives; so it was *witty of Ismail to hire a pleasure boat for our end of film 'wrap' party. It was a Dionysian affair—I speak for myself. Fabia Drake may have a different take to tell. But near the end of it, Jim, in his soft voice and with his sharp brains, said 'I'm so glad you played Mr Beebe for us. It could have been so fuddy duddy and . . . boring . . . and, well . . . It's not.' That's as handsome a compliment as I've ever received.*

When I wrote this piece, I had clearly failed to realise, or was unable to express, how uncommon the Merchant Ivory experience was and is. Of course, not every film they produce is a masterpiece, but they represent a sense of continuity both in personnel and in themes which can only be compared with the work of director-producers like Capra, Ford and Sturges in America, and Truffaut and Renoir in France. That their values are frequently as much literary as filmic is perhaps due to the weight within their organisation of Ruth Prawer Jhabvala, who is not only a superb scenarist but also, in her soft-spoken and withdrawing way, an exceptionally wise and shrewd advisor of impeccable taste. It is almost impossible to say where the contribution of Jim leaves off and that of Ruth and Ismail begins. This shared responsibility extends to the atmosphere on the set, which is often explosive, frequently mutinous, but always democratic. The actors feel part of the whole effort, and there seems to be an intimacy between all the departments—sometimes united by sheer desperation, it must be admitted—that I have rarely experienced in what can so easily be the alienated world of movie-making, with distant and unavailable producers, preoccupied and autocratic directors, remote and hermetically self-involved technical crews. The word 'family,' in all its implications, is unavoidable; in this context, I have used it twice above already. Perhaps its real roots are in Ismail's Indianness—the integration of society, the knowledge that everyone is in this together, the unending wheeling-dealing and striking of bargains, the sometimes reproachful but always loyal attachment to one's own.

This perhaps seems a long way away from Forster's Edwardian world, with its contrasted values of North and

South, English and Italian, though of course the link is provided by *A Passage to India,* the film that Merchant Ivory was destined to make, but was disastrously pipped at the post from producing by David Lean. *A Room with a View* is perhaps the most idyllic of their Forster adaptations, and though the filming was not without its tensions and setbacks, it was an extraordinary experience. The twin locations of Florence and Kent were in their different ways inspiring; the team of Tony Pierce Roberts behind the camera, Jenny Beavan and John Bright in the costume department and Chrissy Iley in charge of make-up was one of the most creative and untemperamental imaginable; and the cast in its range of age and experience alone was unlike any I have ever worked with since. The younger actors were a remarkable crop, from Helena Bonham-Carter, fresh from her first film (*Lady Jane*) with the dark intensity of her looks—so frequently and so wrongly described as those of an English rose—her speed of thought so rapid that to be understood at all she had to be forced to slow her speech down both in life and on film, to Rupert Graves, himself a boyish beauty without a trace of narcissism and a madcap disposition which made him oddly vulnerable, Julian Sands, like a greyhound, lean and muscled, savage and tender, the very image of Forster's George, and Daniel Day-Lewis, who presented a character study filled with the kind of the detail and inner pressure that he would develop in a series of roles which suggest to me that he is the only real heir to Charles Laughton. I was older than all of these, well-known in the theatre though not in film, poised between them and the illustrious generation represented by Maggie Smith, Judi Dench and Denholm Elliott. I knew Julian before the filming, and became very friendly with Helena and particularly Rupert, whom I regarded and continue to regard as one of the most purely talented people I have ever met. Dan was then what he is now, entirely his own man, full of impacted pressures, though with a wild and witty streak, and occasional unexplained rages. Running into me in the grounds of the house in Kent where we were shooting, he asked me what I was listening to on my Discman. It was Bartók, the string quartets. 'Garbage!' he cried. 'That's not music. I don't believe anyone who tells me they enjoy listening to Bartók. *It's not music.*' There was no arguing with him, and his mood tuned very dark. I moved off. A day later, he was all sweet courtesy again.

At the other end of the age scale were Fabia Drake and Joan Henley as the Misses Alan. Fabia was immensely distinguished and rather bossy; she had been married for many years to a High Court judge, and something of the bench had rubbed off on her. Her pronouncements were magisterial, and often magisterially wrong. She had been a classmate of Charles Laughton's at RADA; alas, she could remember little of her time with him there, but when I told her (I was writing a book about him at the time) that he had taught acting for many years, she said, 'Nonsense. Charles would never have done such a thing.' No evidence that I could adduce would persuade her otherwise. Meanwhile, her companion Joan Henley (a life-long friend who often stood in for her in films but who had been allowed this once to appear alongside her) who *did* remember a great deal about Laughton was never allowed to divulge her memories, always being overridden by Fabia. I made a note to talk to Joan away from the set, but didn't really get round to it till the premiere of the film, at which I asked Fabia how I could get in touch with her. 'She's not here,' Fabia said. 'Where is she?' I asked. 'She's dead, dear. Dead, dead, dead,' she replied in the trumpet tones that had so thrilled theatre-goers when she played Lady Macbeth at Stratford-upon-Avon in 1929, and which did not fail to arrest the film premiere audience over 50 years later. While Maggie Smith and I were waiting in the foyer of our hotel for Ismail to take us to lunch on the very first day of filming in Florence, Fabia had been sitting for a while in a taxi on the Piazza della Signoria. 'He'd better hurry up,' said Maggie, 'or Fabia will turn into a monument.'

They were the first words I had heard Maggie utter close to. My admiration for her work in every medium being little short of idolatrous, I was deeply ill at ease with her as we stood by a bowl of bird-of-paradise flowers ('They look as though they might attack at any moment') and fatally blurted out some clumsy words of praise, in response to which she simply exhaled the word 'Oh . . .' and looked off into the middle distance. The conversation was at an end. In the course of sitting around on the set we had occasion to exchange a very few words, but they were not warm ones on her part, and I avoided her. Then came the dreaded day when we would have our first scene together. The moment we started acting together, any anxiety disappeared, on both our parts, I think, and we fell into easy conversation thereafter. To act with her is a heady experience; her presence in the moment is absolute, her focus and relaxation complete. It is as if the oxygen was suddenly richer, life fuller. She is open and alive to whatever you might be giving her. Every scene was an event as she went further and further into the world and life of the character. Very often after a take she would laugh uproariously, though it had not necessarily been a comic scene: just the exhilaration of being someone else to the very extreme of their being had filled her with joy. Once, I got a phrase in a tangle, ending up talking gibberish. 'Cut,' said Jim, and Maggie wailed with laughter. 'So you are human after all,' she said to me, most unexpectedly.

Disappointingly, I had no scene with Judi, but she and Maggie had created a sort of naughty conspiratorial atmosphere on the set which was delicious and relaxed. Denholm Elliott tended to absent himself from these delights; he felt very uncomfortable with what he perceived to be the British theatrical establishment, raging against Peter Hall's attempts to turn him into a classical actor. 'Bloody blank verse,' he'd say. 'That's not my kind of acting. What I like is saying "Good morning" and meaning "Fuck off." ' He was largely dismissive of his own work, noting that 'if you look very hard, you will see that my acting is quite closely based on the Muppets.' (And there was something about his mouth in the open-jawed position, as he liked to demonstrate.) Often he and I would slope off to talk, mostly about sex, which was a matter of all-consuming fascination to him. His needs in this regard were acceleratingly voracious; he had guide-books for the gay haunts of every city in the world, of which he generously made photocopies for me. It was an ecstatic quest for him, a craving for romantic oblivion, and he was increasingly impatient with a world that didn't accept that sex was the basis of all human motivation, the moment of truth that we are all seeking. It was a somewhat Zen-like position, which he acknowledged. When he had read Alan Watts's *The Way of Zen*, he told me, he had thrown the book across the room, not because he thought it a bad book, but because it said everything he had ever believed about life: that only in the truthful moment, the moment lived entirely for itself, are we alive. At other times, he spoke to me at great length about his children, about whom he felt guilty but also resentful, a dreadful combination, as he admitted. 'They want me to show them that I love them,' he said. 'But how can I? I don't have enough love for myself.'

All these conversations took place in trailers or in rooms on the location set, while the screenplay's much more courtly exploration of similar themes was being shot only a hundred yards away. This is highly characteristic of the making of a movie, where the vacuum of time created by the unavoidable hours of waiting are filled with dramas of many sorts. My friendship with Denholm, which carried on and off for some years until his death, was always slightly volatile on his part. One day when we were shooting in Kent, Jim had made a rare comment on the scene we had just shot. 'Denholm,' he said, 'could you do *less*?' 'What does that word "less" mean, Denholm,' I asked, satirically. Denholm whirled round with all the considerable force at his disposal and barked: 'Only his second fucking movie and he's giving me notes. Fuck *off*!' I had only meant to imply that he and I were both not unknown for going a little too far, but he had taken it quite otherwise. I was attempting to apologise and explain, when Julian Sands, that naughty boy, came up and said, 'Oh, by the way Simon, about that note you gave me yesterday . . .' (Giving notes to each other, it should be explained, is the greatest solecism one actor can commit with another.) The other actors—among them Rosemary Leach and Amanda Walker and Patrick Godfrey, about whom I write at some length in the *Manifesto* diary—came and went, now and then part of the family, second cousins twice-removed, but still family. The whole enterprise was supervised by the burly, bearded and genial Kevan Barker, the First Assistant Director, his calls for quiet on the set loud enough to rouse the dead, his instructions often delivered in incomprehensible cockney rhyming slang—'I'll get you on the dog, sir' (dog and bone, phone). It was a most agreeable experience.

The first public showing of the film was at the Paris Cinema, off Central Park in New York. It was my first glimpse of the completed film, always a nerve-wracking experience, but this was in front of a rather distinguished audience, including the painter Paul Cadmus, John Malkovich on the brink of Hollywood fame (he had already taken Broadway by storm) and the innumerable Long Island socialites and belted Earls that form Ismail's social circle. The one reaction I and most of us had not expected (Julian, Rupert and Helena were all there that night, though none of the seniors) was laughter, but that is what welled up from the audience almost from the first lines. My suggestion to Maggie and Helena—the Rev. Beebe's tentative suggestion to Lucy Honeychurch and Miss Bartlett—that they might change rooms was greeted with a roar. I suddenly realised that part of the charm of the movie was the quintessential, preposterous Englishness of these people. Thank God none of us had thought that for a moment while we were making the film. The scene in the Sacred Lake was greeted with applause, and then the combination of Dick Robbins's score (with a little help from Puccini), Tony Pierce-Roberts's beautiful pictures and Forster's quiet assertion of human verities, took the response to another place.

Not bad for a beginner, I thought, smugly, after the releases within a year of both *Amadeus* and *A Room with a View*, both laden with nominations and awards wall-to-wall. Then came the fall.

INTRODUCTION TO
THE 1990 EDITION

Towards the end of September 1987, I was contracted to appear
in the film *For a Night of Love*, to be directed by Dušan Makavejev, shooting in Yugoslavia. Nick Hern suggested that I take
a tape recorder along with me and keep a diary. It might be
useful, he thought, as well as amusing, to record the day-to-
day experience of an actor in the throes of filming, giving a
more complex account of what it's like than is possible in the
average on-location colour supplment piece. It might, I said; but
it might do more than that: it might give an insight into the mind
of an exceptional filmmaker, and thus, perhaps, into the baffling
process by which a film comes into existence. At this, we both
became fired with excitement and the spirit of scientific inquiry.
Leaving Nick like an explorer preparing for an expedition, I
solemnly bought the equipment needed—a microcassette recorder and thirty tapes—and prepared, in a mood of clinical
detachment, to report to myself, Makavejev and The Movie.

The mood was short-lived, as the following pages will testify.
Scientific inquiry was soon replaced by confusion, doubt, and
paranoia: emotions not entirely unknown on a movie set, but
not ones which conduce to the formation of an objective view of
the process. The transcribed tapes were, in fact, dismaying. Never
mind the shattered syntax, the adjectival over-kill, the obsessive-
ness and the repetitiveness, most of which could be accounted
for by the lateness of the hour of dictation and the amount of alcohol by that time ingested. No, what was dismal was the way in
which the diaries were increasingly dominated, to the exclusion
of almost everything else, by the steady erosion of joy in the
work, and the estrangement between Dušan and myself. I

told Nick that I couldn't allow them to be published. Firstly, as they stood, they were almost unreadable; secondly, I would never again be asked to act in a movie. Who needs a fifth column on a film, reporting, criticising, analysing? It's like finding that the commis chef works for the Ministry of Health. Besides, I had no desire to hurt Makavejev, for whom I still harboured great though baffled affection. Nick argued that the very qualities I disliked in the diaries – now known between us as *Dušangate*, because of the tapes – were what made them valuable. It was the incoherence, the inelegance, the repetitiveness of reality: their justification was their unmediated authenticity. As for Makavejev, well, he'd obviously behaved badly, hadn't he?

I wasn't so sure. As I stood back from events, it seemed to me that I had behaved as badly as anyone, if bad behaviour there had been. And I wasn't even sure that the diaries were authentic. They were certainly a precise record of how I felt at one, two, three in the morning, awash with whatever. The very act of talking into the whirring little box produces a feeling which usually conforms to a recognisable pattern: starting with rhetorical bravado, either angry or exhilarated, it steadily declines into depression and bitterness. This seems to be in the nature of the midnight monologue. An interlocutor might break in with a little cheerfulness, or at least force you to question the premise upon which you remorselessly build your argument to apocalypse. As it is, the uncensored bile gushes on, redeemed only by attempts, fewer and fewer as the tape proceeds, to describe outer, rather than inner, landscapes. The result is that heard back, even a few weeks later, the tapes are nearly incomprehensible to the person who dictated them, because they lack a context.

As I ruminated on these matters, I was summoned to Denham Studios to dub the film. This was the first contact I had had with Dušan since filming had ended three months before. I was nervous. We hadn't parted on good terms, and the transcripts were burning a hole in my brain – not that he knew anything about them. It was like having said something terrible about someone and hoping it hadn't got back to them. At any rate, the meeting was formal, almost curt. I dubbed apparently to his satisfaction, and that would

36

have been that, I would have gone home and burned the transcripts, and mourned an experience that had ended without a positive resolution. But the production company, oblivious of any tension between us as it had been oblivious of virtually everything else on the film, had hired one car to take us both back to London, and so we were obliged to spend an hour in each other's company, in the closest proximity. After a slow start, conversation picked up. Makavejev can't resist an interesting fact, and I fed him a few, culled from books I'd been reading about Orson Welles and Eisenstein, and he duly relished them. Finally, just as the car was about to reach my destination, I summoned my courage and said, 'Things were not happy on the film, were they?' 'No, there was . . . something, something not quite right,' he said, dreamily, as if recalling events of a previous lifetime. I continued. 'You know I was keeping a diary during the filming.' 'No, I didn't know that,' he said, genuinely surprised. But he *must* have done. Everybody did. People made jokes about it all the time. At one point of paranoia, I thought his attitude towards me was cooling precisely because of the diary. 'Interesting,' he said, and chuckled. 'Very interesting.' I had an inspiration. 'I'd like you to read it,' I said, 'and, if you like it, perhaps you'd write an introduction.' I had actually thought of this before, discussed it, in fact, with Nick, who thought it was unnecessary but nice. Then I really did have an inspiration: 'or perhaps you'd like to provide a commentary on what I've written. Sometimes, you know, I'm a little critical of you' – I blushed – 'and you could say:' "Well, if you think *I* was difficult that day, you should have seen Callow".' His eyes sparkled at the thought. 'And like that, we might give a real picture of what movie-making is like, at least insofar as the relationship between the actor and the director is concerned.' 'Aha, aha,' he said, delighted, all the formality and coolness of our meeting banished. The car was outside my house by now. I started to get out. He said: 'And pictures, we could have pictures, cartoons, photographs, and perhaps different typeface for your contribution, and different for mine and . . .' As the car drove off, he was sitting bolt upright. Obviously he could see the whole thing in his mind's eye. The only problem was that I would now have to send him the transcript, that dark, vengeful document.

I handed it to him a couple of weeks later over lunch, just before he and Bojana, his wife – and co-fighter, according to the published text of *W.R., Mysteries of the Organism* – took me to a showing of the very nearly finished film. I thought the film rather marvellous, though the sight of myself on screen created a wave of physical nausea. Dušan was very positive, very cheerful and encouraged, quite rightly so, and he and Bojana went off into the evening in a mood of exhilaration, little knowing what was waiting for them when they settled down to read the poisoned portfolio they were so gaily clutching. In fact, Dušan never responded. I had to track him down in Paris where he lives. It was a muted conversation. He asked for more time to consider whether there was anything he could usefully add. I left messages for him thereafter over a period of some months. We met by chance in Telluride, Colorado, at the Film Festival, where he was showing the film to, it must be said, a wildly enthusiastic audience. We stood in front of them afterwards and touched very lightly on the difficulties we had experienced with each other, but any more serious comment would have been misplaced, in view of their unqualified admiration for our work, his and mine.

We went away and had a drink together, slightly mournfully, and then, under the bright stars of the Telluride night, he agreed to collaborate. A week later, back in England, I telephoned and offered to come to Paris for a couple of days to work on the book. As it happens, nearly nine months elapsed before we got together. When we did, the encounter was touched with surrealism. This is usual with Dušan. I was staying at l'Hotel in the Rue des Beaux Arts – the house in which Oscar Wilde died – and we would meet there whenever he was free. There is a tiny lounge in the hotel, with a cream cocktail piano and potted plants, and we would sit there while I recited sections of the manuscript for him to comment on. I would read out paragraphs criticizing him – savagely, devastatingly – and he would nod, repeating the terrible accusations and rolling them appreciatively over his tongue, as if tasting hemlock were his profession. Above our heads loudspeakers emblazoned with the manufacturer's name – Bose, the German, I moodily thought, for evil – relentlessly ground out the songs of Gilbert Becaud and Charles Aznavour. The waiter would bring pots of coffee and pots of tea, until we could bear it no longer, and I would have a glass of wine and Dušan would sip lager. And all through these terrible sessions, the air was rent with the scream of an invisible parakeet. One day, on my way to the lavatory by a different route, I stumbled upon it. It paid no attention to me, however, because it was made of metal. Our meetings had been punctuated by the cries of a mechanical parakeet.

Dušan's own observations were few and somewhat depressed; why, he wanted to know, did I make it sound so dreadful? 'You will put people off making films. Shouldn't it sound like fun?' Moreover, he said, I had left out nine-tenths of what had happened to me. Hadn't I gone to Vienna twice during the shoot? There was no mention of that. And hadn't I gone to Ljubljana to see a play? Why didn't I describe that? Also, I was a funny fellow, always making jokes and laughing. Where were the jokes, the amusing stories? It was nothing but complaints, whining and bitching. This was not agreeable to read. I stammered that I was trying to give a true impression of what it had been like, but even as I spoke the words died on my lips. I felt that I had betrayed the reality that I, amongst others, had lived. I had also confused maundering in the wee small hours with writing. I told him I would re-write it, using what had been transcribed as a ouija-board to summon back the past. Good, he said, he would then respond to what I wrote. As it stood, however . . . And then he said that after reading the transcript he had, to describe me, written down the phrase, 'his ideas are more noble than he is'.

We then went off to meet Eduard Limonov, the expatriate Russian author of *It's Me Eddie*. I wanted to meet him with a view eventually to filming the book, and I had a strange hunch that Dušan would know him, and of course he did, and so we had supper. Eddie – Edichka – and Dušan fell into a conversation which I could only observe from the wings. They spoke, of course, about their respective countries, and about Communism, and Eddie passionately denounced the West and affirmed his nihilism, demanding that Dušan confess that he too was a nihilist. Dušan said that he felt that he was one of the new breed thrown up by Communism who were neither western nor eastern. He was, he said, a kind of Martian. Eddie insisted that western and eastern systems are essentially the same: in either, if you're at the bottom of the pile, you haven't got a chance; in both, when you start to move up, you acquire privileges. And indeed, it's difficult to argue with that. Frankly, I was selfishly chewing over two remarks made almost en passant: Eddie said I could film his book; and Dušan said he'd like to work on the screenplay with me.

It seemed from that, that my relations with Dušan were repaired, if not exactly restored; and that mattered tremendously to me. It felt very important, book or no book. But perhaps there might be a book, too.

Dušan

4 a.m. Simon Callow came yesterday from London to start 'working on a book'. He is staying in l'Hotel in Rue des Beaux Arts, the same one in which Oscar Wilde died (with the words, 'This wallpaper is killing me'). Is he staying in the same room in which Oscar Wilde died? Is he hoping to die in the same bed?

'Can I say about Simon,' I ask Bojana while typing, 'that he is a clown disguised as a philosopher?'

'I am so uneducated', says she, 'that I couldn't judge. There is something very sad in all these skills he mastered and perfected.'

LONDON
22 September 87

The first I heard about this film was a call from my agent saying that there was a director with a name she couldn't pronounce who wanted to see me. 'Doogan Molokov. Something like that.' 'Dušan Makavejev?' I suggested. 'No, no,' she said, 'definitely not that, something else.' It was, of course, Dušan Makavejev.

I was excited. I had seen *Montenegro*, and (as an amateur Reichian myself) had for years unsuccessfully pursued *W.R. – Mysteries of the Organism*, so I wasn't exactly *au fait* with Makavejev's output. The mere idea of making a European film, as opposed to an American or an English one, was stimulating. Unlike most of my generation, I had not done my formative film-going at the local Regal or Odeon, nor on television. I was in Africa for a crucial lump of my childhood, and a showing of *The Master of Ballantrae* at the Victoria Memorial Institute, with the reels in whatever order the amateur projectionist's caprice dictated, was the best one could hope for. My real movie-going started in mid-adolescence at the Paris Pullman, the National Film Theatre, and the Academies, One, Two and Three and it was Bergman, Pasolini, Jean Renoir Lelouch, Agnès Varda; *Elvira Madigan*, *Les Enfants du Paradis*, *Exterminating Angel*. BBC-2 started up shortly after, and then the floodgates were really open: Eisenstein, Donskoi, Fellini. I hardly saw an American film, after the Disneys and Danny Kayes of childhood, till they were of historical interest, part of a Season or a Retrospective, I almost

41

never saw a modern American film as it came out. So although it was very interesting to make the trip down Wardour Street to meet this or that American film-maker when the opportunity arose, I had little faith in my castability nor much sense of excitement at being part of the Hollywood dream factory. To me film was Film, not the movies, or, in the slang of my family, the flicks. It was Art. Snobbish, silly and plain wrong this may have been, but there it was. As a result, my most envied contemporary was Jeremy Irons when, immediately after the success of *The French Lieutenant's Woman*, he worked, first with Skolimovski then with Volker Schlorndorff!

> *Dušan:*
> *'Schlorndorff!' (with the exclamation mark!) sounds so much better than 'Schlöndorff'. With its teutonic growl added in Simon's version, Volker's name sounds as a war-cry, or like a swear-word!*

Little though I knew of his actual work, Makavejev was clearly out of the common run of English and American film-makers: a creator of political and erotic fantasies, someone who *used* film, played about with the form a little. So even though Cannon, who were making the film, wouldn't let me see a script, which one would normally expect, I went off to see Makavejev in the highest spirits. Mention of Cannon added another promising ingredient to the project. Crazy buccaneers churning out mediocre action epics and buying up cinema chains, they now wanted to establish themselves as patrons of the Art of Film. Vain and tacky they might be, but there was something engagingly reckless about these cousins, Golan and Golem, universally known as the Go-Go twins. Their ambition seemed to have rather over-extended itself by this stage, however, and they appeared to be on the brink of bankruptcy. So the question this afternoon was not merely, would I get the part, but would the film ever get made?

Dušan

Golan and Globus, abrasive and obnoxious intruders on the Hollywood and world film scene, have slipped, travelling through Simon's intuitive and fine-tuned inner ear, into 'Golan and Golem' and 'Menahem Golem'. I consulted Britannica.

Encyclopaedia Britannica

golem, *in Jewish folklore, an image endowed with life. The term is used in the Bible (Psalms 139:16) and in Talmudic literature to refer to an embryonic or incomplete substance. It assumed its present connotation in the Middle Ages, when many legends arose of wise men who were able to bring effigies to life by means of a charm, or Shem (a combination of letters forming a sacred word or one of the names of God). The Shem, written on paper, was placed in the golem's mouth or affixed to his head. Its removal de-animated the golem. In early golem tales, the robot was usually a perfect servant, his only fault being a too literal or mechanical fulfilment of his master's orders. In the 16th century the golem acquired the character of protector of the Jews in time of persecution but also a frightening aspect. The most famous of the genre involves the golem created by Rabbi Judah Löw (c.1525–1609) of Prague. It formed the basis for Gustav Meyrink's novel* Der Golem *(1915; Eng. trans. 1928) and for a classic of German silent films (1920), which provided many fine points on the movement and behaviour of man-made monsters that were subsequently adopted in the ever-popular US horror film* Frankenstein.

It was rather hard to find Cannon's offices, which appeared to be deliberately concealed somewhere along Wardour Street, but when I did eventually get in and took the lift to the top I was greeted by Makavejev and his wife Bojana, who work, think and play together and who were, on this occasion, sitting in the dark, the electricity having been shut off as an economy measure. It was a wet, cold summer's day, and they sat there shivering but also laughing because they have a merry attitude to things. This is unusual in film-makers, who generally seek to stress the importance of their position and the greatness of the work they are about to embark upon, and it's an almost certain principle that the more trivial, fatuous and inconsequential the work, the more serious they become.

Makavejev is about my height, grey-haired, grey-bearded, grey-eyed, too. He bobs and weaves, and is very open, not formidable at all. There is no sense of domination about him. He's completely interested in every idea as it comes up. Bojana is much shorter, with a comfortable physique and beautiful, sexy eyes which give everything she says a certain witty edge. They sat roaring with laughter and talking about everything under the sun, and very soon I was laughing too. They had the gaiety of refugees who'd met up with a friend they hadn't expected to see again as long as they lived. Dušan told me how the film had come about – how Menahem Golem had commissioned him to make it on the spur of the moment at the Cannes Festival – and he did so with the crafty eyes and throaty laugh of someone describing how he'd outwitted the border guards. It was clear that he regarded the project as a conspiracy between us – him, Bojana and me – against the producers. This was very refreshing.

Dušan

Simon is a sharp observer. He dictated his impressions into a small cassette recorder. It's amusing to read someone's description of shared events or places. Sometimes it's something absolutely else.

Our first meeting was on the abandoned fourth floor of the London Cannon building in Wardour Street. There were four hundred scripts on the shelves around us (only four were made into films). The year before, I'd seen Otto Plashkes and his two assistants in the same place flooded by these scripts, boxes and boxes of them. It was just after Cannon took over the EMI and Elstree Studios, and Classic Cinemas. Cannon was everywhere (Royal Première included), and David Puttnam was in America, taking with him Ridley Scott, and Hugh Hudson, and Lynda Miles, and whoever he could save from Go-Go. The Cannon invasion was co-ordinated from San Vicente Boulevard in Los Angeles, Tel-Aviv and the Dutch Antilles.

The day after Menahem Golan signed a famous napkin deal with Jean-Luc Goddard in Cannes, Efi and Nitzi Gilad took me to the Israeli reception on the Majestic beach. 'Do you want to meet Menahem?,' they ask me, 'No, thanks,' I say, and see someone in a white silk Superman jacket and Nike shoes, turning around and shaking my hand: 'Hi, Dušan Makavejev. We like your work. I'll give you the same deal as I gave Godard. One million dollars. You do what you want. And you get fifty per cent of France and all of Yugoslavia.' I see a camera in the crowd. We are in a quickly formed circle. Menahem is creating another event. If this camera works for the festival circuit, we must now be on about thousand screens all over Cannes. 'Sorry, we can't,' I hear myself. 'We don't have a napkin here'. 'We don't need a napkin,' Menahem shoots back; 'we shake hands, that's enough.' I am silent. The camera is circling behind us. 'I am getting Brando for Godard, you know that,' says Menahem. 'You can go to Tahiti, and play hoola-hoola for Brando, but you will never get him,' I reply. 'I'll go to Tahiti, and play hoola-hoola, and crawl like that (Menahem shows how he will go on his four legs) and I'll get Brando for Godard!' (The camera is still circling.) Menahem is quick, he knows how to close. 'Listen, Dušan Makavejev (he pronounces my name right), you are a good satirist (he knows my films). Any time you want to work with us, just come.' Off he goes. (The camera was from Gideon Bachman's 16mm crew, working on a film that was never finished.)

(I still wonder if, when King Lear was sold to him as 'a story of a father with three daughters', Menahem was aware of Jean-Luc's awareness that Menahem has three daughters.)

For about two years, Cannon produced a feature film about every eight days, and they were treated as a newly *emerged mini-major.*

After Andrei Konchalovsky made Runaway Train *based on a Kurosawa story, Cannon became 'respectable'. When Ivan Passer signed his three million dollar contract (as his salary for directing and producing six films) (money he never got), I went to Menahem with my Sonia Braga story and got a 'two-picture deal' in five minutes. The first film never happened, the second was* For a Night of Love – Manifesto. *My only condition was to have Ivan as producer of my films. It was granted. Some time later, in the middle of preparations, Ivan was suddenly off, but fortunately not before we had got through him Eric Stoltz and Camilla Søeberg.*

So, here we are, Bojana and I, in London, casting the film. During the next few months, the four-floor building will get emptied in stages. Last to stay was Duško Petričić, in the basement, working on our animated credits. When he left, the building was locked and sold. A few months later, we mixed the film in Elstree Studios, to be sold by Cannon soon after that. London-Cannon production moved to Golden Square for a while then was liquidated. The film was never listed as British, nor was it American. It played in a dozen festivals in Chicago where the film was listed as 'Yugoslavian'. Prints travelled mysterious routes. The company's phone numbers and addresses were changing all the time. Every time there was someone else on the phone.

Most of the film's turbulent background stayed out of the sight of the actors and the crew. The filming was in Yugoslavia, everything needed was provided by Michael Kagan, the line producer, and Jadran Films, under contract.

Dušan talked about *A Room with a View*; I talked about *Montenegro* and *W.R.*, which I pretended to have seen, being too embarrassed to admit not having done so. He was quite genuinely touched that I had heard of him at all because most people at Cannon seemed not to have done. He didn't really talk about the film, except to mention its title: *For a Night of Love*.

'*You should see* Jenkin's Ear *at the Royal Court Theatre,
with a very interesting actor called Fred Molina,*' Simon
said.
      That's how we got Avanti.

– and I'm delighted to say that some of them are
actually in the film. Then I said, 'You must come and
have a meal with me.' And so we went and had a meal,
at the Café Pelican. They arrived an hour late because of
misinformations along the line, but we had a wonderfully
lively time. All this is unheard of among film-makers –
imagine having just met Michael Cimino and asking him
for lunch and knowing that there was absolutely no sense
whatever of you trying to put pressure on him to employ
you, or trying to ingratiate yourself with him. I had just
met a couple of delightful people of whom I wanted to
know more.

Makavejev has a constantly surprising brain and
speaks English idiomatically, only leaving out most of
the articles. The vocabulary is very wide. When Bojana
speaks English she puts in the articles; she also speaks
French. They are fascinating together: Makavejev is an
imp and loves to play with ideas; she's passionate, rather
intense, and I suspect helps to prevent his delight in
invention from breaking all sense of structure. But that's
just impertinent speculation.

My friend and regular stage designer, Bruno Santini
joined us for coffee. I had a hunch that we'd all get on
together, and so it was. They were curious about his
work and life as they are curious about everything, and
they somehow included us in their travelling community
of artists, engendering a distinctly unEnglish atmosphere,
so that, as the Pelican's somewhat theatrically French
waiters swished around us, we could have been anywhere
in Europe but nowhere in England.

The next time we met I went again to the Cannon
office. The lights had been restored. A good sign, I felt.
He said, 'You know, I don't want you to play Wango.
I'm almost certain that he should be an old man. Apart

47

After about an hour of this delight they shyly gave me a script and said, 'Please read this. Don't even think about which character you might play. Well, perhaps you might think – just *think* – about the character of Wango. Think of that character, but basically what we want to know is, what do you think about the script? Do you think it is a good script? Do you think it works? Feel absolutely free to say anything you like.' So we parted on this very convivial note.

I was delighted by the script because it bubbles with mischief and a kind of sophisticated naïveté which seems characteristic of Makavejev and, I suppose, of certain Eastern European films one has enjoyed a great deal, like Forman's early work and other films of Makavejev's own like *The Tragedy of a Switchboard Operator* and even *The Coca-Cola Kid* (both of which I have just caught up with in my crash course on Makavejevianism. Still no *W.R.* yet, though). The script of *For a Night of Love* was mischievous and intellectually playful; sexually playful, too, not out of avoidance or embarrassment, but out of experience and familiarity. Svetlana, the central character, a young woman revolutionary co-ordinating the assassination of a Balkan monarch, seems to walk through an erotic landscape. The role of Wango, the character they told me to 'think about', is not large, but he too is part of the erotic landscape, a photographer obsessed by his wife's body, taking her, as it were, from every angle. I was stirred by the idea of playing this satyr, awash with booze, luxuriating in all the possibilities of the flesh. The kind of character I like to celebrate, though being some distance from it personally.

I immediately phone Makavejev to say how wonderful, how delightful, how delicious. He said to me, 'Now you must help me to cast the film. Please give me a list of actors that are my kind of actors. I want actors who – we can change our plans at the last moment, we can suddenly do something completely unexpected and follow with the impulse, we can improvise the script a little bit, but who are also good human people.' So I suggested a list of half a dozen such –

from that, though, you can play anything you like in the script. Anything. I want you to be in the film and that's that. So really you could play Svetlana if you wanted to.' His eyes lit up. But then he said, 'No. Maybe not Svetlana because, you know, Cannon may be limited in imagination, they wouldn't be able to take that, although I think it would be very interesting indeed. But anything else you want to play . . . There are two clear alternatives. One is Lombrosov, the doctor running the lunatic asylum, tremendous character, who must be full of force and energy and can be as peculiar as you like. Interesting character, you could do it very well indeed. However, it is quite a small part. Or there's Hunt who is really no character at all, but he goes all the way through the film. He is the police inspector, police commissioner, he follows Avanti everywhere. What would you like?'

I said, 'Lombrosov's a wonderful part. A firework kind of part. And Hunt is rather undefined in a way but,' I said, 'for that reason alone Hunt is more of a challenge – more of a meal. Also I'd like to be around you as much as possible. I'm interested in the film, not just what I play. I'd like to see you at work, I'd like to be around.' 'Good. Good. Wonderful. Exactly. Wonderful.' Then he said, 'What kind of characters don't you like to play?' I said, 'Well, you know, the kind of characters I'm very uncomfortable playing are heroes. I hate to play heroic characters.' 'Very interesting. Why? Why? Why?' he said. Knowing that he was seriously interested, I gave the matter a little thought and said, 'I don't think I like to stand up in front of the audience and say, "This is me, I am a totally serious person." I always like to include a little "get-out" clause for the audience whereby I reveal some aspect of the character, a crack in the shell, that gives them a way in. Heroes – I'm using the word in the widest sense – have to have a sense of their own dignity, and I find that very difficult.' 'Interesting,' he said. 'Any other kind of character you don't like to play?' I said, 'Yes, well I'm not very good at playing little men, simple little men.' 'Hah, hah,' he said. 'Oh, good, very good. Well, we'll try to turn Hunt into a little simple hero. Ha ha ha ha ha.' And he laughed merrily and madly.

Dušan

I remember this exchange differently. I asked Simon, in a blind guess: 'Tell me, is there a character you think you could never play?'

'I could never play a person without qualities,' Simon shot back.

'Then you should play Hunt!'

Simon got pale. Very pale.

I knew that something real and right was happening. I was pleased with myself. Felt like a real director. I knew I had found the challenge that could move Simon to areas he thought he would never have dared to enter. He continued, almost in the same breath.

'Do you know what . . . (someone, who?) said about Hitler?'

'What?'

'He believed that he could control the world, as if the world is in a little box.'

I imagined a Hitler-Simon with a shoe-box on his knees, looking into it with a tender care. *Ein Welt, Ein Führer*.

Then Simon quoted W H Auden's 'Epitaph on a Tyrant': 'Perfection of a sort is what he was after.'

We both liked Simon Callow's funny priest from Room with a View, so we called him without thinking specifically about a part for him. He simply should be in our film.

The source of our exceptional cast is Bojana's sharp eye and wit. She is good in making obvious choices too, but she prefers to try the unexpected. It does not mean necessarily casting 'against the character'. It is looking for 'what if'. If we have a very good actor she'll try something with a mask or costume, just to 'unseat' the safe part, to go somewhere between 'centredness' and 'eccentricity'. Of course, we speak about an undefinable process of being 'gently undermined'.

Before Simon got Otto Hunt (or 'Hunt, Otto' as he played him) the part was quite idiotic. Simon built Hunt Otto into a backbone of the town of Waldheim's Law and Ordnung.

He had understood me, understood how to get my juices going. But they soon stopped going while a period of confusion and doubt and despair set in, as usual when a film has been adumbrated, but no contract is forthcoming. There were some rather desultory negotiations, but the entire project assumed a feeling of unreality. We spoke a couple of times again on the 'phone. I spoke to Bojana. I sent him a copy of my book, *Being an Actor*, and in my heart I doubted that the film would ever happen. I couldn't see what Cannon could expect to get out of this film, because the days when they needed artistic credibility had come and gone, and they had failed to get it. What they now needed to make was money, and I could see no way in which this film could make money. It's delicious, it's erotic, it's caviare, I'm afraid, to the general.

However, in due course negotiations over the contract started again. Marina, my agent, very wisely tried to get the money lodged in escrow (which means that whether the film is made or not, or if it collapses in mid-shoot, the money will be paid by an independent third party. The first film I was in, or supposed to be in, collapsed the day before I was due on the set. I'm still owed £16,000 for that: the money was not in escrow). The line producer, Michael Kagan – the guy that sets everything up, as opposed to the grander Executive Producer, who is part of the Creative Team – refused, challenging Marina to cite one instance of Cannon not having paid an artist. She couldn't, so there was no escrow. On the matter of billing, Kagan said: 'Marina! I can't tell you exactly where Simon's name is going to be on the poster, but I'm not going to hide him, am I?'

They are basically carpet salesmen, but they have a sense of humour. In fact the money isn't bad at all – if I ever get it. But it has all – until today – seemed even more unreal than usual. Plays always feel more real than films: they're announced, posters appear, people start buying tickets, and the opening of the play hovers in front of you, half-dreaded, half longed-for. But films often don't appear till a year after you start making them, if at all.

A consequence of this unreal feeling is that I've not built up, as one normally does, any hopes. I haven't in my mind banked and spent the money. I haven't in my mind played the character and received the Oscar for it. And I haven't lived through whatever interesting country it is going to be shot in. I haven't gone through any of that because I lack faith. So it is with considerable surprise and a continuing sense of unreality that I will finally get on the plane for Zagreb on Wednesday.

ZAGREB
26 September 87

The second day of this limbo period of rehearsals and screen tests and so on and I'm in my hotel room looking out on the greyness of Zagreb. Apparently it's only been grey since I arrived. As always.

On the plane one caught glimpses of one's fellow actors and tried to avoid them because in a way one doesn't want the experience to start until it starts. It's a feeling not unlike going to a new school. Whenever I went away to boarding school, I never wanted to meet any of the other chaps before the first day of term. Somehow I needed that little in-between period of not being at home and not being at school. There is a curious feeling when one goes away on a film, anyway, not in fact unlike going to boarding school, a sense of loneliness and separation and undefinition. But I prefer not to tamper with that queasy emotion; I quite like it. So I sat on the plane in splendid isolation, reading the script. There had been some rewrites, which I hadn't looked at until now. They arrived about ten days ago. I sat there reading my script and the man next to me, a jocular salesman, looked over my shoulder and said, 'Not learned your lines yet, eh? Ha, ha, ha, ha.' Then he said, 'That chap up there, a couple of rows ahead, he's an actor, isn't he?' This was Ronald Lacey. I said, 'Yes he is.' And he said, 'I suppose I should know who you are, but I'm afraid I don't. Ha, ha, ha.' And from then on, throughout the journey he made jokes to his chum next to him about my degree of unfame, and when they got up he took a full proper look at me and said, 'No, I still don't know who he is', quite openly to his friend, who found it very funny.

The new scenes Dušan has written all seem to me to be farcical. A sort of Keystone Kops feeling. This delights me. At Drama School, I once played in a Feydeau farce, and I'm inclined to think the performance remains the best I've ever given. The style requires a single-mindedness, a tunnel-visioned quality that somehow came very easily to me. It's not a style often called for. It seems to be what's needed for Ben Jonson, though not at all for Shakespeare. The psychological complexity and human warmth of Shakespeare are what most English actors are trained to look for, and a genuine farce actor – and a genuine Jonsonian actor, for that matter – is a rarity on the English stage. Leonard Rossiter was one. I can't think offhand of another. Certainly I've never been asked to play in that vein since *Le Dindon* at the Drama Centre. So the Mack Sennett dimension of the new scenes immediately appeals to me. In addition, the character seems to be endowed with certain what one might loosely call Germanic qualities, slavish devotion to his superiors and ruthlessness with his subordinates. I began to wonder if it might not be possible to explore the reverse side of that coin. Perhaps he listens to *lieder*, loves dogs and has vision. I mused on this: a sentimental slapstick perform-ance, perhaps, with intimations of a dangerously emotio-nal inner life. Was this what Makavejev had written? By no means. But I knew him well enough to know that nothing is what it seems in his work. Here on the plane, on my fifth miniature of Bell's Scotch Whisky, I was happy to travel down the dangerous path of trying to intuit his darker purposes and assemble some of the possible ingredients for this interesting cypher called Hunt.

When we arrived, a slight young American, pale, freckled, blue-eyed and ginger-bearded, introduced him-self as Eric Stolz. I knew that he'd been in *Mask*, which I hadn't seen. He'd seen *A Room with a View* (my international calling-card: everyone in the world, it seems, has seen it – walking down the street in a suburb of Kansas City, I was hailed from the other side of the street with a great cry of 'Reverend!'. Something similar happened in Marseilles). Eric is in a separate queue for Americans, for whom, it seems, there has been no truce in the Cold War. Obedient to the request and requirement of Her Britannic Majesty's Secretary of State, the customs officials whisk me through the barriers without let or hindrance. I am met at the other end of customs by the film company, the runners and so on, all armed with walkie-talkies, into which they urgently speak in Serbo-Croatian. There is also a slim-hipped, dazzlingly pretty English boy with a London accent and, it later transpired, rings through his nipples. This is Huggie. Here at Zagreb airport, at ten o'clock in the morning, he brings with him the spirit of the discotheque. In the bus on the way to the hotel there is a sense of gaiety and madness, partly self-consciousness, and partly because of the fact they've all been together for some time, three weeks in fact, and we haven't. (*We* is Eric, finally, grudgingly, admitted into the country; Ronald Lacey, the back of whose neck I have already glimpsed in the plane; a sweet-looking girl, a child really, called Gabrielle; and myself. We don't quite make a team, yet.) A lot of in-jokes, a lot of chatter, some awkward silences as the suburbs of Zagreb, the familiar Eastern European mix of Austro-Hungarian ornamental and socialist-realist concrete, flash by. 'Is there a concert hall?' I ask – more or less my only contribution to the gaiety; not at my best in these situations – and am depressed to have pointed out to me a massive grim hangar. I have been here before.

●●●●●●●●●●●●●●●●●●●

Cultural Reflections (Aside)

Physically here, only very briefly, but here spiritually, here emotionally, I most certainly have been. The brief visit was during a Joint Stock tour of Europe in 1977. We were playing at B.I.T.E.F., the International Theatre Festival which takes place every September in Belgrade. The lorry transporting our set got lost in the mountains for three days, during which we were at liberty to discover the city. This was my first experience of a communist country, or of a Slavonic one. At first glance, Belgrade seemed not unlike its twinned city, Coventry, except that where Coventry's bombsites had been built over with vile concrete piles, Belgrade's remained, a permanent reminder of the 20,000 people killed – before breakfast; the raid was at 6 a.m. – in one terrifying blitz. We had, as usual in international festivals, very little contact with the host population. Once, in a bookshop, a man, seeking as I now think to practise his English, discreetly drew me to one side and spoke of the limitations of life in Yugoslavia. This consisted mainly of the oppressive bureaucracy, of petty harassments and stupidities. One could say more or less what one liked, he said, as long as it wasn't against Tito. But he seemed to have some respect for the old boy, as he by then was. He also spoke warmly of England, because of the war. That being so, I was doubly surprised and disturbed by an incident that occurred a day or two later.

We found – actors always find – the place where all the restaurants are, a street of food called Skidarlje. The menus were exotic: cheese from the isle of Pag, roast boar, roast bear. These last two didn't concern me, as I was at the time a vegetarian, and had, to prove it, a handwritten note which said, in Serbo-Croatian, 'I am a vegetarian'. The phrase was, 'Sono vegetarianisch'. Unfortunately, it meant nothing to the waiters, having been invented by a professor in some university.

Dušan:
It was not in Serbo-Croatian. It was in Esperanto.

So they would gaily bring me steaks, chops, sides of beef, which I would send back, invariably settling for an omelette, a regime which had later, dire, consequences. Meals were accompanied by the playing of a small band, sometimes just two musicians, sometimes more. They played a cycle of tunes known as 'The City Songs', the words to these tunes being learned by the citizens of Belgrade at their mothers' knees. They progress from lively, brisk numbers to increasingly slow and intense ones, till a point is reached at which the tension can no longer be borne, and everyone in the room smashes their glasses on the floor. This phenomenon is known as Sverdet. Well, one night we were eating in one of the restaurants, laughing, arguing, guzzling, when I became uncomfortably aware that the leader of the little three-man band, the violinist, was staring at me, as he dug deeper into the melodies, screwing the tension tighter and tighter. He was facing me directly, seeming to use his violin as a weapon, training it on me. I fell very silent. The others could see what he was doing, too, but thought it funny. Not me. The idea of being destroyed by music was upsetting. It was as if he wanted to wipe me out with it. Eventually when the tension reached its climax, the sverdet was dispelled by the smashing of the glasses and he sloped off with his fellow-musicians to have a drink. I got out as quick as I could, after the usual arguments over the bill. I recounted the incident to someone working for the festival, who laughed. 'He thought you were German,' he said. I was partly relieved, but also partly unconvinced. Do I *look* German?

Dušan:
Two new beautiful words I would like you to keep: Skidarlje *(Belgrade street of food).*

It is an old part of Belgrade called Skadarlija, a cobblestone covered street leading down to Bajloni Market. The street is actually behind the old, once famous, Bajloni brewery. This is the street of gipsy music and grilled meat, the best grilled meat you can find in Belgrade. Simon's 'Sono vegetarianisch' sign, even properly translated, could not possibly be understood there. It would be as if someone entered Montegui boutique with a badge: 'I wear only Capuletti socks'.
Sverdet *(special state of the soul, after midnight).*

It must be 'Sevdah'. There is an even worse state of the suffering soul called 'Kara-sevdah' (from the Turkish kara, meaning black). It is something like very sweet non-aggressive 'amok'. You are not actually after anybody's throat. You just break all the glasses you see in front of you. The most prominent feature of these evenings is broken glass flying everywhere, and sound, in the morning, of shoes walking on a broken glass (as the sound of walking on the gravel on old railroad stations, just a little scringier).

Apart from that, what I principally remember about Yugoslavia from that first visit is shoes (every other shop seemed to be a shoe-shop), churches with inscriptions in Glagolitic, ancient and strange, and a rather disgraceful incident at the British Embassy where I threw up on the doorstep. ('Not to worry,' said Lady Stuart, the ambassador's wife, 'we had the Rolling Stones here last week.') No, my sense of familiarity with the landscape that was shooting by came, not from memories of this country, but from my six months' sojourn in Prague, acting in the film of *Amadeus*. The same shabby, neglected beauty, the same brutal concrete blocks, often unfinished, the same pervading air of depression. My heart sank a little.

●●●●●●●●●●●●●●●●●●●●

We got to the hotel (the Inter-Continental, as in Prague). There's a message from Fred Molina, who's here already. We're old chums, though we've never worked together. We had a noisy telephonic reunion, then went to a meeting which was most peculiar. Dušan had been working with half a dozen of the cast, and when I walked into the room he embraced me with huge Slavonic explosiveness, which was very touching but also a little embarrassing. I desperately thought of some way of justifying the welcome I'd got; failing to do so, I sat down awkwardly, blushing. Dušan continued the little talk that they'd been having, which was about how exciting the photo tests were, how various little things had happened and how much they'd pleased him. The man is eternally enthusiastic, but it's not offensive because it's always specific. It's always something, some little thing, which has stimulated him and excited him, making him – 'guffaw' isn't quite the word, he 'ho, ho, ho, hos' – chuckle huskily with delight. He's a gnome really. He walks with the movement of a woodpecker, which adds to the merriness and mischievousness of his general presence. The dialogue coach, a lady with the Shakespearean name of Elizabeth Pursey, sporting an unashamed and ill-fitting wig, her face heavily powdered, began to speak in a mystical way about some of the things that had happened that morning, and there was complete bafflement on every face. At this point Fred ordered champagne. We all drank it greedily and desperately, and things started to free up a bit, and Dušan told some extremely funny stories about Yugoslavia, which he clearly regards with mingled affection and despair. He told the story of a steel-worker whose face appears on the 1,000 dinar notes. 'Socialist photography, he says, likes the look of steel-workers – and their metal bars.'

During a crisis, the 1,000 dinar notes were demoted, the whole currency was deflated by a hundredth, so two noughts were knocked off the value of the note, and this miner, a genuine Stakhanovite who had been made a people's hero on account of his magnificent output, got terribly distressed. He became a drunk. And he began to get strange delusions. He wanted to get a royalty for every note with his face on it because it drove him crazy to think of all these people getting this money and him getting nothing. So he sued the government. It was a dreadful case. They told him to go away, and he went mad and roamed the streets of his native city, railing against the government. This, according to Dušan, is quintessential Yugoslavian behaviour. He claims, incidentally, that the word slovenly comes from Slavic.

> *Dušan:*
> *On Jan 1st 1990, after more and more inflation, three noughts more were knocked off. The former million is now one dinar. The steel-worker, in the meantime, died. Initially, when his face was put on the note, its worth was about 2.5 dollars. Now it is just a fraction of one cent.*

Most of us withdrew. Eric Stoltz, Fred Molina, Drew Kunin (the new sound man), and I, went off to have a meal in the folksy hotel restaurant. The problem of Eric Stoltz's vegetarianism reared its head but eventually he managed to get a bowl of vegetable soup, and some cheese and salad (no omelettes for *him*), and I had a perfectly pleasant meal which consisted of consommé and a large salad and that very same cheese from the island of Pag which I remember from Skidarlje, rather like parmesan, delicious. I began to realise what's since become patent, that Yugoslavia is not Czechoslovakia – Czechoslovakia, where the vegetables ran out in the third week of every month and everything was either pickled or done in aspic. Here there is an abundance of good food. The shops are full of commodities such as you might find, I suppose, in Coventry or maybe somewhere a bit dingier, Derby perhaps: not quite up-to-the-minute, dowdily packaged, and monstrously over-priced. You can pay for them with credit cards. Yugoslavians themselves have credit card accounts. I don't know why, but credit-card communism seems a contradiction in terms. Again, unlike Czechoslovakia, there are none of the constant offers to change money, none of the surliness, none of the bureaucracy. It's all perfectly straightforward, it's a very nice place to be. And the meal was excellent. Drew and Eric know each other, have in fact been adrift in Europe for some while, staying in an apartment in Rome, where there were, apparently, riotous goings-on. Eric is Anglophile and stays with friends in Muswell Hill, of whose dialect he does a brilliant impression: 'Muswew Iw.' One drank too much, and one's good intentions of going to bed sober and early, to make up for the time loss (we're two hours ahead of London) and one's utter and complete exhaustion from promoting the Laughton book, talking too much about the same things over and over again, were all in vain. It was already midnight, or twelve-thirty or something, when one went to bed and the next morning one was up at seven thirty and off to the studio for tests.

Then the thing started in earnest. I went first of all to the costume designer and then briefly to the make-up supervisor. The make-up supervisor is called Mary Hillman, a very pleasant, skilful Irish woman, whom I know from *Maurice*. She has an assistant called Jeanette, who seems rather severe. There's Boris, who is a tall, willowy, stubbled Yugoslav wearing cling-fit hot pants and a tee shirt with padded shoulders. He also wears a discreet layer of make-up. Strangely, the impression is not camp, because of a certain passionate intensity about him. There's also a bearded Englishman, whose name I didn't get, who was hovering around in the background making coffee, which was very welcome. Again the coffee is perfectly pleasant.

The studio itself is full of greenery, being tended by a number of young men of quite exceptional handsomeness, stripped to the waist. Both the men and the women as far as one can tell at a first generalising glance have striking physical qualities, somewhat Slavonic – large eyes, high cheek-bones – but mediated by Mediterranean softness and sensuality. (This description fits neither Dušan nor Bojana; so much for generalisation.) The studio has none of the characteristic odour of piss which hits you round the head when you work in the Barandov studios in Prague (where there is no paper in the lavatories, only old scripts; one has sometimes felt uncharitable towards some of the lines one has had to speak, but this is going to lengths). Here the work is done in neat little portakabins, which have been very well equipped. Mary Hillman is clear and good and sensible although she does suffer, in the nicest possible way, from the tendency of all ancilliary artists on a film to make assumptions about your character without consulting you and without necessarily consulting the script either. 'Well he'd do this and that', 'Well he's that kind of man isn't he', 'Well he's one of those sort of men who . . . isn't he?' Which is upsetting because you sense decisions being made and assumptions being made about, really, about the whole process of the acting, as if it were all absolutely cut and dried. This feeling is fuelled by the fact that one doesn't altogether know oneself what one's going to do with the character. I mean, they seem to know more about it than I do. In a filmscript, the lines, the dialogue, give you much less than they do in a play. In a sense, the dialogue in a play *is* the play; not so at all in a film. For one thing, in a film, it's usually much scantier. A big scene may have no more than a dozen lines in it. One looks for clues as to the character's physical and indeed emotional life in the directions (which are usually referred to, funnily enough, as the stage directions) or in some outside source, if there is one – if the script comes, for instance, from a novel, or is based on real events. That's a great help. Without any such help, one is to some extent thrashing around. Thrashing around, another word for what in the theatre is called rehearsal, of which, in the usual sense, there is on a film little or none.

The sense of things being arsy-varsy persists at this first make-up session. In the theatre ('*In the theatre*'. I wish I wouldn't keep saying that. But it's really the only way I can describe the strangeness of film-making) in the theatre, make-up is very nearly the last thing that you come to. After four or five weeks of rehearsal, during which you start to sense the facets and dimensions of the character you're playing, you have quite a strong idea of the way the guy looks, and, more importantly, how he feels; what it feels like to be him. Here, it's a lunge into the unknown. What's almost paralysing is the knowledge that if you get it wrong by the first take, there's no going back on it. You're stuck with it. No technical runs, no dress rehearsals, no previews on a movie. *Alea jacta est*.

I have no clear idea about how Hunt should look at all, and I have to try to find out in front of the mirror. So, everybody's standing around, hovering about, make-up in hand, apparently ready to burst into action, to create this thing called Hunt, and I've no idea who or what he is yet. They say absolutely categorically that his hair must be short. I'm not sure about that. I have no hesitation about having my hair cut (at the moment long, grey, and curly; I also have a dark brown beard) but the question is, what happens if we change our minds and they've cut it all off? I'll do anything at all, I mean I'd be perfectly happy shaving my head completely. I've no objection to that, as long as it's right. The only thing is, there's no going back on it. They seem to have an absolutely fixed and certain idea, though. So they start to hack away at it, and because my hair is very curly they start to brush it in a rather romantic way, which seems to me to have absolutely no bearing on any conception of the character. Mary sets to work on my beard. She cuts off the side panels which I had only grown in so that she could look at them. The moustache has now grown very long and traily so we start to wax that up and to practise topiary on the beard, until it has a sort of Napoleon III look about it, which again is totally unsuitable as far as I can see. Dušan comes in full of expectation and delight, but I see immediately from his eyes that it's not the way he sees the character at all, though he's hesitant to say how he does see him. Instead, he opened up a discussion on character. He wants one to take as much from oneself as possible, to use the person one actually is to predicate the character, not to impose something on top of oneself; but at the same time, he's interested in contrast, he doesn't see character as an organic entity, more, I suppose one might say, a dialectical arrangement whereby you present, within the character, its opposite. A Brechtian approach. A non-serious Brechtian approach, I think he called it.

These are treacherous waters for me. I find the questions raised of the utmost interest, intellectually, but I'm not at all sure that they do my acting any good. So to avoid the deeper discussion I said to him, 'I think the beard should go.' He said, 'I think the beard should go too.' Mary said, 'Fine,' and she shaved the beard off leaving only the waxed moustache and immediately something much more interesting began to happen. I said, 'Look, couldn't we really pomade the hair down, couldn't we really stick it down so that it almost sticks to my scalp.' We try this but, because it's so curly, it keeps popping up and we won't be able to stop it doing that. Mary accordingly applied first of all a spray and then pomade, which slightly darkens the hair as well – and suddenly, there he was, Otto Hunt; or at least someone who was not Simon Callow, someone very different from the person who had walked in to the make-up van.

Dušan was as thrilled as a puppy. 'Marrvelloos, marrvelloos, incredible.' Seeing this other person in the mirror began to make me do things, and what was so suitable about the make-up, so suggestive about it, was that there was a kind of moon-faced innocence behind this would-be stern moustache, this would-be fiercely controlled hair. It was a good moment. Everyone realised it and went about saying how good it was and how marvellous and how extraordinary, and of course one was pleased at their response. But on the other hand it's not altogether a nice sensation being praised in that way because one just feels like a . . . it's churlish to say so, but there seems to be an element of patronisation in it, and you feel all the time as an actor on a film that people are treating you like a child, it's something to do with dressing up and all of that. It's like being told by your mummy and daddy that you look really nice for the party and how everyone is going to be impressed by the way you look. This feeling, that of being treated like a clever child, is a feeling which is at the heart of the experience of being an actor, so I should be used to it by now.

Anyway, off to the studio for the tests, in the costume that Marit Allen, the costume designer, had acquired for me in London. Marit is a walking advertisement for her job, slim, gamine even, wittily and elegantly attired, the off-beat accessories perfectly right. She was fashion editor for *Vogue*, and she looks exactly how you would want a fashion editor to look. She's been a huge success since moving out of words and into frocks, as it were. (Her work on the Greta Scacchi film, *White Mischief*, was widely acclaimed.) We had had a jolly time in London at Morris Angel's the costumiers. She was completely open to any suggestion, and the assistants were dispatched again and again to the basement to try out our whims. I was just as much in the dark about what he'd wear as what his face would look like, but Marit and I eventually devised something that was at least very positive, our idea of an Austro-Hungarian police chief's uniform. As I'd hoped, the costume was in fact too tight and gave the impression of the man bursting out of it all the time. I stood in front of the camera and was filmed by the assistant cinematographer, an informal screen test.

Dušan arrived and was very appreciative of the costume though a little worried about the, so to speak, uniformity of the uniform, again seeking something contradictory in the character. Not to create a more complex character in the usual sense but in order, I think, to throw the character into some sort of relief. He said to me, 'The make-up is incredible, I never expected you would find it straightaway like that. You went so quickly to find it!' Then, without stopping, 'I'm worried that we have nowhere to go, I mean, the moment I saw you looking in the mirror like a dog I knew it was perfect, but now where to go?' I went upstairs and put on the second costume, the hunting costume. It has a cravat, which I threw on rather aimlessly. The effect was definitely incongruous. The hunting costume is very formal, and the cravat created a raffish element, and Dušan was thrilled. He thought it was absolutely perfect, including the boots which Marit had chosen, which happened to be a rather light shade of brown, almost orange, and he loved that. I sat down to have my photograph taken by the stills photographer, and the continuity woman introduced herself. Nada her name is, and I leaned forward and said, 'Hello,' and then I got back, as it were, into the character, and Dušan ran over and said, 'The moment you leaned forward to shake hands with Nada, there was something marvellous, it was marvellous, because for a moment you were just nice, behind this terrible stiff uniform, this terrible stiff face and so on and then you were just suddenly very very nice. It was incredible, wonderful. We must find something like this, something very easy, very human, because these guys, you know, they must have off-duty moments.'

Following his train of thought (I hope) I said, 'Perhaps we could show him sleeping. I'm always touched when I see people asleep, people that one perhaps doesn't immediately warm to, a meths drinker, or a thug of some kind, or indeed a policeman or a soldier. Sleepers always look as if they've earned their sleep.' 'Yes, yes, very good, perhaps we could show this. It would be nice, but – another thing, perhaps, you know, he's at a party and he picks up this illegal thing, something he shouldn't eat. Perhaps he picks up a Mozart ball, and, now there's a Brechtian moment for you. How long did you play *Amadeus* for?' 'Two years,' I said. 'How wonderful. You look at it, you, Simon, having played Mozart, look at the Mozart ball, you are going to eat yourself; but it is also Hunt looking. It gives something else. Something different, something that cuts away from the character'

I said, 'Right, yes.' I don't quite know what world we're moving into but I love it. It's delightful. Not an in-joke but some kind of a stepping out of the frame of the picture. Interesting, wonderful, he's got an extra-ordinarily lively sense of film. It's a shame that he and Kundera didn't work together as they had planned to do in the seventies; 'ludic', Kundera's favourite word, descri-bes Makavejev's approach. We later talked about the same sort of thing when I'd got into a second uniform, the one Hunt wears at the party. There's something odd about the shoes, and he loved that, too. Marit and I had worked out a costume that is something like what a Purser wears at the Captain's table, a cross between an officer's uniform and a waiter's. Trousers with stripes down the legs, a little bolero-like jacket revealing a great expanse of bum, and a dress shirt. I was hoping to get the highly-starched dicky to roll up like the lid of a sardine can, as in the old silent movies. Dušan very happy, revelling in all the contradictions.

'Yes,' I said, 'once you've established the central principle of the character you can do almost anything and contain it. In the case of Hunt perhaps it's interesting to think of him as having a secret of some kind. You know, not exactly a secret life, but there's just something that is not apparent on the surface, that fuels him and is his poetry. It is his dream, or whatever. His secret.' We talked about how necessary it is for children to have secrets and how one of the first indications of healthy autonomy in a child is when he tells his first lie, because it is something he knows that his parents don't know. Dušan talked about a paper recently published by Masood Khan about the importance of secrets in psychoanalysis – the patient must have secrets from the analyst and so on. Makavejev is interested in everything, and it's wonderful to work with him because for him everything is stimulating, especially paradoxical things. Anything that is even remotely paradoxical entrances him. I told him my story about the murderous violinist in Belgrade. Dušan adored this because of the paradox: music, which is beautiful, trying to kill you, destroy you.

'What a wonderful paradox. We must use it in the film,' he said. I don't know whether we will or can. Except that he would like to use everything that is lively in his film.

When I was in the prop room I picked up a fan and played with it and suddenly thought, 'Yes, if we saw Hunt giving in to some femininity for a moment that might be quite interesting.' Dušan wasn't so keen on that idea. I don't know why. I think he thought it might be seeming to say something, to add a layer to the character which is not what he wants to do. He wants, as I keep saying, to contradict the character in some way. But that's exactly what I think this little gesture might do, so perhaps I can persuade him of it.

At another point he said, 'Eric doesn't want to wear any make-up at all. And that's very good. Now,' he said, 'the equivalent for you would be not to do any acting at all in the film, so it creates a tension'. Quite innocently, Dušan created an immediate tension in *me*. Reminiscences, no doubt, of Milos Forman, forever roaring *'There will be no acting in my film!'* Either the remark is mystical, in which case I entirely approve of it, or it is another way of saying, act differently or act better, in which case, why not just say it. To approach a character with the negative thought that one mustn't act is impossible. Milos gave the same note to Roy Dotrice on *Amadeus.* 'Roy! You are acting!' 'Right,' said Roy. 'Sorry. I'll do it again.' When Roy started the scene again, Milos bellowed:' *'No no no!* Now you are acting *not-acting.'* It is bound to happen. On the other hand, part of me knows perfectly well that my acting is inclined to be over-ebullient, and I am eager to refine it. So, we'll see. Even more wilful men than Dušan have failed to achieve this no doubt desirable result. But, we'll see.

Once in costume, I came into the adjacent room where the cameraman and various other members of the team have a chance to react to it. This costume parade is again faintly embarrassing because of the 'child' feeling, as if one were in fancy dress and expected to do something funny or outrageous. One just longs to get out of the costume as soon as possible and become like an ordinary grown-up, like everyone else. It does sometimes seem as if the acting is light relief in the process of film-making, the huge corporation which has been convened to get the film together being concerned with more serious matters like building the set and making the camera move in the correct way and making the costumes and all the rest of it. And the actors are just, well, perhaps the fairy on top of the Christmas tree. Eye-catching, ornamental, but sort of optional. It's a curious feeling, and again, quite unlike the costume parade in The Theatah (sorry), where the actor brings his accumulated knowledge of the character to the costume, and informs the one with the other. Here it's like a party game where one puts the frock on and hopes that something will happen. Of course sometimes marvellous things can and do happen. The self-consciousness probably derives from the feeling that they should.

On the way back to the hotel, Ronald Lacey (a twinkling, poetic sort of chap, plump but featherlight) and I travelled in the van with the dialogue coach Elizabeth Pursey – she of the extraordinary perruque. She is a very pleasant woman, a fussy sort of creature but very pleasant, and she has a theory. Her task in the film is to create some kind of unified form of utterance, which is something we could certainly do with. The undoing of almost all international films is that nobody has any real language. The later films of Visconti, Bergman's when not working in Swedish, and to a certain extent Dušan's (*Montenegro*, for example) all seem to take place in a linguistic limbo, the characters all citizens of no man's land. In this film there are Yugoslavian actors, there are English actors, there are Australian and American actors all playing characters of the same nationality – presumably (this has not yet been discussed) Yugoslavians. How are we going to talk? In what accent? Elizabeth's theory is that the accent is in a sense immaterial; what is important is to observe the way Yugoslavians move and understand the resonance of their voices when they speak and then to proceed as normal. This is theoretically interesting, but I can't in practice see how on earth it's going to work. She's been having sessions with the actors.

The very suggestion of working with someone called a Dialogue Coach made me bristle so intensely that I think I must have put out violently hostile vibrations to her. Once she'd explained her theory to me, she quickly said, 'But I'm sure that it'll work on your creativity, and so I shall have to do nothing but just watch you on the set, and I'm sure I shall be applauding heartily at everything you say and do. I am sure you will get it in one go straightaway.' With that she stood well back from me. I was prepared to make a strong speech to her about how I am more than eager to work with anyone who has some special skill to impart to me – something that I don't know about: fencing, riding, acrobatics, singing, whatever – but dialogue is supposedly my special skill, that's what I know about. At least I *should* know about it, and if I don't know about it then they should really get another actor for the film. Handling the text is not only what I am supposed to be employed for, but it is what gives me pleasure. I don't want anybody else tampering with it, and above all I don't want a lot of other would-be experts on my plot, because you cannot start to talk about text without talking about interpretation and character, which is the exclusive preserve of the actor and the director. I was, as I say, building up this rather shameful head of steam in my mind, when she skilfully deflected it with her very charming remark about getting it in one. So whatever else she has or hasn't, her intuition is very strongly developed.

Dušan:
Elizabeth Pursey was hired primarily to deal with non-English actors. She channelled away a lot of angoisse and uncertainty. She played the role of a warm blanket or hot tea on a cold, uncertain night. Elizabeth was a charming, reassuring Dialogue Nurse. There is a lot of static electricity on film sets. Some professions (wardrobe, make-up, camera, sometimes even grips and gaffers) act as lightning rods, they massage auras and clear the static. Simon's private 'electromagnetic field', being atypical, he felt 'invaded', so he 'bristled'.

She is in a difficult position. She's been working with the other actors, and they have taken to it fairly reluctantly; Ronald Lacey just exploded because she's starting to give him inflections and line readings and so on. I suspect this will be a recurring issue.

Lindsay Duncan has arrived, to cries of delight and joy from Fred and me. She is a beautiful, a kindly, and a witty adornment of our profession, but *I* remember her when we were children, still at Drama School, and she was staying in my friend Richard Quick's flat, and we all smoked each other's cigarettes and drank gin from the bottle and thought that getting a job in a good rep was the best thing that could ever happen to us, fat chance. And now she's the toast of Broadway. Or was, until last week, when *Les Liaisons Dangereuses* closed. I haven't seen her for months, maybe years, except glancingly. The last time we really sat down and spoke to each other was when we did Howard Brenton's TV film, *Dead Head*, in '85. I don't know where all our social lives would be if it weren't for work. So, we all went and had a meal. I was keen to display my modest knowledge of Zagreb, where with Joint Stock I had played one performance after the ones in Belgrade. I remembered a restaurant called, I seemed to think, Lovacki Rog, meaning The Hunting Lodge. I remembered a vast room, with chandeliers, long tables and a pianist playing Strauss, Johann and Richard. It was on a large square. Investigation reveals that there is such a restaurant, but it's not Lovacki Rog, which is somewhere quite different. We make for Lovacki Rog, supposedly the culinary jewel of Zagreb. It is dingy and fairly empty, but the food is wonderful. Now unashamedly carnivorous, I eat bear steak, preceded by boar soup. Fred joins me in these, though he addresses the wine more daintily than Lindsay or I. He has lost a stone in weight, and is determined to lose more. He is the glamour in this film. I'm the comic relief: girth can only be a plus.

The walk to the restaurant was really our first glimpse of Zagreb. We strolled past the Opera House, a lovely nineteenth-century confection, the Palais Garnier writ small, past the Mimara Museum on the left, newly built, but equally nineteenth-century in style, down the main shopping street, the shop-windows characteristically arched, the trams rattling by, people milling about in clusters, the whole scene lit by weak street lamps to lend everything a ghastly yellow glow as if it had been drawn on parchment. I remember Peter Shaffer's joke about the whole of Prague being run on a 40 Watt bulb. In Zagreb it's up to 60.

In the restaurant, despite the exotic menu, and the Serbo-Croatian badinage of the otherwise unoccupied waiters, we became just British actors sitting round as we might have done at Joe Allen. We talked about our childhoods. About Fred's remarkable Italian mother – subject of many wonderfully funny stories. (One day he bumped into a friend who said: 'Sorry to hear you've given up the business, Fred.' 'What?' said Fred. 'I saw your mother the other day,' the friend said. 'She told me you'd joined the R.A.C.') When she died, I wrote to Fred to say how much I'd miss her, though I had never actually met her. And Lindsay's mother who, though completely conventional in most of her attitudes, is delighted at her having become an actress and never, ever, suggested that her proper function was to get a serious job and settle down and get married. And my mother, thrilled that I'm directing now, because acting is such a menial job, always being told what to do. While we chatted, despite the bear and the boar and the unfamiliar wine, Zagreb faded as we wove a web of English life around us.

I've been feeling as if I'm wearing a new face. I arrived in Zagreb wearing long hair, long curly grey hair, with a bushy beard, and now I'm somebody completely different with my short hair, my long trailing moustache and my little boy's face underneath it all. I don't think it's necessarily unattractive, but it's just another manifestation of me to which I cannot relate – like all the other manifestations of me. I see myself in a mirror, and I see myself reflected in a shop window, and of course I recognise myself – him again, I think – but I simply don't identify with . . . him. And I think that's infinitely more the problem than thinking that I'm not attractive to look at, because even when I do think the image of me is attractive it is remote from me. It is as if I were a room which I could constantly rearrange but which somehow isn't mine. It's somebody else's. Where does that stem from? I don't know. What are its implications? I don't know.

It's now 4.30 in the afternoon and I'm about to go and have a first session with Dušan and Fred, working on the text with the famous Elizabeth in attendance. So we'll see.

I should add, as a little post-script to my semi-drunken musings on the plane, how I see Hunt, at this moment. I have really the most unrelated impressions. His attempt at self-control. His desire to impress Avanti – even his love of Avanti. His extreme seriousness. An overall tone which is rather Chaplinesque – not Chaplin himself, but some of his boobies. It is the world of the silent movies. There's an eagerness about him and a capacity for running into brick walls, which is rather touching, and I have a sense, which Dušan immediately fixed on, that I will probably base a lot of him on Brunge, our dog.

● ● ● ● ● ● ● ● ● ● ● ● ● ● ● ● ● ●

Aside About Brunge

Brunge, his name adapted from the Dutch for Rupert Bear (Bruntje Beer), is a brindled boxer of great character, alternately noble and psychopathic, melancholy and skittish, omnivorous and fastidious, but always absolutely committed to his appetite of the moment. His twin projects in life – to eat all the food in the world, and to destroy all the cats, tasks which he selflessly and tirelessly performs on behalf of humanity – often exhaust him to the point where he has to sleep for some hours at a stretch. When he sleeps, he sleeps more deeply than seems compatible with continued life, but when he wakes he is *élan vital* incarnate. His secondary project – to smell all the smells in the world, and presumably to catalogue them – instantly possesses him. His limitless curiosity in this regard was responsible for his nick-name, Brunge of the Yard – which is partly why he comes to mind when I think about the policeman Hunt.

I said somewhere, in some interview, that I lived with the best movement teacher in London, and the best acting teacher. Who are they? the interviewer eagerly enquired. Brunge, I replied. And it's true: his bodily movement is an object lesson, not only in gracefulness and strength, but in economy of effort. Not a muscle used that isn't needed, not an iota of unnecessary tension in the whole body, and when he falls, which isn't rarely, because his curiosity leads him to take such insane risks, he has the relaxation of a drunken man. Once he fell thirty feet down a loose trap on a stage, and leaped straight up onto his feet, rather thrilled with his flight through the air. As to the acting: when he pretends, which he frequently does, to be angry with you, he exactly reproduces the physical symptoms of anger, the blazing eyes, the bared fangs, the body poised to leap at your throat. To an onlooker, even a couple of yards away, there could be no question but that a savage and possibly rabid dog is about to disembowel you – but, though his jaws close around your arm or your ankle, his teeth never actually make contact with your flesh. He holds his jaw in a vice-like grip to avoid hurting you. Now that, it seems to me, is a perfect paradigm of exciting acting, completely real, and completely in control. Equally, if he knows he's done wrong – knows it intellectually, but doesn't, of course, believe it: there is never any remorse, only appeasement – his body contracts, his eyes widen, he starts to whimper and to shiver, even, in extreme situations, to pee. A flawless impersonation of fear, so fascinating – and maybe this is the planned effect – that you lose your anger immediately. I suppose it's a ritual designed for use with another, larger, dog – doggy white-flag waving. Except that the fearless Brunge would rather die than acknowledge another dog's superiority.

His only real flaw, as far as I can make out, is that he lacks a sense of humour. His general benevolence (at least towards the human race, especially little ones) and sweetness of temperament make up for that. But his lack of a sense of humour makes him an even better model for Otto Hunt.

● ● ● ● ● ● ● ● ● ● ● ● ● ● ● ● ● ●

27 September 87

Five hours later. Midnight. When I walked into the room there were the unmistakeable signs of a crisis. Fred was puffing away at a cigarette and saying to Dušan, 'Well, I can do it any way you like, but you must tell me what you want. I'm here to do what you want. I want it to be the best it can be, and, if you tell me that it's not good, I'll accept that, and I'll do something better, but I must know what it is you want.' And Dušan, to whom such talk is obviously anathema, was on his feet, also puffing away. He was a little red in the face, but obviously only because he's distressed Fred, which isn't what he wanted to do. He said to me as I came into the room, 'Look, I have a little problem with Fred. We've reached a little crisis, which is that he did so many things in the reading which were so good and were so funny, that made me laugh such a lot and were very very skilful and it was marvellous, but it was acting. It was good acting, it was great acting, it was great *theatre* – but I didn't feel the fear that I always experience in the presence of real life. When Fred and Gabrielle were doing the scene together on the couch here they did it very charmingly, and then they did it again, and then they did it again, and then – just for a moment – there was a feeling of real sex, there was a real danger that this little girl would be deflowered and abused and in some way that she was inviting it as well and it was terrible to watch and it was wonderful. [He was referring to the scene in which Avanti seduces a thirteen-year-old girl who's selling ice-cream.] Anyway,' he said, 'this is something we'll have to sort out.' Then he sat down.

This was even before we approached the question of the accent. Elizabeth was sitting on the other side of the room chipping in with words of agreement, completely redundant phrases like, 'Oh, I do so understand what you mean. I really grasp what you mean, Dušan. Of course it's marvellously true.' I think this was an attempt to pour oil onto these troubled waters but in fact was merely annoying.

Dušan said, 'I must explain again what I mean. I must try to make this very, very clear. There was a moment when Gabrielle and Fred were acting together when the ice-cream which is in the scene suddenly became complete-ly real, and the scene sank to the level of the ice-cream, and then it was wonderful. What we have to make sure is that the acting doesn't aspire upwards to sensuality, but it climbs downwards to sensuality, and then everything becomes interesting, everything becomes surprising.'

Dušan:
When someone is trained to whisper Shakespeare's words so they can be heard properly in the third gallery, how could you possibly convey to him extraordinary importance of a drop of sweat in an actor's eyebrow? How do you explain to him that everything is acting on the screen? Melting ice-cream in cones in lovers' hands forces them to lick it quickly, or in time, while their eyes explore each others' faces, and their lips produce small lying phrases. They can do everything wrong in so many ways, while the ice-cream never lies. And, yes, you have to climb up to the bottom of it, or slip deep deep down to the very top of it.

As Dušan was saying these things, Fred was slipping into a decline, doing what actors always do in that situation: staring at his text, reading it over and over again as if the answer somehow lay hidden on the page, as small children, asked a difficult question, search the ceiling for the answer. Dušan said, 'I've said enough. Maybe I've said too much. I don't know why I chose to say that just now, but I wanted to say it. So. Let's read the text.' Fred, trying as always to rise to some jocularity, to break the atmosphere, said, 'You know, Dušan, this is a very important moment for Simon and me. We've never acted together before. This is a historic moment. And it's a very difficult moment for me. I hold this man in some awe. I have to warn you.' And Dušan was thrilled with this, delighted, excited! We read. It was a tiny, tiny scene. Then we read it again. Dušan gave a couple of little notes, and then we read it for a third time. Dušan said, 'Absolutely fabulous, lovely, it seemed perfect to me. The dialogue is marvellous, the accents and everything.'

I said, 'But, Dušan, we're doing completely different accents. I'm doing some sort of lower middle-class English accent, and Fred is doing a foreign accent, a more or less Italian accent. Which do you want?' At this point Elizabeth weighed in metaphysically, and we started an enormous discussion about the kind of language we were going to use in the film, cast as it is from actors of so many different nationalities. Dušan said, 'I don't know why it's happened that way but it has. Cannon think this is a commercial film.' We all roared with laughter at the absurdity of the idea, no one more so than Dušan, and he said, 'They want to make the film in Europe because it's much cheaper. But they have not interfered creatively, they see me as a creative man and they want to have this creative person in their family, in their fold. However,' he said, 'there is a great problem. There are Yugoslavian actors in the film, there's a Danish actress, there's an American actor and there are English actors, and we just don't know what is the correct mode of utterance for them.' Elizabeth said that her brief from Menahem Golan had originally been that it should be Trans-atlantic, to which she had said, 'Well, that is really no accent at all.' (Bravo, Elizabeth.) Next time she phoned, he said that it should be a 'standard' accent. She wanted to know, was that standard English or standard American? Then she and Dušan had together conceived the notion of creating what they called Film Sound: a universal language, the language of Waldheim (Dušan has naughtily named his middle-European town after the embattled Austrian president and ex-Secretary of the United Nations). Elizabeth and Dušan told this story with great relish. They seem to get along together very well.

Fred said, 'I must make a speech. I will do anything you want us to do, but at the moment we are wasting precious rehearsal time. We need absolutely every moment we can get. It's unusual enough to have rehearsal time. We must use it properly, and we are just messing around. This decision should have been taken weeks ago, and I must say, Elizabeth, with respect, it is not for you to make the decision, nor is it for Simon and me to make the decision. Dušan must make the decision.'

Dušan looked appalled and said, 'I, I, I must make the decision. Hah. OK. Well, you must give me 48 hours.' He looked quite ill at the idea of making a decision. He then said, 'Fred, I can see I've confused you. What I don't understand is why you are uncomfortable being confused. I've been confused all my life, but I try to be comfortable about it. My job is to undermine you, so I'm succeeding in my task. But I'm terribly upset that you aren't pleased to be confused.' To which there was, to put it mildly, no reply.

'Now I'd like to make *my* little speech,' I said. 'I agree with what Fred says, but I believe that you, Dušan, are an unusual film maker. You are not like other film directors, and I trust you. I don't necessarily want a decision immediately from you, but whatever decision you make has considerable implications, and we must know before you make your decision what the implications are. I think that the script is remarkable. The more I read it the more remarkable I think it is. It's poetic, it's disturbing, it's funny. It also has stiff intellectual content. It mustn't be destroyed. My fear is that if we all speak in would-be middle-European accents all its nuances and its originality will be destroyed. The whole thing could easily become ludicrous. There's a great danger that a generalised accent would create a generalised perform-ance.' Dušan said, 'Let me hear you do it, both using foreign accents.' So we both did it with more or less the accent that Fred had done, and Dušan roared with laughter, and the girls (i.e. the continuity girl Nada and Sasha, Dušan's assistant) thought it was wonderful.

I said, 'We can do it lots of different ways. We can do it American.' So we read it American and Dušan roared with laughter and said, 'Yes, I see. You can do everything with such skills, such skills.' You are never completely sure whether he is being satirical or not, but there is an endless flow of good humour and mischief about it. I don't feel, if it is satirical, that it's destructively so. He says, 'You see, Elizabeth, we have here two giants, two giants of acting. They can do anything at all, anything whatever, but they just need to know what to do. I see, I see. I must make a decision. I must make a decision. But, you know, there is another problem. There are varied levels of skill in this cast. There are people who are better actors than other actors and there are people who can use the English language better than other people. There are lots of ways to adjust the balance. I mean I can cut, for example. I can cut three-quarters, nine-tenths of anyone's part, if they're not good enough, or if somebody else is very, very good but has a small part, I can build up that part, I can do anything I like.' Though said without the slightest trace of arrogance, there was something chilling about this Promethean claim. 'That's the way to achieve the balance. I just hope it will all fit together and make one film which makes sense. You know, this is the most coherent script that I've ever written. My early work, which I prefer, is much less coherent. I don't prize coherence. My two last films, *Montenegro* and *Coca-Cola Kid*, are much more coherent than the earlier stuff and they are much, much more successful, but I have the feeling that the more coherent I get and the more commercially successful I get, the less creative I am. It worries me terribly. Still, we have this script and we must try to serve it. I said to Fred earlier – it disturbed him very much – that I hate writers. I was talking about myself, the writer, the man who wrote this script. The trouble with words is that they pretend to have answers. They don't, especially my script. It's translated from Yugoslavian into English, and then there are some bits which I tried to write in my own clumsy English, and it's very unsatisfactory. I won't have the words dominating us. I won't let them do that. What we're trying to do is to create real life, something real must happen on the screen.'

When he speaks about 'real life', it is the nearest that he comes to an ordinary or obvious thought about the film, or indeed life. It's interesting to compare him with Milos Forman, whose idea of real life is doing it his way. To him, that is real and natural. Whereas Dušan is talking about something fundamentally anarchic. He wants to create something on celluloid which is truly alive, not just lively. He wants to capture the very moment of contact between an actor and his character, not a dead finished thing, 'the performance', nor anything as crude as simply capturing an emotion or an impulse or a gesture. He wants, perhaps, to find the moment of paradox, to capture the very moment when the paradox occurs. He talks about having constantly to break down the frame. I find myself unable totally to support Fred, because I can imagine that Fred might want to do something much more straightforward than what Dušan's talking about. There are few directors in the world like Dušan, and it would be madness to try to force him into being another kind of director. Presumably the pressures from the front office and so on will be trying to make him into an efficient, brings-the-film-in-under-time-and-under-budget kind of director. He's completely open about his relationship to Cannon. He doesn't despise them in the least. He's not taking the money and running. He regards them with good-humoured affection, as people who must be mad to have given him the money to make the film anyway, as people who have no possible notion of what it is he is trying to do, but who are nonetheless well-intentioned, trusting and even enlightened people. He was saying in the Cannon office for any Cannonite to hear that the only reason they had given him the money to do it was that they wanted a classy film at Cannes next year. So it had to be made now, straightaway: it's a tiny budget but nonetheless we've got to get this quality product out, and they rely on him to provide them with it.

Something the meeting revealed was that he is a real collaborator. Like Brecht, he is not interested in authorship as such. He embodies the principle of his work, is its conscience, and doesn't in the least mind who contributes to it, either in words or in scenic ideas or whatever. Brecht's was the central intelligence which assembled it all together and therefore it was his work. In the same way Dušan acts as a constant watchdog over the ideas that go into the film, but he's very happy for anybody to suggest anything. He said to Sasha, 'Do you remember I asked you to write the story of the film because I wanted to know what it was like, just out of interest?' This of the script that he himself had written. She fished out a piece of paper and read from it. What she had said was, 'The characters in this film bear no relation to any character living or dead and the train only begins to exist the moment it enters the film. After the film has been made these characters will only ever exist as quotations from the film *For a Night of Love*.' He listened to this with delight and wonderment. Nobody could quite see why he'd mentioned it at that point or what we were supposed to think about it, but he was enchanted by that contribution. On a film it is very usual to say to the director, 'Maybe I could do such-and-such.' But with Dušan it is quite different. The level of creative participation is much higher: you must begin to think like Dušan, to absorb the principle of Makavejevianism. It's nothing whatever to do with creating a many-layered real character. It's everything to do with constantly alerting the audience to the playful possibilities of any given situation. But he doesn't want to make that happen, he wants it to come about of its own accord. I begin to see that, just as he wants me to do away with my acting, he wants to do away with his own directing.

Despite these vistas opening up – *because* of these vistas opening up? – the meeting ends indeterminately.

Lindsay and I went to a restaurant where we ate fish, very nice, and about half-way through the meal one of the waiters came up to me and said, 'Tom, tom'. I don't know Serbo-Croatian and had no idea what he meant. The other waiter, who spoke a little English, came up to me and said again, 'Tom, tom', 'Sorry,' I said, speaking too loud and too clear, 'I don't understand.' He said, with explosive beer-drinking gestures, 'On television, Yugoslav television, programme Tom Chance.' Gracious. *Chance in a Million* has hit Yugoslavia. They like it, and, apparently, me, to judge from the happy smiles and light applause generated by my presence. I went off to the lavatory after we had more or less finished the meal and while I was gone this chap who had been sitting near us and eavesdropping on our conversation, laughing when we laughed and smiling delightedly at the jolly English folk, started up a conversation in reasonably good English with Lindsay. He was, it appeared, a salesman of dishes, by which he meant saucepans, and some advanced form of German cutlery. He produced his catalogue and showed us this stuff with which you could cook, as he said, 'except water, except oil' (without water, without oil). He said very solemnly, 'I don't see myself as salesman. I see myself as missionary for the health-food culture. It's very hard in Yugoslavia because the rich people aren't interested in it and the poor people can't afford it, and the idea of the health food hasn't convinced the Yugoslavians at all. There is one health-food restaurant here. It is terrible.' Yugoslavia is not a destitute, third-world kind of country at all. Everything is a few years behind what you would find in a western capital, there is no Mayfair and there is no Bond Street, but the standard of living seems really quite high. But the idea of health food obviously seemed insane to the Yugoslavs. Busy trying to make up the gap between the West and themselves, they were baffled by an antidote to excess. In this context the salesman's excitement and zeal, his missionary fervour were rather magnificently doomed. We found ourselves poring over his catalogue. Simultaneously, without saying anything, Lindsay and I saw the scene – two English actors sitting in a fish restaurant in Zagreb being shown non-stick saucepans by a vegetarian salesman. We caught each other's eye, but we didn't laugh. It was touching, quixotic, even, and somehow very sad, the thought of him roaming the country with unwanted improving products.

Today I had my obligatory session with Elizabeth – the drill, as Dušan calls it. She was a little tense and told me about how difficult she had found her work with the actors on *The Unbearable Lightness of Being*, particularly with Dan Day Lewis, who was violently opposed to the producer's idea of using a Czech accent. The director was far from keen, either. 'Mr Kaufman,' she'd said to him, 'how do you feel about the idea of a dialogue coach?' 'My dear Elizabeth,' he replied, 'anathema.' She'd overcome that, and eventually it had all worked very well. Of course in that film they'd decided to speak with Czech accents, which is at least a real accent. For our film she's devised this Waldheim tongue. Frankly it sounds like 'stage foreign'. Of course she's a phonetic expert (teaches at RADA), and she's analysed it in terms of phonemes and whatever, but it just comes out as semi-Slavonic foreign. I suggested to her that she should devise a sentence which contained all the characteristic Waldhei-mian sounds which we could use as a reference. That's the only way that I have ever got hold of an accent: by imitating somebody to get the actual sensation of the sound; to find out, in fact, what it feels like to be that person saying that thing. She thought that might be quite handy. We didn't look at text at all, so we ended up really very pleasantly and she said how grateful she was that I'd come and spent my time and all the rest of it. I still feel with Fred that one should make a virtue of pushing the accents further and further. Dušan's films are so fragmented and deliberately dislocated that I think it could be another fruitful dislocation. But I think he's frightened that Cannon won't buy it. Not that they're much in evidence; Michael Kagan isn't here; there's a chap called Peter Cotton, English, formerly married to Jeanette of make-up (he seems to be on our side); and there's another chap, an Israeli, who finds it hard to utter the most elementary courtesy. I'm not sure whose side he's on, though apparently he used to be Menahem Begin's bodyguard.

BLED
1 October 87

I have been away for three days in Vienna and Munich. The *Evening Standard* have asked me to write the first in their series on Great Hotels of the World. I had suggested the Royal in Scarborough. 'Oh, no,' they cried, 'what we had in mind was The Raffles in Singapore.' I was all for that, until it turned out that they weren't actually prepared to pay the fare. So then, knowing about the film, I said that I'd pop over to Vienna and stay at one of the great hotels there. They chose the Imperial, and I accordingly set off for the airport. Fifteen hours later, I arrived, having spent some ten hours in Munich, three of them having lunch at the Four Seasons restaurant, which is no hardship, admittedly, but something of a surprise when you're expecting a 50-minute flight. The reasons for the re-routing were never explained. Now that *is* ominously like Czechoslovakia.

On arrival at the hotel, I found that, unfortunately, due to an urgent state visit, they could no longer accommodate me, but had booked a room for me at their sister hotel, the Bristol. Well, I'd write about that, then. But no, apparently the *Standard* still wanted me to write about the Imperial, so lunch and a guided tour would be provided the following day. The Bristol is a splendid hotel, very twenties in feeling, full of black marble and elegant chrome fittings. The Imperial, infinitely grander, also seems somewhat more vulgar with its bourgeois-baroque splendour; it might be better named the Hotel Faninal. Lunch was excellent – Wiener Schnitzel, inevitably, but most acceptably – while the manageress regaled me with the slightly melancholy tale of the hotel's history. It was built as a palace, but the Grand Duke discovered the moment he took up residence that the famous Ringstrasse was planned to pass directly under his bedroom window, so he sold up in disgust. Hoteliers snapped it up, it was quickly adopted by the royal family as a sort of overflow annexe and awarded the accolade 'kaiserlich und königlich', imperial and royal. (K.u.K = Kuk in German = just exactly what it equals in English, a fact with which Karl Kraus made much play.) The Hapsburgs often lodged their guests there, and, since their demise, the republic has similarly used the place to put up heads of states. It's allegedly the Queen's favourite hotel in the world. During the war, less regal guests were in residence: the American liberators, who apparently ripped out half the furnishings. By the early fifties, it became a hotel again. The guided tour was informative, though not without its French-farcical moments, as when we discovered a couple *in flagrante* (we had the wrong room – or perhaps they did). I was photographed all over the place, up the stairs, in the lobby, on the pavement. Later, I walked in the Prater, I walked along the beautiful blue, well, the beautiful, Danube, I saw *The Bartered Bride* done (to death) at the Volksoper. Among the photographs of past Intendanten on the walls was the unmistakeable bald dome of Otto Preminger. Preminger directing operetta! Fun! I ate ravishing food and drank exquisite wines and felt that I hadn't penetrated the city's mask one inch. I spoke to no one, sat in perfect solitude in various restaurants, reading the new Peter Ackroyd, *Chatterton*. I might just as well have been on a luxury liner. I didn't feel as if I was in Vienna, I obviously wasn't in England; and I certainly wasn't in Zagreb. I felt, in fact, as if I were in a novel, a novel about a solitary man reading his life away. It was a most pleasant sensation. The whole interlude however has served to distance me from a film which has already been so unlike any other as to have acquired a dream-like feel about it.

Arrived a couple of nights ago in Bled where about three weeks' filming is going to take place. It's a magic little wonderland, like Lucerne, built on a lake, surrounded by mountains. There's a castle, and a couple of beautiful eighteenth-century churches, one of which is on the island in the middle of the lake. The lake itself is small enough to walk round in about an hour. I have a view of all this from my window. I can see the Alps from here even as I speak, I see the castle, I see the church. I also see the sports stadium whose roof is a horrid scarab of corrugated iron poised just below my window but apart from that all is loveliness. Fortunately it doesn't seem to have the same claustrophobic feeling as Lucerne because the mountains are cosier and smaller, and anyway it's goldenly beautiful weather.

The hotel is called the Krim: the Hotel Krim, Bled. It is designated five star, but so was the Hotel Bristol in Vienna. Stars are relative things. This is a cheap tourist hotel. It is claimed by the production company that they settled on Bled as a location at the last moment, and this little jerry-built shoe-box of an hotel was the only one which could accommodate us. Well, maybe. Mutiny is widespread among the actors, who have all found something wrong with their rooms, either because they are near the lift or because there is no room service, which is indeed tedious, or the lighting's wrong or whatever, so they are agitating to move to other places. A couple of people – Fred, Eric, Camilla – have elected to transfer to a nearby apartment block, where they have their own kitchens. As a culinary paraplegic this option holds no charms for me, though their promise of inviting me over for delicious home-cooked meals does. My natural greed and equally natural delight in the efforts of others makes me the perfect guest. In fact, I am thrilled with my little cell and its huge window. The room is full of light and there are wonderful vistas. And the plan is that I should do some serious writing though my fingers have not exactly been trotting over the keys these last few days. I must try today.

I find myself in the usual place of an actor making a film – limbo. I did that day of work, that is to say the work on the make-up, and the tiny little bit of work during the discussion with Dušan about the character, the accents and so on, which seemed to open up exciting possibilities, and then it was all switched off. Juices started flowing, and then all those juices were summarily stemmed, and I am undefined again as to my work. I haven't acted for what seems like a lifetime; two years, in fact, during which I've directed and written and fronted documentaries, but not practised the profession which was once my entire *raison d'être*. In my long walks around Vienna and my long walk around the lake yesterday, great paranoias about who am I, what am I, and so on. Above all my attitude to writing and how serious about it I mean to be, or whether I'll just be an amateur at that too. But none of this is relevant to the filming or the film.

The other actors begin to declare their identities a little more strongly and start to engage in rituals of courtship and aggression, staking out their territory and claiming their women folk. It would appear that Camilla Søeberg, who is all Danish loveliness, tumbling hair and copious curves, has a sweet temperament, but it's very hard to know because she is an international film all on her own. You can't tell how well she speaks English. She speaks it with a slight Californian accent, laced with Scandinavian vowels. She stares in wonder at much that one says: is it unfathomable or merely incomprehensible? However, from tiny traces of eccentricity (roaring with laughter at unexpected moments, for example) I suspect she's quite spirited and that her temperament probably isn't anything like what her face and her body suggest. She certainly doesn't seem to be a narcissist. And she's struggling with her waistline, I can see that she's longing to pile into dumplings and such like things but somehow manages to resist. Eric remains quirkily determined on his image as a vegetarian non-drinker, non-indulger. His anti-carnivorousness has become a good-natured joke, even to him. I wonder if that's new for him. I wonder if people laugh at it in California? He and Camilla would seem to have forged a friendship, which was demonstrated, in an oddly old-fashioned kind of way, over the supper table. He has a trick, old Eric, of folding the napkin in such a way that he can put it on his head so he looks like a Dutch peasant woman. In a moment Camilla snatched it off his head and put it on the table and then they engaged in play with the napkin, losing themselves from time to time in each other's eyes, sometimes nearly touching, pulling the napkin this way and that way. It was choreography. It seemed almost to have been rehearsed. Most elegant and charming it was and while it was going on the three of us, Lindsay, Fred and I, continued a vigorous and lively conversation with jokes and impassioned outbursts against this and that. And when Camilla and Eric sloped off to their separate dorms and the rest of us gathered together to have the Imperial Torte that I had brought for us from Vienna, we all simultaneously remarked on the business of the napkin. So we'd all taken it in, we'd seen everything, the whole ritual, all three of us, although apparently totally immersed in each other and in the conversation. Actors!

I think actual filming will begin tomorrow and I find it awfully hard to focus my brain on it. That's the problem with filming. It becomes so diffused. You don't really feel part of it. I'll go down to the set at lunchtime and try to catch a bit of the film – just as one might catch cold?

Evening. About midday I set out for the railway station where they're filming, but I must have taken a wrong turn, because I walked for miles in the stated direction without coming upon anything remotely resembling a train and certainly none of the tell-tale signs of a film unit: cables, caravans and caterers. The landscape I walked through was dramatic, all gorges and ravines. Eventually, at about two, I knew that I was lost. And hungry. I had passed several clubs – country clubs, they must have been – and determined to go into the next one and try and find some lunch. But suddenly the supply of country clubs dried up. There was a camping site of sorts, however, and I walked down, down, deep into the valley, past empty chalets and abandoned assembly points; the place was obviously out of season. Clearly I wasn't going to eat here. But then, like a mirage, a large wooden cabin equipped as a kitchen and run by a short, fat, rather hairy woman, loomed up. It wasn't a mirage. A very real smell of cooking was now assailing my nostrils. What was odd, though, was that there seemed to be nobody eating there at all. At a nearby table were half a dozen women of the same age and size as the cook, making merry with a bottle of brandy; but they weren't eating. I asked the cook in my restricted German (oh God, are they going to try to aim another musical firing squad at me?) whether one could eat, and, yes, one could. She pointed at a huge fish lying there: 'Forelle,' she said, and shortly afterwards served up the Schubertian morsel, deliciously cooked. It was too big even for me, so I shared it with a cat that came from nowhere, unceremoniously demanded some of my food, and then bitterly complained when there was no more. So there I sat, scoffing freshly-caught trout in this sun-drenched valley, surrounded by empty chalets and a great deal of forest, as the cook and her friends shrieked with laughter, laughing as women only laugh when talking about sex. The cat hissed and I got glowing drunk.

How am I ever going to acquire a sense of reality?

2 October 87

Reality strikes. My first day of filming. It started fearsomely early. We assembled in the car at 6.00. We were on the set at 6.10. Tremendous wave of excitement and urgency hurled one into the make-up chair and from there into wardrobe, from which one emerged panting at 7.00, not to appear in front of the cameras until 12.00. So it's already a typical day's filming.

The station is tiny, but situated up the hillside to give a panorama of Bled: the lake, the church, the castle, the island. Picture postcards exist because of views like this. The weather remains golden, though it's a bit nippy. We sit in the station waiting-room and start to make tentative contacts with the crew and the extras, all of whom are very friendly, and many of whom are eager to practise their shamingly good English. That shot at 12.00 was just to ride a bicycle up and down the platform twice, but it took half an hour partly because of the steam, and other mechanical things, but also because I am introduced for the first time to my agents, the actors playing my police agents. Dušan has had the entirely Dušanian notion of my being constantly accompanied by six agents, all of them having identical moustaches to mine. They range in size from the very tall Tom, a film-maker, apparently, and an anarchist, to others as small as or smaller than me. One of the men is, he tells me, a ballet dancer. He's very handsome and lithe, but nothing else about him would make you think that he was a ballet dancer, except, perhaps, for a slight air of wide-eyed boredom. The others are extras, apart from one who is an opera singer. This is rather an unusual line-up. I'm keen to form a good relationship with them – they're my little army – but language is a big problem. Only the ballet dancer speaks English, but he's so haughty that only a few terse words at a time pass his lips. Socialising with people who don't speak your language is hard enough; acting with them is almost impossible. They have an occasional line which they do in heavily accented English, not really understanding it but that is not so bad as their not understanding what I say, as I'm giving the orders. It proved difficult this morning to co-ordinate ourselves. No doubt things will improve. I'll learn a few words of Serbo-Croatian; they'll be told what it is I'm saying.

This little scene is historic. It's the very first thing I've done in the film. It's rather nice that it's not anything too demanding but probably later, when one was a little more certain of what one was doing, it might have been a moment that one might have made something more of. In truth, I was quite happy to do it just deadpan.

There was a long wait until the next scene – my first scene in the film, as it happens, where Avanti arrives on the train and Hunt greets him, only to be reprimanded for blowing his cover. He is then doubly confounded when Christopher, the young mailman, calls on him to receive some top-secret packages. It was a complicated little setup, and we were already suffering from lack of time and the loss of the sun. It had been bright and warm in the morning, but by afternoon the sun had gone, and it had in fact become very cold and overcast. So there was a problem of continuity, in addition to the scene being quite elaborate to stage. Avanti arrives, Hunt goes to meet him. As Hunt is meeting Avanti, Svetlana, to whom Avanti really wants to talk, is coming out of the train; she's being met by Martin, the stable boy, who secretly loves her. Christopher, who, equally secretly but more romantically, also loves her, is at the end of the carriage collecting the parcels.

All this in one shot. It was a tracking shot, always somehow the most exciting thing in film, the quintessentially cinematic shot. (I suppose the opening track in Rick's American bar in *Casablanca* was the first time I became aware that I was watching a film, rather than a photographed play.) It's quite a complex thing to stage, and when the staging's difficult it almost certainly means that you start to make compromises in the acting. You have to do things, as they say, 'for the sake of the shot'. The greatest difficulty for an actor in a film is that no matter how much you study the script, you can't know what the shot is going to be like. You don't have a shooting script. The chances are that nobody does. It's probably more or less improvised on the spot. One must simply be prepared to do anything that's asked of one and somehow keep hold of the character and the situation. I'm still enough of a novice not to feel entirely confident about this. I keep trying to learn to think cinematically. Bearing in mind something Alec Guinness had once said to me (that when he played the leading part in a film, he always insisted that the first shot of his character should be full-length, to establish the entire character; details could then be elaborated from that base) I had hoped that the first glimpse of Hunt would be of him standing waiting for the train, sweating. Just a still, sweating figure, eagerly waiting, longing to serve, who is then thrown into turmoil. That couldn't be because, Dušan explained to me, they had already shot points of view from that angle (as the train pulled in) and in those shots there was no one on the platform. I would therefore have to, as it were, make an entrance. Fair enough. That was alright, that was fine by me, I hastened into the scene sweating and mopping myself down and then presented myself to Avanti, though I was dimly aware that Hunt's first appearance in the film was, as a result, off-centre, and that all that one saw was his incompetence and not his efficiency.

Fred as Avanti presents an extraordinary sight. He has lost another stone since Zagreb and is dressed dapperly in a suit, cream with baby-blue stripes. He carries a cane and wears a hat, the very image of suave elegance – not something he's been accused of being the very image of before. The greatest transformation is to his face. He's bearded, and his very fine, very dark hair falls elegantly over his brow, highlighting his big brown eyes, which gaze out of his sexy, powerful face with erotic melancholy. Can this be Fred? He's always been a handsome, if sometimes rather substantial, man, but the make-up (the trimmed beard, the curled hair) brings out very clearly the fact that this cockney wit is not English at all. His dad's Spanish, his mum, of beloved memory, Italian. We see his face now for what it is: dago, wop, foreign. His slightly broken nose only adds to the impression. He's almost unrecognisable, and yet this is definitely him – he hasn't replaced his face with another face: this is one of the faces of Fred. Fred could go around looking and behaving like this. It wouldn't be false. It's the Fred he might have been. The Fred he *is*, however, breaks up when he sees me, looking like a bulldog whose owners have squeezed it into a uniform.

So far, so uproarious. The moment we open our mouths, though, there is a problem. Dušan said straight away, 'Isn't the accent too strong? Isn't it too strong?' It seemed to me to be exactly the accent we'd used before, just a mild, generalised, middle-European accent. Elizabeth, who was straggling along with a portable headset over her wig which made her look even more bizarre than usual, came over and offered some observations, which I did nothing about. We rehearsed the scene again, and she came up and congratulated me on the improvements. Then we shot the scene.

I was very conscious of the fact that it was my first scene and that I wanted some indication from Dušan of his approval or whatever. Yet none was forthcoming at all. Of course he is under great pressure: we are already behind, the weather is bad. (The weather is always a foe, rain or shine. It doesn't matter what it is, it causes problems unless it remains absolutely constant.) Those things apart, however, he seemed worried, and I got depressed because we did about five takes, and none of them seemed to satisfy. I would have thought, generally speaking, that they got better and better though one is still in limbo as far as the accent is concerned. The convention of two people speaking their own language to each other but with an accent means that there is no attitude to language. If someone is struggling with a foreign language then that gives a multitude of hesitations and difficulties. Here though we're not talking about someone having difficulties, he's supposed to be absolutely fluent in the language, and yet to have this accent. That is still a slight poser.

As I say there was almost no response from Dušan. I fell into a mild depression, and then we sat, Fred and Ronnie Lacey and I, talking about this and that, and finally I went down to shoot another little scene with Eric Stolz. That was interestingly done, interestingly talked about, but I by now began to feel that in some way I was disappointing Dušan, that he was Saying Nothing, that somehow he'd expected more, or better, or less, or God knows what, but different. So when he said to me, 'I'd like to talk to you for a few minutes after this about interpretation', I was relieved, though I felt like a schoolboy being held behind after class. When we spoke he said, and this is absolutely typically charming of him, 'I have some problems. I want you to help me with the problems. I have here Fred who is the comic lead in the film. And I have Camilla, playing Svetlana, who is the romantic lead in the film. And I'm really making two films: one is a political comedy and the other is a thriller-romance, and I hope that they will mix in and that everybody who's playing either a comic character or a romantic character will just play them, and it will all blend perfectly well together. But today I was a little worried when you had the accent quite strongly, which made you seem comic. Then I hear Christopher playing the accent very strongly too and it worries me that my romantic male lead is becoming a comic character. What am I to do about it?'

I said, 'As far as I'm concerned, I don't actually believe that Hunt is an inherently comic character. I think that he's a pathetic character, because he wants so much, he's so emotional, he yearns to fulfil his duties.' And I explained to him why I had hoped that there would be the still moment, and I said that I would really love it if he could find as many still moments for Hunt as possible. And he said, 'Yes, but you see, what you do, you're such a wonderful comedian, it's so comic, your comedic ideas, the little things that you do are so funny, it's brilliant, maybe too funny. But I don't dare to come to you and say "Hold it down. Don't be funny".' I said, 'I'm not trying to be funny. Of course it's very nice if some of it is funny, but that's not at all in my mind. I took very seriously what you said the other day about the uniform and the make-up being powerful and effective in themselves. All my efforts are directed towards doing something as simple as I can possibly make it'.

He said, 'Yes, the mask is incredible, it's so powerful. I was astonished because it was so perfectly, unbelievably, right. But Fred's mask wasn't at all like I expected. I expected this kind of D'Artagnan, this rather swaggering figure. I was amazed at what he invented, but I just didn't know whether it was right. What I was worried about was that it was strong, powerful and funny, but could he be attractive to women? So I mentioned it to the women on the film and they all said, "My God, yes, of course, he's so attractive". And I said, "But you know, I wouldn't want to go to bed with this man", and they said, "Yes, yes, yes, yes, of course we would all want to go to bed with him." Why is this? It must be a resistance in me. It must be a jealousy in me because I'm clumsy. I've always been clumsy. Even when I was at school or university. These guys would come into the room, and they were smartly dressed and they were suave and elegant and we laughed about them and said they were stupid, but all the women wanted them. What is it?' 'Narcissism,' I volunteered. And he said, 'Yes, but it's a certain kind of narcissism which is attractive. And why are women attracted to narcissism? And there are narcissists that are not attractive.' I said, 'Well, it is absolutely true that there are narcissists who are not attractive but no one who is attractive is not a narcissist.' And he laughed and said, 'Yes, yes, yes, I think that's true. Anyway, we'll talk more about it.'

I want to question him rather closely about the more abstruse ideas, the theories that he adumbrates from time to time. He said something today which was interesting. I don't think he even had time properly to formulate it. He said, 'Long shot is always a kind of choreography but the wide angle is something else.' I really didn't know quite how he was going to finish that. I must ask him about it. He also decided to cut a couple of lines of dialogue in my scene with the seven agents. 'I'm turning it from a theatrical scene into a film scene,' he said. 'So we just see the agents we know. We learn about it by visual means.' For such a complex and contradictory man it was almost banal. Surprising.

He likes to look through the lens. He is very attentive to his cameraman, Tomislav Pinter, who is a lovely chap, gentle, slow in his movements, with a face whose apparent tiredness is contradicted by his sharp eyes. He's worked a great deal in Europe, speaks English well and is uncommonly courteous to actors. He has filmed with Dušan before, though their relationship doesn't seem to be entirely without tension. Dušan gets right up onto the crane, he tries out the shots. I suspect he's got a very good, sharp and clear eye. He doesn't talk to the actors at all, really, except to express these curious reservations which always come from a position almost of embarrassment at having the audacity to talk to them about their art. This of course is very charming, but sometimes it might be a little easier if he said something a little clearer before the scene, to which you could react one way or the other. But that's what he wants to avoid.

The caterers come from England. Very nice chubby fellows. And they're doing their best. As usual one is fascinated by the privilege we actors have in being fed free with all this plentiful and fresh food, while the passing populace looks on. I'm reminded of an occasion during the filming of *The Good Father*. We had a rather élite catering firm, because there were so few of us. We were filming in the Temple, and they devised a wonderful spread for us which they laid out just behind the caravans, on the pavement beside the Embankment Gardens. At this, a dozen or so tramps emerged from their benches or wherever and formed a semi-circle of awe around the food, like forest animals drawn by a camp-fire. We took our boeuf bourgignons and our glasses of claret and all the rest of it and sat on the bus surreptitiously watching as their lunch arrived and they were served bowls of soup from a travelling soup kitchen. They'd drink their soup and then go to the end of the queue again to get a second bowl. And this went on until the soup was exhausted. It was a ghastly, shaming juxtaposition. No such thing here, of course.

That was the last filming I did that day. After lunch here in Bled, which came too early – 11.45 – and was over too soon – 12.15 –, we spent hours and hours and hours on the set doing nothing so I read a novel. You can only read about eighty pages before you really have to stop and try to make conversation with someone, make some kind of human contact. The anecdotes are spread around. All quite pleasant, and of course the surroundings are absolutely gorgeous so one really has nothing serious to complain about except the odd feeling that one still doesn't really know what one's doing with the part and yet the film is being made – irrevocably.

Postscript. Fred and I had a conversation during the day, about American actors. We looked at Eric. I'm fascinated by his kind of self-protectiveness, the way he looks after himself. We thought of American actors that we'd worked with and how aloof they keep themselves from their fellow actors, that is to say from those who are not also stars, and how superior in that regard the English profession is. On an English film set a kind of spontaneous ensemble is quickly formed, partly because the English profession is much smaller, partly because it still remains largely based in the theatre, partly because everybody knows more or less who everybody is, what everybody's status is, and that's respected and observed. It is something of a paradox that the hide-bound traditional English acting profession is more democratic than the American one. It's hard to get close to American stars – perhaps because stars are the secular saints of America, and the American public wants to be able to touch them, to hold them and as it were catch their magic, their holiness. So it's necessary for a star in America to erect protective barriers around himself. It is still possible in England for Maggie Smith to walk down the street and be spotted or spoken to by members of the public without her being engulfed by them. That probably isn't possible in America. Eric – the starting point of these reflections – is very nice and friendly. But both Fred and I were struck by the way in which, like most young American actors, he is preparing himself for stardom. But then everybody in America, it seems, is in permanent readiness to deliver their Oscar acceptance speech. Everybody, not just actors. The Oscar Award ceremony is religious, the culmination of the year, the high feast of American life, and the idea of being acclaimed, acknowledged, validated by everybody, and thanking all those who have contributed to one's being acclaimed, acknowledged, validated is at the heart of the American dream, holding the same place in American awareness as canonization does in that of pious Catholics. American actors are all preparing themselves for eventual stardom and they are shrewd and canny about it in a way that almost no English actor ever is. They are wise and sharp about the motives of producers and directors. They know about their best angles, about how the light falls; they immediately and skilfully get on good terms with the cameraman and the sound recordist. All this is of course sensible and good. But there does seem to be a certain lack of innocence about it all. It may be that American actors are passionate about the art of acting – some are, some aren't. But they are all intensely loyal to their careers.

On reflection, I realise that what I'm saying is that American actors are more at home in film than English ones. English actors are just as canny about the stage – we all know where best to stand, how best to be heard, how to make the most of ourselves. We form, if we're wise, relationships with the designer, the lighting designer and the stage manager. Of course we do.

Second postscript. We discovered a restaurant, very expensive by Bledian standards but with an amazingly diverse menu – yoghurt soup and all kinds of fancy things. Bled is a holiday resort and still, almost at the end of the season, a little festive. (There are, incongruously, some package holiday groups with unmistakeable South London accents. Quite how good a time they're having is questionable. 'The way I look at it,' Lindsay overheard one middle-aged lady to her companion, 'it's only two weeks.' 'Yes,' said her friend, "I suppose there is that.') Dušan and Bojana were there finishing off their meal, and they acclaimed Lindsay for her rushes, which they said were simply wonderful, and they flooded her with sunlight. I felt mildly paranoid about not being praised. How could I be praised? My scenes haven't been seen in rushes yet. But I detect – I'm sure I detect – a certain coolness towards me, which I naturally attribute to disappointment. After all, they were both incredibly warm – until about yesterday.

Stupid. Terrible. Typical. (Of me.)

3 October 87

Back to the location to do the scene that we very briefly rehearsed last night. Up at 7.00 this morning and on to the set at 7.55, so for once there was no waste of time at all. As I approached the set Dušan said to me, quite briskly, 'Whatever we actually discover from the rushes of last night's scenes, I think it would be very good for you to do less. The same comic energy, just less.' At which I froze. I said, 'OK', and he heard the silence and didn't break it. I moved away and began to sink with startling speed into depression and a kind of sulk, thinking, 'Right, OK, I'll do less. I'll do nothing, if that's what you want. Actually, I know very well what you want. You want to inhibit what I am doing, you want to deny my contribution, you in fact would prefer that it wasn't me at all, you want me to be somebody else or you want just to use me but you don't want to use my energy.' I slithered deeper and deeper into that mire, concluding, as if by an inexorable logic, 'OK, so I'll give up acting'; and then, as an inevitable progression of that, quite seriously asking myself, 'Is there any way of my being able to get out of this film?' Actually considering possible ways of leaving. And alternative ways of making a living.

Dušan:
I had a problem with Simon, and it has to do with his genuine belief that actors should act. Being an actor he already was OK for what we needed from him, what the camera needed, what 'Kodak' needed if you wish.

Unfortunately 'being' is not good enough for him. If he does not 'act' he does not feel all right. So I was getting him, 200%. He could not understand it. But I ask, Why should an actor 'act'? Acting in film is done simply by actors (or whoever is placed in the 'role' of an actor) being in front of the camera or doing what they have to do. 'Acting' is, most of the time, an unnecessary 'plus'.

The less acting the better. The secret of Marlon Brando's famous 'acting only 40%' is based on the fact that almost anything in front of the camera is too much, especially if you have a charismatic actor. The more he takes away, the stronger the impact on the public. So, while I was seeing any trace of 'acting' as intrusion, Simon was getting panicky and feeling deprived, not knowing that lens and lights and Kodak, and editing style later, all produce actors 'acting' in the final film. The actor in front of the camera, defending, or covering for a tiny segment of the final film's length, does most of his work by being as clearly as possible present in the scene. Ten hours of daily work on a film produces about twenty minutes of actually 'shot' film (20 minutes of images) to be cut down to 2 minutes in the final film.

Dušan had, probably quite accidentally – or was it? – pushed a button which is marked: do not use except in case of extreme emergency. The word 'less' has dogged me all my life. I am always being asked for less: less noise, less energy, less laughter, less talking, less feeling, less trouble. He wasn't to know, but it upsets me terribly. It makes me feel awkward, foolish, clumsy, out of control. It must have something to do with childhood. Whatever it is – and I just don't know – it goes straight to my centre. So, with me in this frame of mind – on the edge of a nervous breakdown, that is to say – we started to do the scene between the mailman and Hunt – Eric Stolz and me. I start the scene by removing the wrapping from the portraits of the king, realise what they are, try to conceal them, then take out the telegram, read it to him and ask him to look after the packages. He cheekily looks at the king's picture and says how nice it is. A simple scene.

The first time we did the scene the packaging wasn't right, which meant I had to tear at it. This, Dušan said, made it a violent, dramatic action, which was not what anybody wanted. So I explained to the assistant director several times the kind of wrapping it should have, and then we went again for a take, and again it was exactly the same, and so I did what I loathe to do – it was only a mark of my self-irritation – I shouted, 'I asked three times if the packaging was correct and it still wasn't.' So there was a ritual burst of anger from the assistant director towards the props man, and they all ran off and finally brought another one. In this way we did three, four, five takes. As we went on, somehow or another I managed to convert my negative feelings into more careless ones. I can't say I enjoyed playing the scene, but I didn't really give much of a fuck any more, which has in the past been quite a creative state for me. I don't know whether it is now. We shall see.

Somewhere in the middle of some take or another Dušan sensed that I was very switched off from him and from the whole thing, and while the wardrobe women were brushing me down and the make-up woman was checking my face, he and Bojana came up and praised my costume, my make-up and how marvellous I looked. I can't pretend to be anything but paranoid, but it did seem to me quite obvious that they were trying to think of something nice that they could say to me. 'Oh, marvellous costume. Oh, God, how wonderful. God, the buttons are so good.' And again one feels like a little boy, a little person being encouraged, being lured out of his little mood. But I wasn't to be lured out of it. I was in the grip of the totally impossible feeling for an actor of being required to not do something, to be not loud, to be not emotional, not forceful. Now the chimaera, the monster, the King Charles' head, that is raised, is that of Film Acting.

● ● ● ● ● ● ● ● ● ● ● ● ● ● ● ● ● ● ●

My Life as a Movie Star (Aside)

What Dušan is saying to me, I know, is that I am not giving a Film Performance. The idea that there is a qualitative difference in the kind of acting that is needed for film and the kind required for the stage, is one that sharply divides people. Some – including for example, Alec Guinness – deny it, saying that there is only good acting and bad acting; others insist that there is a profound difference, which you ignore at your peril. I find, after a certain amount of experience, that I belong to the second camp. Now, this is a nearly indefinable thing, though I believe that I understand what it means as a sensation. It seems to me that stage acting is always an art of projection and movie acting is always an art of introjection. The sensation of a movie-actor is of swallowing the camera, of drawing the camera in. In the theatre, no matter how small the audience or the auditorium, you are always projecting something to the audience, giving them something, and in some way magnifying yourself, even if the magnification actually consists of talking very, very quietly. But in film it is totally different. There isn't the audience *out there*. The audience has to be taken in to you and into the character and that is nothing whatever to do with the volume of expression, either of voice or of gesture, or indeed of characterisation as such.

The idea of two different kinds of acting obviously exists in film-makers' minds. For years I would have the most delightful meetings with directors who had specifically asked to see me and who declared their profound admiration for my work – on stage, of course – only to watch the blood slowly drain from their faces as they encountered me in the flesh. 'How', they were plainly thinking, 'could I put this over-loud, over-energetic, over-opinionated creature in front of a camera? The lens would shatter, the celluloid melt. There would be altogether too much acting. It would be – ', and then an involuntary shudder would run through their bodies, 'theatrical.' And with barely concealed relief that the nightmare vision that had unfolded in their imaginations need never happen, they would bid me a fervent goodbye, and 'I'm afraid it didn't work out', would come the message from the casting director, who had warned them, anyway.

I didn't disagree that there were two different kinds of acting, but there was no reason that one person shouldn't be capable of both. French and German are different languages, but bilingualism is not unheard of. All that's needed is a little intelligent thought about the differences, and a little practice. But Catch-22 is at work here: until you've appeared on film, no one believes that you can possibly do it. So what it needs is a giant leap of faith on someone's part. For me this came from James Ivory and Ismail Merchant, who never seemed remotely troubled by my enormity. They saw me in *Amadeus* on stage, we met and then, one day, they offered me a part in *Heat and Dust*. I was shocked by this transgression of all the usual rules. I hadn't made a film yet – how could they want me to be in one? Hadn't someone explained this simple law to them? In the event, I wasn't in the film because the play that I was in ran and ran. (They have a somewhat unusual attitude to casting, it must be admitted, because as I recall they also suggested that my mother – who has never been on stage, let alone on screeen, in her life – should play one of the senior mistresses in the maharajah's harem. The loss of this performance, I suspect, is a greater blow to the history of film than mine would have been.)

Later, they asked me to play the Rev. Beebe in *A Room with a View*, a part which, failing at first to appreciate the richness of the character, I turned down again and again, until, after one final glorious curry, I could turn it down no more. It was in that part that I began to get a sense of what film-acting might be, despite, or perhaps because of, the part's relative lack of definition. Beebe weaves a gentle path through the film, starting a scene, swelling a progress. His essential task is to exude benevolence. It was a question of being rather than doing.

Before that, I had been involved in the film of *Amadeus*, which had greatly increased my store of anecdote, but had done little to advance my education as a film actor. Milos Forman had cast me out of sentimental considerations, and I was never quite able to fulfil his notion of the character (though he used often to cry: 'I wish I could change the name of the character to Simon Callows! Be yourself! Be yourself! Don't act! There must be no acting in my film'). And I didn't really understand how to relate to the camera. In *Amadeus* I'm still dictating to it, projecting. I should say, in self-defence, that I was playing an extravagant actor-manager. But in *A Room with a View*, *The Good Father* and *Cariani and the Courtesans*, Leslie Megahey's charming film for the BBC, I think I give filmic performances. They felt like it at the time, and they look like it now. They may not be wonderful performances but they are filmic performances. So when Dušan said to me, as if I'd never done a film in my life, 'It's a really big close up. Your face is very big in the shot, you know, a screen is very big and wide, so you must be economical with what you do', I bridled intensely inside. I like him too much to show it, though what I must have shown was just a switch off, a blankness.

●●●●●●●●●●●●●●●●●●●●

Back to Bled. In all those other performances, I did, on the whole, know what I was doing. Here, the director's intentions are protected under the Official Secrets Act. I got a clue as to what they might be from Elizabeth, in whom Dušan seems to confide things that are more usually – and perhaps more usefully – said to the actors. She had rushed up just before we shot to observe that I was rolling my R's a little too much. Afterwards, when as far as I know I had done nothing different, she congratulated me on having corrected it. Then she said, 'Oh, it's all so terribly, terribly difficult. I really don't know quite what to say, but I think I understand what Dušan meant when he said to me that he's written all these eccentricities into the character of Hunt but that it is very important that Hunt isn't aware of them himself.' That was a kind of clue; but why couldn't he say it to me? Alas, I have to report that, when he does say something to me, Dušan isn't finding the words that release anything, so I am in despair, really. I am very distressed. It's an unhappy experience, this. I feel as if I'm failing, failing to please him and failing to give the performance the film needs. In the long term I'm no doubt letting myself down, although I feel that what I am doing is not untrue, it's just wrong. Presumably. He should know: it's his film. Perhaps he should be a little more communicative about what it is that is right. He is scrupulously, wilfully, determined not to impose anything on the actors.

He gave Eric some notes. He said, 'You seem to be aloof. You're treating Hunt in a very aloof way. There's a kind of innocence about Svetlana, which I think Christopher should also have. We should see that in his kindness. He is a very nice man. He is very polite. He may disagree with Hunt politically, but Hunt is nonetheless a person; he is always nice and kind to people, so here too he is very sweet.' He said to Eric, 'You have blue eyes and that's very good. We want it like you're sort of from another planet, you're too good for this world. We should have that feeling about you.' Good notes and very positive, but they clearly baffled Eric completely because Dušan seemed to have said something completely different a day or two before. And just before the shot, Dušan urged him 'Be organic. Be a tree or a cloud.' As Eric staggered away from the set, utterly confused, I said to him, 'No-man's-land, without an interpreter', and he laughed.

Yesterday Fred shyly and rather shamefacedly confessed that he'd done much less work on the part of Avanti than he had on anything else he'd ever played, and he'd found it much harder to work on. He'd done much less work, for example, than when he was playing Halliwell in *Prick up your Ears*, and I said, 'Well, of course, there's so much to go on with Halliwell; there's so much to do, there's so much research and background reading. You have a great treasure there to draw on. Whereas Avanti is a sort of deliberate cypher, because Dušan is not interested in an organic, many-layered character in the sense in which Stanislavski or most American film-makers would understand it.' 'What is he interested in?' Fred wondered. A meeting-point, I suggested, between Avanti and Molina, and that's what he's getting. I suppose that's what he's not getting with Callow and Hunt. In a way I think an underlying problem is the one brought up when he said to me, right at the beginning, 'What kind of characters do you find it hard to play? What kind of characters don't you like to play?' and I said, 'I can't play heroes or little men'. And it is probably the case that he conceives of Hunt as a little man. I suppose I'm being too colourful and passionate for his purposes, in which case we are probably in quite big trouble, because I'm not sure that I know how to play this little man. I'm contemplating writing a letter to Dušan, because I think the position should be stated very clearly, and it should be got in hand, and yet I don't want to take him away from his other concerns. A letter might be the easiest and neatest way of broaching the matter, and I will probably express myself better. On the other hand, letters always have the nature of an ultimatum about them so I'll write it and I'll have to decide later whether it's advisable to send it or not.

On the set today Bojana took over the job of the make-up woman, who had gone off to hospital to have her eye looked at. While Bojana was putting glycerine on my brow to stimulate sweat, I said in a bedroom voice, 'Fais-moi suer, Bojana', which made her laugh. This brought Dušan over. He said, 'Ah, so Bojana, you've become the make-up girl. That's very good. Are you a good make-up girl? Have you done the make-up properly? Ha, ha.' And he gave make-up instructions to his cigarette box as if it was a walkie-talkie. Then he said, 'You've found a new profession, Bojana. That's good. They say that everyone should have four professions in a lifetime. That's apparently the average now.' I said to him, 'How many have you had?' And he said, 'Half a profession'. And Bojana said, 'Yes, half a profession of being a schizophrenic.' Whatever else, he's still unlike any other director that I've ever worked with.

Fred has discovered in conversation with Tom, the tallest of my agents, that Dušan had made half a dozen revolutionary documentaries before he started work on his first feature film, the name of which I can't remember. *Man is a Bird*, I think it's called. If he was a documentary film-maker, just like Milos, making films with non-actors, of course it's going to be terribly hard for actors to work with him, or at least for me. I think he has the same misconception as Milos, that in some way I am going to be the same person on the screen that I am in life, and there'll be *no acting*. Acting is just as dirty a word for Dušan as it is for Milos. It's a very tough thing for

108

me. I find it extraordinarily hard, because I feel my performance being deplored and regretted all the time and him feeling that there are glimmers of it that are possibly nice and real and then others which are not. He makes me feel as if I were a highly calculating, technical and contrived actor, whereas I am in fact giving absolutely free play to whatever I feel. Within the rather strict limits of the camera movements I try to let whatever will happen happen in the moment, you know, some new thing with a bit of paper or whatever. I absolutely don't work out and polish and hone my effects, I just try to let the character rip in the moment of shooting. So there's a complete gap between our visions, our views of my performance, of film-making and indeed of acting itself.

Tomorrow we shoot Hunt's last scene in the film. Let's see if I can fuck that up too.

Apart from the ongoing trauma there are fascinating characters to observe. There is Sasha, who sometimes gives one the calls. I'm not quite sure what her function is – apart, that is, from writing synopses of the plot. She has a highly dramatic face with prominent front teeth and a deep, 40-a-day voice, and she tends to make every simple statement into a crisis of the utmost drama. 'You are wanted on the set' becomes a desperate panic: there's why you weren't there already and how quickly can you be got there and everything is being held up until you are there all implied in her tone. Of course, in the event, you get there and have to wait for half an hour. It is, it must be said, a problem for us that we are filming in a foreign country with largely foreign technicians and indeed a lot of foreign actors (foreign to us, not foreign to themselves, of course; they are in their own country, but the film is nonetheless being shot in English, and most of the principal actors are English-speaking). One doesn't know what's going on technically at all, although Dušan and Tomislav, the cameraman, go to great lengths to try to remember to talk English. But inevitably as soon as anything at all complicated comes up, they must speak

Serbo-Croatian, and they do, laughing and talking and despairing and apparently doing imitations of us, and the result is a maddening sense of exclusion, which is a hazard of film-making at the best of times. There's also difficulty in scenes where there are Yugoslavian actors who are told to do something in Serbo-Croatian and you don't know what it is. There is a great deal of laughter. At what? We haven't the faintest idea.

Another very pleasant member of the team is Huggy, he of the nipple rings and the unbounded energy. He is apparently the boyfriend of a Golan daughter and has recently given up alcohol, which may explain the energy. Unfortunately, in cracking his drinking problem, he has acquired a talking problem. He is aware of this and constantly enjoins one to tell him to shut up, but this becomes a little tiresome in itself, however gratifying to begin with. He is capable of asking one how one is ten times in the course of an hour. This, it seems to me, is reasonable grounds for homicide: culpable courtesy. Then there is the constant supply of coffee, which, if refused, provokes the anxious enquiry, 'You alright?'

He is not clever in his dealings with the Yugoslavian crew, talking to them like a crazed colonialist, speaking too loud, rolling his eyes, berating them like children. They regard him with ironic amusement, rightly judging him to be harmless, with his heart in the right place. He, and his good nature, are indestructible. Non bio-degradable, one might say.

They've given him special responsibility for Gabrielle, the seventeen year old who's playing the thirteen-year-old ice-cream seller whom Fred has to seduce. This seems a little like getting a nice friendly fox to look after the chickens, and indeed, he seems to have fallen in love with her, but she can handle it. She has sat around day after day expecting to be called, or sent home, but neither has happened. She pines for her boyfriend and the discos of London – she and Huggy can sit for hours comparing notes on the scene, and which of their friends is going out with whom this week – but her self-possession is remarkable; as is her beauty. Her father is Indian, and

110

his influence on her features is strong. It is astonishing that there is no one *in loco parentis*. Perhaps Huggy's not such a bad chaperone, then. He'd fight anyone else off, and I don't think he'd force himself on her.

The other day I shut him up for quite a while. I called him Hugh. I mustn't do this too often or it'll wear off.

Walked round the streets of Bled yesterday. I spent a lot of time wondering and thinking, trying to review my entire philosophy of film-acting and, as often, asked myself how, for example, Alec Guinness or Peter Sellers might have played the part, and though, no doubt, Sellers would have been more comically extreme and Guinness probably more inventive, I can't see that I'm really picturing anything quite wrongly. Yesterday, as I walked along the street, I saw a dog doing what dogs are supposed to do but which I had never actually seen before: chasing its own tail. It was an Alsatian, and it had a very big tail, and it madly chased the tail and got hold of it from time to time, bit hard and was then startled by the fact that it had hurt itself, which only made it more determined to chase and punish the tail. It occurred to me that it was a perfect image of myself at this moment.

At about five-thirty I drifted into the hotel bar to get some espresso coffee. It's a sort of greenroom; the extras and whoever's not needed on set tend to end up here. I ran into the great Yugoslavian actor, Rade Šerbedžija, who's playing Emile, the bailiff with a strange sexual hold over Svetlana, and we had a verbally slender but emotionally thrilling conversation. I understood that he wrote poems, that he would give me a copy of them; also that he sang, and he would sing me his songs. I graduated onto wine -- a mistake -- and then scotch. By now, Tanya Boškovic, the saucer-eyed beauty playing Wango's wife, Olympia (how the name suits her, Olympian, Olympic, the Olympia in Paris), had joined us, with a friend. They were going to the theatre, in Ljubljana. Would I like to come? We leaped into Tanya's friend's old banger, and clattered off. As we went, they told me about their theatres, which one was up and which was down, which was in, which was out, how they would follow such and such a director from theatre to theatre, whole companies, sometimes, moving from one side of the country to the other. They told me about the different languages spoken in different parts of the country.

There was a fervour about their discussion, a sense of the importance of acting and the theatre, which was not, I think, a note one would often hear among a group of English actors. It seems that Zagreb's theatre is really down in the dumps, hopeless, but that Belgrade's, which had been very old-fashioned, is now in the forefront. They talked to me, too, about the state of their country, of the collapse of central authority since Tito's death. Each section of the Yugoslavian federation – and that's what it really is, seven countries, with seven different languages and cultures yoked together – takes it in turn to provide the prime minister, who holds office for six months at a time.

The result is that no one can point a finger at anyone any more; the buck does not stop. Their mood as we rattled through the darkened fields on the way to Ljubljana was sombre: they could only see the imminent collapse of the entire structure. The most ominous development was the ever more militant Albanian population in Serbia, demanding autonomy, separate status. A civil war was in progress, in all but name.

We arrived in the harshly and intermittently lit city, of which I saw almost nothing. We drove to the studio where the play was taking place. It was, Tanya told me, the second part of an adaptation of Dostoevsky's *The Possessed* spread over two evenings, the first dealing with the political aspect of the book, the second with the sexual. This was the part we were going to see. 'Good,' I said. The title of the play was on the poster: *Bludnje.*

What did it mean? A vigorous discussion ensued. 'It means,' said Rade, eventually, 'like making sex without love.' 'Ah,' I said, 'what we call lust.' 'No,' said Tanya, 'also if, for example, you teach without love. You know

– bludnje,' she said, expressively showing empty palms. But I didn't know, and I still don't, really, though it would be worth trying to find out, in view of Goethe's remark that the untranslatable words contain the soul of a language. The production didn't enlighten me, wonderful though it was in a familiar way. It was exactly what we mean by East European theatre: the action framed with repeated rituals, sweeping, stitching, climbing, the scenes punctuated with bursts of very bright light and very loud music, the acting emotional and physical, not in the least cerebral. The actor playing Stavrogin was bald and massively still. He never spoke above the brink of audibility, and so brought you to the edge of your seat, even though, in my case, what I heard would mean nothing to me. Tanya said she thought he was too quiet, and when I agreed, she told me that I must tell him. We went round to see her chums after the show. The bald man, called Cavazza, born in Italy but brought here as a child, was even more impressive off stage than on, and no louder, but I didn't dare to tell him.

Back in the car, then off to have supper in a mountainous suburb of Ljubljana with the adaptor/ director of *Bludnje*, another Dušan (Dušan was the great King of the Serbs), Dušan Jovanovič, leading playwright and director, Rade's special friend, director of his famous *Titus*. He and his wife received the unexpected addition of an English actor to their supper table with charming delight. They prove to be great friends of David Gothard, director of the theatre in Leicester. The fact that every leading theatre artist in Europe knows and indeed loves David should really cease to surprise me by now, but it never does. Odd what a good start to a conversation with strangers it gives to find that you have even one friend in common; the name becomes a mantra as you spend five minutes passing it back and forth. In fact, though, our common love of the theatre had already dissolved any strangeness that might have existed between us. Rade held forth gloriously, laughing, singing, embracing, rushing off at ten minute intervals to make telephone calls of an emotional nature. Not one word of any of this did

I fail to understand, though it was not in any language I spoke. At other times we talked of all kinds of things in pidgin English. I enquired after new writing, new developments. Jovanovic was thinking of doing a production of *The Kiss of the Spider Woman* and was thrilled and amazed to discover that I had acted in the play in London. I wanted to ask him about the situation of homosexuals in Yugoslavia, but there finally the language barrier defeated us, and we passed on to other matters. I left laden with texts, some in English because a play of Jovanovič's had been performed, with Rade, on an international tour, and in America translations had been provided. The food had been delicious, nothing more so than what I suppose was a kind of lard, a local delicacy, made by leaving the fat from the pig on a ledge inside the chimney for several months. This had been made by Jovanovič's mother and was as full of flavour as anything I've eaten all year. As we drove back, Tanya told me that there are witches who practise in the country towns around Ljubljana. Mrs Jovanovič, Milena Zupanačič, (prominent Slovenian actress), had gone to see one who had predicted that their house would collapse totally. They laughed; it was as solid as a rock. A week later, when they were away from home, a freak earthquake made it crumble and fall. The witch's other prediction was that Dušan J. would die in a car at the age of sixty. He is fifty now and drives like a maniac, blissfully certain that for ten years he will never have an accident. 'But what if he kills someone else?' I asked. 'Yes,' said Tanya, wistfully, 'he never thinks of that.'

And so to Bled.

Tuesday 6 October 87

We started at 5.00 this morning. Actually on set at about
9.00. It was a scene in which Hunt and Avanti in a boat
push the bodies of Christopher and Emile into the stream.
It's a beautiful scene but it took a lot of sorting out. We've
moved from the station to a location over an hour away
from Bled, a tiny town, almost a village, called Škofja
Loka, which means, one of the locally recruited extras
tells me, the Bishop's Town. Here they speak a dialect
different to that of Bled. The bishop's palace, now a
museum, dominates the town; at least it normally does.
Now the film dominates the town. This morning's
location is on and around the bridge that spans the fast-
flowing river. The banks are steep, and lined with
hanging trees. An idyll, especially with our mechanically
induced mist. The third assistant director, Dubi, slight,
handsome boy, all eyes and smiles, tells me that the river
is totally poisoned from an upstream factory; nothing
lives in it at all. At a certain point when we were standing
on the bank a woman appeared, wailing tragically.
Apparently we were in her garden and had trampled all
over her flowers. The film had trampled over her flowers.
She made an extraordinary progress down the steps,
mourning, keening and shaking her head from side to side
in disbelief. An apparition of woe.

She was bribed to contain her grief, and the work
continued and went very well. It was very high spirited.
Amazing how one sustains the energy, considering we've
been up seven hours, even though it's only eleven o'clock.

Before we had actually started the filming Dušan had

come to me and said that he'd seen the rushes and that they were 'marvellous, marvellous, unbelievable, fantastic. Everything very good, the appearance, everything. My worries are halved now,' he said. 'I didn't believe it was possible to act in such different styles, but apparently it is. About the accent: it makes you kind of Greek if you go over on the accent. Well, just take it down, take it down, take it down. Less, less, less.' I said to him, 'May I say something, Dušan?' 'Of course.' 'It's not useful, advisable, to speak to actors exclusively in negatives.' He said, 'Ah, you mean, "don't do this, don't do that." Yes, I see.' I said, not pompously but from the heart, 'It's so much better to tell actors to do something rather than to not do something.' 'Ah, good, yes, OK, well you will be very strong for me today, yes. Hah, hah.' Off he went.

We did the scene on the water, a rather Wagnerian affair with Fred and me being slowly rowed across the river to separate the intertwined bodies of Eric and Rade. It was fine, though it took a very long time. Then lunch, after which, my last scene in the film, where the bodies are stranded on the beach and Hunt explains to Avanti his version of what has happened: the official police report. I played it very formal and deadpan. Dušan came down and did what he almost never does, he gave a note. He said, to Fred and to me, 'Both of you are as stiff as the corpses. Well I suppose that's quite interesting, but I think you should move, move, move and point to him and point to him and so on, and so on. Hunt, you are excited, you are thrilled, you are proud you have discovered the answer.' I said, 'Ah, you think he really genuinely does believe that he's solved the case.' 'Yes, yes, of course. Very proud.' I said, 'Well yes, OK. I just thought the opposite.' And he said, 'No, no, no. Policemen are very proud, and it's not good to be very quiet and to throw it away.' So I said, 'Fine'.

And I did it, I think to his satisfaction, though God knows you would never tell because immediately after the shot a huge row broke out between Dušan, the cameraman Tomislav Pinter, and Dejan, the first assistant director. And the row raged here there and everywhere and so far as I know continues even at this moment of speaking – that is to say midnight. But my little discussion with Dušan was a significant one. There are twenty different ways you can play almost any scene, depending on what emphasis you want to give it, what the most interesting choice is, and so on. Not for Dušan. He, like Milos before him, assumed that there was one kind of obvious way, and he couldn't really understand why I wasn't playing it that way. The irony is that the scripts of both Milos and Dušan are often (not *Amadeus*, as it happens, but elsewhere) so slight as texts that there is almost nothing you can derive from them. They are scrappy pieces of dialogue that can and should be used in whatever way one chooses. However, it's all perfectly pleasant with Dušan. There's no unpleasantness about it at all; he doesn't roar with disbelief and accuse you of emotional dishonesty when you don't do it exactly as he imagined, as is the case with Milos. He's just baffled.

During the row, Fred and I withdrew and sat in a caravan. We stayed there for three and a half hours before being told that we were free. On the journey back, we had a gloomy discussion about how nothing seems to be happening from within, nothing seems to be flowing spontaneously from us at all. I said that one has the feeling that every time one's been instructed on a scene, done a scene, played a scene to Dušan's satisfaction, one has just contributed another bit of mosaic without knowing how it will be used. There's no sense of the continuing life of a character. Maybe that's simply job satisfaction, and why should one feel entitled to that?

Supper. Lindsay, Fred and I went out with the Yugoslavian actors: Tanya, Radej and Svetozar, the star of *Montenegro*, who's playing Rudy in our film. They all come from different parts of the country, and each belongs to a different theatre company. Sveto speaks English very well, Tanya less well, and Rade least of all; but this grizzled handsome man with his blue eyes and bass voice and explosive movements conveys more with his handful of words than the others with their careful syntax and good vocabularies. (One's shame, as usual, at knowing nothing of the local language. Not quite nothing actually: I do recall two phrases from the 1977 tour: 'Pušenje zabranjeno' – no smoking; and 'neme probleme' – theoretically meaning no problem, but actually signifying that nothing at all will happen.) Despite verbal problems, there is a definite *esprit de corps*: what is it that all actors everywhere have in common? Ego? Exhibitionism? Well yes, I suppose so. But even more central to the actor's being is an attitude to events, to people, to social life. We're always looking at behaviour and seeking to analyse it, capture it for future use. Most actors' stories, apart from simply being funny or effective, contain some view of human nature, which our art preserves. Or can, if it's allowed to. Shakespeare's claims for us are very high, but it is true, an actor's life is a long-term project to record the reality of human life in living flesh. We sat here in Bled and exchanged, in fractured speech, fragments of experience, poring over them like archaeologists sharing their finds.

We also, of course, told jokes and boasted about our work: past performances, past productions. The three Yugoslavs have all worked together at one time or another. Both the men are very big stars in their respective companies. Svetozar, tall and blond, is ascetic in appearance, a Slavonic archangel. He doesn't drink. Rade, who does, who drinks, in fact, for Yugoslavia, says, with rough humour, 'Sveto's a good actor, a very good actor, but I can't love him because he never gets drunk.' He takes me to his heart, though, as I match him, glass for glass, bottle for bottle, brandy balloon for brandy balloon. Rade's most famous role is Titus Andronicus. Apparently, the others tell me, he made his first entrance on a motor-bike, riding it round a Wall of Death. It all sounds very Michael Bogdanov to me, but I'd travel far to see this theatre warrior in action.

We English actors, feeling rather tame by now, talked about the film, expressing our dissatisfaction. Interesting theories were advanced. Rade's theory was that Dušan is preoccupied with technical matters to the point where he's temporarily forgotten about the actors. He's apparently very worried about the cameraman's work, the frame is far too clean, it's far too classical, he wants odd random things in it, he wants a dirty frame. Tomislav Pinter is a highly formal cameraman. Svetozar said no, that was exactly what Dušan had said on *Montenegro* (also shot by Pinter). The real problem is that Dušan likes one's work but sees no need to say anything. Then Sveto told a little story about how, after the first day of shooting between Fred and me, Dušan had said 'God, I like it so much I don't know what to say. I daren't tell the actors I like it so much so I don't just know what to say.' 'What is Dušan's background with actors?' I wanted to know. Sveto said, which came as a surprise to me and even to Rade, that Dušan started in the theatre, graduated as a theatre director, even acted in the theatre, but all his productions were banned by the government so he never actually brought anything in front of an audience on stage. Then he turned to making documentary films. Fred pointed out that as the whole film is being made by Serbo-Croats in Serbo-Croat, except for us the actors speaking English dialogue, we never pick up, overhear, those stray bits and pieces of conversation which might enlighten us. Tanya, who was also very unhappy, had eaten a banana split to cheer herself up (a sylph of an ex-dancer, with a dancer's permanently wide open eyes, really a great beauty). She was quite cheered up by the fact that we were all in such trouble. I said that basically I found the man delightful and exciting, and I loved his movies (compliment here to Sveto, whose physical transformation in *Montenegro*, I now realise, was astonishing, from the grave iconic figure sitting opposite me to the swarthy, muscular peasant of the film). However, everything that Dušan had said to me suggested that we would work in a mood of playful collaboration, trying all the while to delight him, but at the moment there's no sense whatever of him being delighted, there's no sense of reaction at all. It is as if he were playing roulette: sometimes it worked out well, sometimes it worked out badly, but you obviously didn't say anything to the roulette wheel or to the ball.

Our new friends listened politely and with interest, slightly baffled. They obviously don't quite follow. Perhaps they're attributing this to some problem of translation. Even I, I must admit, am beginning to wonder about what it is I'm trying to say; but Lindsay and Fred know what I mean. We don't seem to be involved in any active way in the making of the film. As we walked back, down the sloping path that leads to the lake, through sleeping Bled, and back to the hotel, Fred mentioned something Dušan had said to him yesterday: 'There was a fantastic moment, a stunning moment when you were on the boat and the boat was swaying and you nearly fell into the water and fifty people held their breath and it was incredible.' I said to Fred that I could now define Dušan's ideal actor: a very interesting person to whom happy accidents occurred in front of the camera.

7 October 87

The idea was to do the scene in the square in Škofja Loka in which Rudi Kugelhof, the teacher, played by Sveto, is arrested. That was to be the only scene, because we had apparently dropped a scene from yesterday completely. So we were up at 7.00, not monstrously early at all, and were to start in the square immediately.

It was raining quite heavily, and there was mist. Lindsay was already there when we arrived. She had been got up by mistake at 5.30 in the morning and had therefore been there for an hour and a half by the time we arrived. She desperately wants to get back to England tomorrow for a break. She eyed the rain with dread, because it meant maybe we wouldn't shoot the scene after all. I asked Sasha what we would do, and she said she couldn't possibly say because no one from the production team was there yet, and in fact it wasn't until an inexplicable 9.00 that anyone from the unit arrived on the set (Škofja Loka is only forty minutes away from Bled). I was made up, and my hair was done and all the rest of it, but half the cast weren't there so there was absolutely no possibility of us really working until 10.00 at the utter earliest. Lindsay and I repaired to the communal caravan (we don't have individual dressing rooms). Fred turned up after a while, and we sat there and talked, and I read and so on, until 11.30 when it was decided that they would try to slip in a scene with Camilla. I knew that would take until lunch so I went up to the museum, in make-up, but not in costume, and looked at the pictures. It's a rather wretched museum, a dozen or so poor

Renaissance paintings, some by the not-so-masterful Master of Škofja Loka, local copies, I'd guess, of paintings in the Cathedral at Ljubljana, and a few more interesting nineteenth and twentieth-century canvases, the latter including a very personal series, dream-like fantasies of some power, again, presumably by a local artist. There are needless to say no postcards of his work, and no catalogue to speak of. Photography is forbidden, so I shan't, I'm afraid, be the one to carry news of his talent to the outside world. Elsewhere in the museum, an exhibition of Škofja Loka in the war. Usual scenes of suffering and misery, with, as always, in the midst of it all, someone laughing, oblivious – in love, perhaps, or just finished making a good chair.

I descended again to the caravan area, a parking lot at the foot of the castle, just a few minutes away from the square. There's the make-up van, the catering van, our caravan, and a large tent which serves as a dining room. The make-up van has very quickly become a haven. Mary Hillman calmly presides over it with Jeanette, who *can* be severe, but is also very witty and addicted to good black coffee, supplies of which she has brought from London; from Fortnum and Mason, to be precise. Coffee matters a great deal to her. On her last day off she and Mary went to Trieste to get some decent espresso. Trieste! Visions of James Joyce and the last days of the Austro-Hungarian Empire loom up. It's a mere two hours drive away. For that matter, Budapest – for which you can catch a train from the tiny station in Bled – is no more than half a day's journey. Yugoslavia seems to be round the corner from most of Europe.

The man with the beard who made coffee for me on the first day turns out to be her boyfriend, Doug, and he ensures that the machine is kept constantly and cosily brewing. The make-up van is, in fact, home from home, which is the way it always is on a film set. The make-up artists are the people with whom one has the most intimate and, hour for hour, the longest contact on the film. One spends more time in front of the make-up mirror than in front of the cameras. Rising before dawn, the actors and the make-up team generally travel on the same bus in the same state of dumb vacancy. We slowly come to life together, in front of the mirror. They tend and shape our features. Our faces are their canvas, their poem, their song. They are also their bread and butter. The make-up chair, like the hairdresser's, is a great releaser of secrets and innermost thoughts. If anyone wanted to know what was really going on on the film, this is the van they should bug.

Boris, the exotically epicene Yugoslavian make-up assistant, has got hold of a copy of my book, *Being an Actor*. His English is excellent, and one has intense conversations with him in which little is stated, much implied. His make-up has been getting thicker, his pants hotter. He is given to sudden throaty laughter accompanied by meaning glances. I think I know what the glances mean, but I'm pretending not to.

Outside, there is the catering van, which fuels the whole operation. At meal-times, they are besieged. It is interesting to note that there are always some members of the crew who have a sixth sense about when the meal-breaks are going to occur. These clairvoyant diners appear nonchalantly ahead of the stampede to secure the most succulent pickings. Actors – the leading actors, at any rate – the director, and the cameraman, are brought their meals by assistant directors, which is very nice. I prefer to eat only salads and cheese, and thus never form very warm relations with the caterers, who feel subtly criticised. I'm very happy with the food here: there's an abundance of fresh fruit and an array of cheeses, though none, as yet, from the Isle of Pag. We don't eat in the tarpaulin refectory; we have our own caravan.

The one here is not quite like the normal caravan. The favourite kind is called Winnebago (after a Red Indian tribe. Why?) It contains a lavatory, a shower, and a bed. None of these is to be found in ours, which is basically a white box on wheels. There is, at the back, a raised section where there's a sink, and at the other end, an arras behind which one changes. Marit has extended her responsibilities. Not merely content with making herself look beautiful, and us look interesting, she has decided to make the caravan look like somewhere, rather than nowhere in particular. Potted plants, flowers, magazines, drapes have arrived; a cassette player is promised. Despite all this, the mood in the caravan today between Lindsay, Fred and me is heavy, insane. At about 2.30 or 3.00 Lindsay was told that the rain was persisting, and they wouldn't after all be able to do her scene. She made a joke of it but clearly was heartbroken because it probably won't be until Friday that she gets back to London. She has it actually specified in her contract that she must have two breaks in the course of filming, having come to the film more or less direct from two years of *Les Liaisons Dangereuses* on two continents. What she needs now is a holiday, a long one. While she was in New York, I sent her the script of *Shirley Valentine*, which I was to direct in London. It was not what one might call type-casting, but I'd known Lindsay for many years, and I knew that underneath the peaches and cream of her aristocratic complexion lurked a varied and surprising past. In this particular instance, I was thinking of the year she'd spent as the conductor of a bus in Bristol. She was tempted by the glorious text but turned it down, partly because she thought it would just be too much of a stretch of the imagination for the public, but mainly because she was *tired, tired, tired*. And she still is.

We had made a lark of our lunch, got some pineapple and cream buns and potato crisps. But then we hit a slump. It's the sitting around. I finished *Chatterton*. I couldn't quite face starting another novel immediately. I couldn't look at any more of the town. I couldn't tell another story. I couldn't take another photograph of Fred from a funny angle. It's just impossible.

Anyway, after Lindsay went back to the hotel, it was now 3.30. Finally we got the message that we would do the scene in the post office. Fred, Tanya playing Olympia, Eric playing Christopher, and me. It was a scene for 'weather cover', a standby scene for when the weather makes the scheduled scene impossible to shoot. We got made up. But now we had a crisis with the lavatory. The lavatory in the make-up bus, the only functioning one on the set, had broken down. There was no lavatory one could use, and Fred had thrown a little wobbly, which had been overheard by Dušan, who admired it very much and promised he would do something about sorting out a lavatory.

After about half an hour he came into the dressing room. There was Fred, Eric and me. He sat down and made a little speech about how the Yugoslavian film company, Jadran Films, which is providing all the facilities and a number of the personnel for the film, had made lots of successful co-productions, but until now it had always been the parent company from whichever country that had provided the entire staff. The Yugoslavs had been merely people who sharpened pencils, but they had been given names like Unit Manager, Production Manager, Production Co-ordinator, and frankly they weren't up to the job at all, and it was utter chaos and it was dreadful and he was ashamed and embarrassed. Now, though, he thought he finally had the problem cracked because at least he'd defined it, and he was so deliriously happy with his cast, he couldn't have a better cast, except – he said, with typical openness in front of Eric who is particularly fond of her, although Dušan may not know that, though I shouldn't think there's much he doesn't know – for Camilla. The only person in the cast who was not exactly an actor was Camilla. She was so exciting to watch on screen, so fascinating, so interesting. She was, however, completely uneducated as an actress and knew nothing, and he had to be very careful about which part of her anatomy to put the focus on in any scene she was involved in. But as for the rest of us we were, he said, ten Cadillacs who had been forced to ride over a bumpy road and the road must now be cleared up. He said, 'The only problem I have is a slight problem with the accent.' He said to me that somehow, with my character being so comic, it did sort of work, but he was still slightly worried about Eric's accent. It remained something that he thought might stand in the way of the film. But essentially he had no problems. He was very happy, if only everybody would use the accent the way Fred was using it. To his ear (though he admitted that being Yugoslav he couldn't really hear subtleties of the English language very well) Fred had more or less no accent (which is quite absurd because Fred is using a distinctly foreign accent. I remembered a day during the shooting of *Amadeus* when Milos and Peter Shaffer descended on me simultaneously from different sides, Milos saying' 'Isn't your accent too English?' and Peter saying, 'Your accent is so American!'). 'But anyway,' he said, 'anyway let's go. Now we can shoot the scene in the post office.'

The scene in the post office is just a three-minute scene, but the set-up took hours and hours and hours. It was pouring with rain which was a problem, even for this scene which is supposed to be weather cover, partly because the different levels of rain made a different showing on the camera lens but most particularly because the sound was heavily affected. Anyway we sat in a little street in Skofja Loka for many a long hour, attended with fascination by the local populace, some of whom were actually involved in the shot, and thus in costume. Finally I got to rehearse my bit, the second half of the scene, which we did for camera movements. I was a little troubled by the way Eric Stoltz was playing the scene with me. He was, in effect, ignoring me, dismissing me. Not me, but Hunt. And in so doing, he was destroying my power, Hunt's power. Dušan gave a little note to Fred, a tiny note to Tanya, and then said this to me, 'Now, for me Hunt is still far, far too strong. I don't understand why he is so strong. Is he too vocally loud? The whole thing is too much and too comic.'

I said, with a little irritation, 'I don't give a fuck about comedy in this part. I'm not in the least bit interested in making anyone laugh. I just want to try to play the scene in the way in which you want it to be played. That's why I'm here. That's what I want to do. So let's try it another way.'

He said, 'Well, it's much better if it's a bit sinister, that's what gives it such a marvellous quality.'

I said, 'I am sorry. Maybe this isn't the moment' (there was terrific pressure on him; there are all the cameras; the crew waiting; time is money, all of that pressure) 'but we have got to sort out certain fundamental things about this character. Now, he is the Chief of Police, for example. He is the most important and most powerful person in the town. How can it be that this young postmaster simply ignores him?' As Christopher was turning his back on me, brushing me aside, I said to Eric, 'you cannot completely undermine me. If you regard me with complete indifference then I become a totally unimportant person.'

Now this is very tricky territory. Every character (this is as true of plays as it is of films) is defined by the other characters' relationship to him. It's a tired old truism that it isn't the actor who plays the king that makes the audience think that he's a king; it's the way all the others treat him that does it. We must then have some consensus among the actors as to their relative status. The person whose job it is to produce that consensus is the director. It's very difficult when the actors have to do it among themselves. I was very conscious of treading on Eric's toes – though he bore no signs of resentment. I sounded, as I spoke, distressingly like the American actress who shall be nameless (Kate Jackson) who, at the end of each rehearsal of the scene we were playing together summoned the director over and murmured her notes, which he then conveyed to me. 'It would help me very much if . . .' Finally she tired of this procedure and got rid of the middle man. 'For Christ's sake,' she exploded, 'will you just look me in the eyes.' I was playing a man on the run from the C.I.A., frightened for his life. But she wanted the eye contact so she could pop her pretty little eyes during her close-up. Now was I behaving the same? I certainly wanted Eric to look at me. I said to Dušan: 'I hate to talk about another actor's performance, and I even more hate to ask you to adjust another actor's performance, but the truth is that if you want to see Hunt a strong, clear, simple Chief of Police, a lot of that depends on the relationship he has with other people.

127

They will create that for him. Now, with Eric, if I say to him, 'Christopher, my young friend, I want a word with you', and he turns his back on me then I'm completely destroyed. I'm either not the Chief of Police or else I'm a totally ineffectual one. Unless I turn him round and bang his head against the desk, which might be a possibility, I'll never recover my authority. It depends on him as well.' Dušan said to Eric, 'Yes, yes, yes. That's absolutely true, that's right. You must relate to him. You must also like him, even though you don't like what he stands for.' So in other words we went through some of what we'd been through the last time Eric and I worked together, a couple of days ago.

I continued relentlessly with my attempt to nail Hunt down. 'We have to say, don't we, that he's stupid.' Dušan replied, 'Ah, perhaps he is stupid, but maybe I want to love him because he's stupid, and I don't want you to be telling me that he's stupid.' That's a very important thing for him to say. It's what one needs to hear. It is a trap you can fall into very easily: patronising, judging the character. He said to me, 'You being intelligent perhaps despise this man, but I don't want you to despise him. I want to be able to love him, I want to love him for his stupidity, I want to love him for his eagerness and so on'. I said, 'OK, let's try it again'.

I tried it again and he said, 'The last line was very, very good. I would like the whole scene to be played at the level of the last line.' So, completely artificially, I tried to do it at the level of the last line after which he said, 'Well, it was a little better but I'm not happy. I'm still not happy, I must say. But maybe it'll be all right. I wasn't happy about what you did the other two days but when I saw the rushes I was much less unhappy than I thought I would be.'

I said, 'Well, that's really marvellous. As long as you were less unhappy. That's so encouraging.' I tried to control my sarcasm. 'Please let me tell you how I see this man. I see him as an intensely emotional man, a man who has a longing to serve the king, to serve Avanti, to do well. And he is so emotional that it stops him from thinking clearly, so he has these brilliant ideas, as it seems to him. He becomes incredibly excited about them, but he doesn't think them through, so it only takes somebody very simple like the postmaster to spoil them. He thinks "I'll go to this boy. I'll say to him, 'I'm a great friend of Rudy Kugelhov's, and I'm going to take some letters to him. Would you please give them to me first.'" And it never crosses his mind that his ploy might not work.' Now it must be said that this is intolerable behaviour on a film set. Nobody has time for this. The acting is something that is expected just to be there, anyway. You're not supposed to rehearse on the set. But I didn't care.

Dušan stopped me in mid-flow, and said, triumphantly, 'Ah. Now, when you just did that, when you just told me about the scene, that was it. That was perfect. That was the character.' So I said, 'OK. Let's do it. Let's do it now. Let me just do it.' I tried to do it much more directly, I suppose, much more straightforwardly. He said. 'Yes. That's much better. Much better.' I said, 'OK. I'll do it again, immediately.' And he seemed to like it. I said, 'Could I now do it without the accent?' 'Yes, yes, yes,' he said. So I did it without the accent after which he said, 'It has much less pressure in it.' I said, 'Do you want less pressure?' 'Yes, yes, yes,' he said. He seemed to be clutching at things. All that he knew was that he still wasn't really happy, and in his unhappiness he'd veer from one thing to another. Anything that he could cling on to. At one point he said, 'It's really sinister, and that's what's very good.' And then he said, 'It's really touching. That's how it should be. I should be very touched by this man. Very moved by his stupidity. I should love him.' Then he said, 'I think perhaps I should say nothing more to you because I always speak in contradictions. That's all I ever do, speak in contradictions.' At which everybody laughed. But I stuck at it doggedly, anxiously; I was utterly determined to get somewhere with this, because the pain of being bad is just too much to bear. When I did it without the famous Waldheim accent I did it in a London accent, an 'off', lower middle-class accent and of course it came into much, much greater focus. He said, rather surprisingly, 'Ah, yes. That's much more casual. That's the word. Casual. Casual is how this character should be.' I had another stab at the scene. He said, 'He is very powerful. You must remember about the Mafiosi. How quiet they are. Maybe that's how he works, through being very quiet and not even looking at Christopher.'

So: he is sinister, loveable, powerful, stupid, quick, slow. I suddenly felt very stupid and rather tearful, as if I were in a dream and had been set some unsolveable puzzle and wouldn't wake up until I had solved it. It was Alice in Wonderland.

Dušan:
Alice in Wonderland! Thanks for the image! Alice is the sweetest and most sensual depiction of this beautiful confusion called life. Uncertainty does not cancel beauty, it makes it fragile and credible.

Both Eric and Fred came over to commiserate. Fred said, 'By now I would have lost my temper completely. It's incredible. Listen to me, Simon. Don't change a thing, because it's lovely what you're doing, it's absolutely perfect.' But I know it's not lovely. It's not quite right. Perhaps it's quite wrong. I am completely baffled. It all becomes academic at this precise moment, anyway, because, fortunately, there is some insuperable technical problem, and we can't shoot (or perhaps unfortunately, I don't know. Perhaps it would have been nice just to get it onto celluloid once even, so then they could see the rushes and make some sort of decision about it). Anyway we can't shoot.

I don't blame Dušan. He's not being clear, but neither am I. I'm doing something which he doesn't like, and I'm just digging in my heels, not because I believe in what I'm doing, but because it's the only thing I can think of to do. What's fundamentally wrong is that I have no picture of the character in my mind. Any performance of the slightest value that I've ever given has stemmed directly

130

from my giving in to an image firmly lodged in my brain. I don't give my good performances; they give themselves. In that sense people, like Bill Gaskill, who have described me as an inspired amateur, or sometimes as just an amateur, are quite right. I have no technique, alas. Or I have a technique of using images. I seem to be incapable of constructing one in this situation. On *A Room with a View*, I had a very good idea of how Edwardian middle-class people behave, largely derived from my grand-mothers. I had a sense of how Anglican priests comport themselves, from the Oratorian fathers – Catholic converts, actually – who educated me. And above all I had a very strong idea of a man whose whole emotional life resided in his aesthetic sense, a kind of aesthetic sublimation. I knew about that, because that could have been me. In *The Good Father* I knew about barristers (as a child, I wanted to be one). I knew about yuppies. I knew about those terrifying young stockbroking sharks who work out in my gym. Whereas with Hunt, if I really think about it, I have no point of reference. Finally, I don't know him. He's not a policeman in the professional sense, in any realistic way. It doesn't seem to be written that way. But what way is it written?

The character is attractive and amusing, but I suppose I have seen him as a theatrical stereotype. I am not locating him in anything but a dim memory of certain kinds of performances. This is a script where you can derive nothing from the text in terms of background. You can derive nothing from it in terms of rhythm or energy. It's one of those scripts where the words are something that you can use once you've got everything else. It's a script written by an entirely original and visionary film-maker. His vision we are here to serve. It would be absurd of me to tell him that I know more about the character than he does, but he won't tell me what he knows. And there is no 'ur-text' to which to refer, no original source to discover. Three of the films I've been in are derived from novels, the fourth from a play in turn based on real people. The slightest descriptive phrase in a novel can open up casements on the character; and if it's based on a real person, a character often falls into place when you discover a detail in a biography, an incident omitted from the screenplay. But it's impossible to research a character that has sprung straight from its creator's mind. I am actually going from minute to minute and from second to second hoping that I'll meet someone who *is* Hunt, which is absurdly against the odds. Having this operetta accent has compounded the problem. It makes me give an operetta performance. Dušan is terrified of the operetta dimension in the film. He wants to avoid it totally. He must cut against it with what he calls reality. I understand his problem, but understanding it is no help to me. I am completely at sea. So it was, I suppose, ultimately a relief when they decided at two minutes to eight that there was no further joy at all to be had. We went home.

Dušan:

Out of a dozen characters, Svetlana – with Avanti, Rudi, Christopher and Emile (her four lovers-to-be, all four to be also lovers-to-die) – forms a principal set of conspiratorial activities. Hunt, Otto, leader of the second echelon of characters with his constant mis-reading of the events, succeeds professionally, not in spite of his incompetence, but because of it. While everybody around Svetlana dies happily for a cause, Hunt, Otto, must be credited for keeping it all out of sight. Because of him, the world stays beautiful, uneventful and safe.

What I am stating now about the character of Otto Hunt was, it seems, visible from the script. However, what followed after our first meetings in Wardour Street, on locations in Bled, Škofja Loka and Zagreb, was something more complicated than the simple search for a character. Reading Simon's diary, it is clear to me that I, as director, was stubbornly 'refusing to explain' whatever I was asked to, or I was 'talking about something else', or 'explaining anything but'. It seems as if, to use the same old anecdote about Dustin Hoffman and Laurence Olivier ('Why don't you just act?') that I, as director, refused to ask the actor to act.

Of course, I know what I was waiting for. If I feel a resistance, if the scene does not 'happen by itself', if there is an insecurity and doubt, something is wrong. You can't fix it with words. I expect the actor to find his own ways to 'disappear as an actor', by relating to other actors, or using some prop, whatever. What is important is to get rid of the 'acting'. I know that it sounds contradictory, because we are talking about acting. But we are talking about 'film acting'. What we see on the screen is 144,000 still photographs for a film show a hundred minutes long. These 144,000 still photographs will last on the screen fifty minutes. For another fifty minutes the public sits in a total darkness, filling in the movement, emotions, thoughts, drama. There are no actors on the screen, only pictures. Of course, the Anglo-Saxon tradition that calls a film a 'photoplay' has tried for the last hundred years to treat 'film' as pure technology, as a registering system. There is the play in front of the camera mechanically registered. The Screen is understood as a window through which you are watching the 'play'. In the film the actor has to, in front of the camera, disappear as actor, get caught on film in a still photograph (series of still photographs) to 'reappear' as an actor when the film gets projected on the screen. What is projected on the screen is not what was shot on the set. What are the several months of 'editing' for? From the wider selection of say ten or twenty to one, each piece is measured against others, plus sound and melodies, tempo and rhythm. Director and editor produce a certain amount of 'acting' for each actor, if not much more, than what was done on the set during the actual shoot. Selecting and improving what was originally done is only part of editing. So often it is changing the meaning of what was done, or using pieces in places that they were not intended for at all.

So far then, I have actually shot on two days. Both of the days have been a complete waste of time, which is unfortunate, since they show the beginning of my character and the end of my character. Somehow I have got to sort out the bit in between, otherwise I will have wasted my time and wasted Dušan's time. I want to work with this man. I want to do something new for him, to work in a new way. But apparently it's impossible. If this were a play in rehearsal, however short the period, even if it was two weeks (more likely it would be three), we would have had time to explore all of these questions, test all of these things out. On a movie set you are expected simply to come up with everything. It's incredibly good luck if you happen to get a script which you understand perfectly. I don't understand this one at all. I thought I did, but I don't. As I would have said to Dušan in the letter that I never wrote, 'This is the only time the script *For a Night of Love* is ever going to be made. It is the only time Otto Hunt the character is ever going to exist. We must get it right.' So what I shall do is to go through the whole script again and again, trying to discover something that can play me instead of my playing it. And it must be something deep in the heart of the character. Dušan lightly says things like, 'You represent order and control', and all the rest of it. And at the point where I bump into Tanya, 'Of course you are Mr Macho.' This is not at all how I had seen it. I had seen a sweating, hopeless, trying-to-keep-up kind of figure. But to Dušan every possibility seems equally legitimate as long as he believes in it at that moment. That produces a kind of unbridled liberty. It opens up a range of choice that is ultimately oppressive. But I must crack it, otherwise I am going to have such misery. And Hunt is a wonderful character. Somehow, in my bones, I know that, even though I can't play him. He has such a wonderful line through the film. I don't know. I really don't know. And then of course one is so tired one can hardly think at all.

Jill Gascoyne, Fred's wife has arrived in Bled for a couple of days, to his great joy, and they give a little dinner party for Lindsay and myself, and once again we are suddenly back in England for an evening; certainly Fred, a master chef, cooks as though he were at home. Jill laughs at our stories about the film, and that puts things into some sort of perspective.

8 October 1987

The day started early at 7.00 and, having failed to read the script as I had wanted to the night before because it was too late, I read it all the way on the bus, twice, and still failed to find any real substance in it. I hoped to find that somehow I had overlooked something in the stage direction, or that somewhere in that script some clue was screaming at me. But I never found it.

Made up. Then went in to meet Lindsay who was also fully made up. She is not a happy woman. She talks about the Broadway run of *Les Liaisons Dangereuses*, which had left her drained as only a long run of a play can, brain cells blown out from the increasingly desperate attempt to find meaning in words repeated in exactly the same order, to exactly the same person, on exactly the same spot, eight times a week. And she's been doing this on and off for two years, at Stratford, in London (twice), and now on Broadway. What she needs is not so much a rest as a fortnight of continuous sleep, followed by three months in Barbados doing nothing, and then, and only then, the leading part in a witty and glamorous comedy shot in the South of France. What she needs least of all is to play the increasingly crazed and bedraggled revolutionary school-teacher, Lily Sacher, in *For a Night of Love*, shooting in provincial Yugoslavia (Bled, Split and Ohrid, the three loveliest resorts in Yugoslavia). But the part spoke to her, and here she is. For her first scene, on the train, the one Dušan and Bojana had so loved, she had had her face covered in grime from the funnel of the train; now she's in her plain-jane ordinary Lily Sacher make-up. The face's beauty is impossible to suppress completely, but they've had a very good try. Straight brown hair, no make-up at all, flatties and a slack blue dress do not spell glamour. Lindsay is gazing at her features with active dislike, but more than that, bewilderment, as if the Marquise de Whatever in *Liaisons* had been hijacked, stripped of her cosmetics and accoutrements and imprisoned in a caravan, waiting on her cruel captors' pleasure. In fact, she is just desperately willing her scene to be finished before we lose the light.

What happened was that though it was raining in Bled it was sunny in Škofja Loka. (Sounds like a Harold Arlen number.) I immediately predicted that the sun would prove as much of a problem today as the rain had proved yesterday, and so it did. But not before we got in a quick shot of Hunt and his agents peering behind the monument – that was the wide shot at the arrival of Svetlana. Then there was a long pause. Fred arrived. We sat in the dressing room telling tales of past glories, past laughter. We talked about the kind of actors we were, Fred not knowing exactly who he was as an actor, thinking of himself as a comic actor in the disparaging sense ('clever little comic actor'). Me saying that this film could change his view of himself and perhaps the whole world's view of him: in this film he cuts a very elegant and attractive figure, amusing but not comic. He wasn't sure.

What about me? How did I see myself? What parts did I want to play? I couldn't think of much, because, as I told him, I've been in crisis about my acting for some time, ever since, in fact, *Kiss of the Spider Woman* at the Bush Theatre a couple of years ago, which was as near to perfection as I ever expect to get. That is to say, not only did I think it was accomplished, but in playing the character I had drawn on things in myself which enabled me to interpret and not merely play him. I was able to bring my understanding of the world to the part and say something about the forms that love takes, and about the power of art – the only two things in my life that have mattered a whit. Now, odd though it may seem, this was something of a breakthrough for me. When it happened,

I realised that my lust for performance had died. I no longer wanted to act for the sheer exhilaration of it, but because I could say something about a specific individual, his nature and how the world had shaped him. I think what has happened is this: when I started acting, or to put it more precisely, when I discovered acting, it gave me a wonderful opportunity to go behind the mask that I had forged for myself as a means of surviving socially and exercise all the other possibilities within myself that I had rejected. As time went on, the mask – which I still retained, naturally, when I wasn't up on stage – had become me, had gone deeper. Now I really am me; before I was merely posing as me. Now, I wanted to show something of what was inside.

In the nature of things, there are few parts to which one can bring that kind of insight. Most actors have only a certain number of such performances in them; perhaps it is a definition of great actors that they have more such performances in them than most of us. Perhaps that's true of any sphere of artistic endeavour: most writers can expect only to write a handful of really good books; most painters will only paint a few good paintings. Of course, you can never be sure which one it will be, and it may be that twenty years will separate two exceptional pieces of work. In the interim one has simply to keep forging away, so that when the moment arrives, one is ready. In the matter of my acting, however, I agreed with Orson Welles when he said that there was no point in making a film which wasn't going to be a great one. There was no point in giving a performance which would not be a great one – and by that I didn't mean one that was greatly admired, but one that I had filled with specific truth. Part of this feeling stems from my close study of one of the greatest actors of the century (Laughton) but it's been lurking for a long time. The exact moment of revelation occurred when I was playing the role of Richard III on the BBC's World Service. It was a part I had longed to play from the time, aged eight, that I had seen Olivier's film. When I finally came to it, I found that I had nothing whatever to say about deformed psychopathic regicides.

I could not muster an ounce of relish in the role; and without relish, there was no point. (The fact that my brilliant contemporary, Antony Sher, was at that very moment eating up the stage of the Barbican in the same part, reinventing bravura acting, underlined my feeling of impotence.) I felt empty and foolish in the face of what should have been a glorious opportunity.

It would be silly not to admit that I feel disappointed by acting, that it has let me down. I pursued it with the abject ardour of a lover, lavishing my entire being on it, but somehow I've never felt that it had loved me back in the same way. Somehow there has always been a disparity between us. It's never quite clicked. The earth has moved, to be sure, but never quite how I imagined it would. But now, with *Kiss of the Spider Woman*, having known true bliss, I won't settle for anything less.

Well, said Fred, if I wasn't going to be acting – an idea which he had some difficulty getting hold of, in view of my hitherto nakedly carnal relationship to it– what was I going to do? I rehearsed the usual things without much conviction, because, feeling something of a failure in my present profession at this precise moment, I felt no real right to do anything else: get this right first, then we'll talk about my ambitions. Oddly, though, the one ambition I mentioned that seemed to be at all feasible, and that really stirred juices in me even as I talked about it, was the desire to direct a movie. The moment I walked on the set of *Amadeus*, I thought: 'there's only one job here,' and I've set my mind to it, not talking to anyone about it, but simply willing it. An indication that something might be stirring now was given when Jerry Epstein sent me the script of *At Freddie's*, asking me to play a certain part, which I refused because of various weaknesses, which I detailed, in the screenplay, and he wrote back and said 'your criticisms are spot on, would you like to direct it?' I would. And I've brought the novel with me to write a new screenplay.

I was called. On the set earlier today Dušan had said to me, 'We'll have to talk later about what we said yesterday, but meanwhile will you do . . .' such and such. He suggested one or two things, which I did. Then when we came to shoot the scene he said, 'Don't do this, don't do the other thing, it's funny.' My blood rose again because he seemed to be obsessed with the idea that I wanted to create comic effects. I wanted to say to him, 'Neither do I want to be funny, nor do I expect ever to laugh again after this.' Fortunately I restrained myself. I don't at all want to hurt Dušan or to be rude to him. It is simply that the frustration continues. Anyway, he said, 'I want to talk to you,' so we went off. He said, 'I love almost everything that you're doing. There are just certain things that I am not happy with. I want to keep everything that is there, just add certain other things. I realised,' he said, 'that of course a lot of the things that you spoke about yesterday, about him being stupid, about him getting things wrong, are to do with his relationship with Avanti. Now, he is one kind of man with Avanti, but with other people he can be somebody else. So with Christopher, he can be stronger, more powerful, mafioso and so on.'

I said, 'But do you realise that you've written virtually every scene of Hunt's so as to start with him being made a fool of? He may not be stupid, he may not think of himself as being stupid, but he certainly is made a fool of and knows that he is made a fool of. We have a word for it in English: "wrong-footed".' 'Wrong-footed,' he said, absolutely thrilled with a new word. 'It means like two left feet, or something?' 'No. It means not being in a state of readiness for action.' He wanted to know the etymology. I improvised wildly, because I don't really know. 'I think it comes from cricket. If you throw the ball when you are on the wrong foot it simply doesn't work. Your body is a complete mess.' 'Ah. Wrong-footed. Very, very good. Yes, OK. Yes I see. Wrong-footed. But then we should see him recover. We must see him actually put the right foot.' Trying to communicate by means of a phrase which neither of the people using it entirely understands was beginning to shed darkness rather than its opposite. 'Well, yes,' I said. 'I can certainly do that.

That's not a problem.'

Somebody came up and said he was needed for filming. He said: 'Use this scene where you distribute the agents about the square to show how efficient you are, that it's only Avanti that undermines you, that makes you appear foolish.' I said, 'I'll be delighted to show that, but please,' he was running off by now, but I had to vouchsafe my great insight, it seemed that it might solve the whole misunderstanding, 'let me say one last thing to you. I am just as keen as you are on showing the contradictions of Hunt, but you can't make contradictions until you've made a statement. There must be some initial statement of the character which reveals Hunt, which is the centre of Hunt. From then on you can go off at any tangent you like. You could just do any fucking thing you like.' 'Oh,' he said, 'very interesting.' And then ran off.

I didn't see him again until I got onto the set. Strange to talk about a town square as a set, though as a matter of fact it is just the sort of thing someone designing a Sigmund Romberg musical might have run up. It's sixteenth century, about the size of a school playground, with a church at the end. It's impossible to say what's real and what's ours. All the signs on the shops have been specially made, of course, and the shops themselves have in some instances been commandeered. A number of local people have become extras and seem perfectly at home in their 1920's costumes, sitting outside the Bierkeller drinking beer, as if this is what they do every day of their lives. I talk to a group of lads who look particularly of the period: their faces, lightly bearded, blue-eyed, belong to another age. It's not the features, it's the expressions, that ring a familiar, distant bell: open, hopeful, young. Faces of genuinely young, young people, such as you see on almost no one of their age in the west. Faces one has seen staring out of a thousand sepia photographs. Peter Shaffer was moved by the extras on *Amadeus* because they were so unlike extras – professional extras, that is. They made no attempt to act, but simply took delight in dressing up and were wholly absorbed in the acting of the principals, reacting to it with complete naturalness. The same is true here. I ask the boys where they're from. Here. And what they do. Students. And what they want to do. Teach. Where? Here. And I am as ever amazed – silently, of course – that everybody in the world doesn't want to get out of wherever they come from. They were very keen on England and the English. One young man had actually had a holiday there. He principally remembered the National Gallery, the discos of Brighton, and rain.

As well as the extras, there are a couple of feature players in smaller roles. Here, for example, is a huge fat man playing the baker. He has a brief exchange with Camilla, preparing for her the traditional loaf with a file in it. This scene isn't due to be shot for a couple of weeks, so I'm not sure what he's doing here,

Dušan:
Simon, it's called continuity.

but he has been standing for some hours outside his (newly converted) baker's shop, covered in flour from head to foot, his hair greased into curls, onto which the flour has settled to give the look of an eighteenth-century perruque. I'm told that this chap is one of the most famous comedians on the Serbo-Croatian stage, but to me he's a baker, seeming to have stood behind that counter, or dawdled at that shop door, all his life.

We did the scene in which Hunt arrests Rudi (Svetozar) at the head of his crocodile of children. While we were waiting, the children were swarming all over me, very sweet. (This, too, I remember from *Amadeus*, where one take was spoiled because one of the kids got over-excited and shouted out to me, 'Simon!', in the middle of the scene.) One maniac of a child hit me and tried to tear off my jacket and pull off the crowns from my coat, seized my hat and did all this with a concentrated intensity of purpose that made me feel that I was a surrogate for someone else – a parent, a teacher, a policeman? Or perhaps he just hated me. The other kids were very sweet, but I liked my assailant best. And so the day trickled to its close as the light ran out. Dušan seemed perfectly pleased with the scene as we had played it. Svetozar and I had sorted a little something out, a little interplay, and Dušan seemed completely pleased with it. That cheered me up quite a lot. I went off to cheer Lindsay up. She had begun to realise that she was not going to get out of the country tomorrow either. I saw a long, distant look of dismay on her face when the assistant director made it clear to her that she wasn't going to shoot today. She went straight to her caravan. I stopped off on the way and popped into a pub and got her a double scotch and thrust it into her hand without a word before we went off – a noble and truly Christian and beautiful gesture.

Flushed with eleemosynary elation, I plucked up the courage to address a few words to a striking young man that has joined the catering team. He's Croatian, very tall, black-bearded, with glinting, fiercely humorous eyes, and a thin, burgundy-coloured mouth that is always sardonically smiling. He would be striking enough as it is, but what makes him horribly compelling is that, clearly visible underneath the beard, and around the edges of his eyes and his mouth, are deep burn scars, which are also in evidence on his arms and his hands. I have wanted to speak to him for some days, but have lacked courage. I make some feeble quip about the catering, to which he responds with a bark of laughter, his eyes flashing. This is more attractive and more frightening than ever, because the tightness of the skin on his face produces an involuntary contortion that is beautiful and painful in equal measure.

I discreetly ask Sasha about this man. Her round face, with its protruding teeth and huge eyes, surrounded by lank hair, seems to fill with emotion. The eyes get bigger, the teeth take an even sharper angle to the face, and the whole physiognomy assumes the look of a tragic mouse. 'I know him very well,' she says, in a thrilling bass-baritone. 'We were at university together. He is a little crazy.' I was not altogether surprised. Insanity has always been an aphrodisiac for me. 'But he is brilliant scientist. He was trying chemical experiment, using new chemicals, when he have his accident. He nearly died. Also, he is political agitator. But very, very intelligent.' I asked his name, but couldn't somehow catch it. I can't even spell it. Nem – something. Not, surely, Nemo. For some reason, I immediately associated him in my mind with Nikola Tesla, the Yugoslavian Faust, inventor in this century of AC/DC current, and melancholy dreamer of many of the most revolutionary departures in electrical physics. A native of Belgrade, he went first to Paris, then to America, where, in partnership with Westinghouse, he made a fortune (a tenth of the size of Westinghouse's, of course). Increasingly eccentric, coprophobic – he always dined alone, wearing a pair of white gloves for fear of contamination – he died in New York. When he died, they discovered a wardrobe full of the white gloves. I'm not entirely sure why I link this eccentric figure with Nemo, but I do.

When we got back, we – Lindsay, Fred and Marit, with Drew and Mark, the sound men – all went out for a meal to the Villa Bled, very imposing, in fact a converted palace which Tito had used as his summer resort. After his death it became a hotel, but certain party high-ups got their eye on it, and it was re-converted into a resort for . . . certain party high-ups. Other party high-ups resented this, and lo, it became a hotel again, which it now is – and very grand, too, ablaze with chandeliers. There are three other diners, and literally a hundred empty tables.

Earlier, at the Krim, Dušan, having come back from rushes, said to me, 'Oh, a very sad face.' I said, 'I do have a sad face but I'm not thinking sad thoughts.' 'Ah, yes,' he said. 'Like my friend. I have a poet friend. He has a most peculiar face. It's not exactly ugly but it's just strangely put together. And he wrote a poem saying, "I'm not sad, I am just ugly".' I said, 'Very good. That's what I'll say in future whenever anybody asks me if I'm sad.' He said, 'You know the rushes were very, very good. We are very pleased with the way everything goes together but we haven't filmed half of what we need to do. But it's just looking splendid.' Of course I was delighted to hear all of this, but as I wasn't actually in any of the rushes, it was somewhat academic information. However, I am genuinely glad that he is very pleased. I hope the film will be wonderful, and I'll be the only blot on it. Oh, *shut up*.

9 October 87

I am not sure whether I remembered from yesterday the extraordinary moment when Dušan had come up to me and said, 'I want to have my photograph taken. Must have my photograph taken with agents and with you.' So we stood, Tom, my chief agent, on one side of him, me on the other, and Tom produced some handcuffs and waved them, and Dušan said, 'Put them on me. Put them on me.' Tom said, 'You mean it?' 'Of course, put them on.' And so he put them on, clicking them shut. Just at that moment, the assistant director said, 'We are about to shoot,' and so Dušan, still attached to Tom, ran over to see the scene. They couldn't find the keys to release him, so he watched the scene still handcuffed. I think this should happen to more directors. The director as convict.

Today there was a very simple scene, the arresting of Rudi. It proceeded without any particular hitch and without any observation whatever. Dušan just said, 'Right. Now we do the next shot.' So then there was a wait of a couple of hours, three, four hours, and I came back and rehearsed a little line to the children of which they now wanted a close-up. The line was, 'School's out, boys, you can go home now.' I said it more or less as I'd said it on the master shot. Dušan came over and said, 'Now we have to see that Hunt is really enjoying his power. He knows what to do. This is efficient Hunt. This is Hunt who is in charge, in command.' So I said, 'Yes. I'd like to be sweating, to be wiping the sweat away at the end of the line.' 'I think sweaty Hunt is something we should keep for scenes with Avanti, yeah? Now you should be nice. I want to show here that he's happy, full of happiness.' I did the scene and without any comment he accepted it and then passed on to the next shot. And I resigned myself to the fact that there is really absolutely nothing I have done as this character that has struck him as being right. By now I am reduced to giving merely mechanical impersonations of the character. Nothing comes at all from within. There's no flow or juice. I have no doubt that it looks as dead on the screen as it feels doing it, because I can't find any through-line, any reality, any sense of life in the man at all.

P.S. to the 9th

The designer, Veljko Despotović a sly, bearded man with a nice line in cravats, told me that he has erected in the middle of the square of Škofja Loka two statues of saints and a statue of a horse and rider, all made from polystyrene. A couple of the local people asked him if he could possibly leave them behind because they improved the square so much.

Back at the hotel, trying to banish the voices of paranoia and despair, I finally start to work on adapting *At Freddie's*. Penelope Fitzgerald is an author new to me, writing about mild, low-key events in such a way as to make them surprising and moving – a Chekhovian gift of finding the universal in the ordinary. It's the precision and originality of her tone that is exhilarating, and that, of course, is the hardest thing to transfer into the film. I say this like a veteran, but of course I know nothing whatever about writing screenplays. I've *read* a few, however, in my time, and many of them were adaptations. I've only volunteered to write this one to find out what kind of film I want to make and, perhaps in the process, learn something about thinking filmically. I'm just writing down everything in the book I think should somehow find its way onto the screen. I'm fascinated by how much the previous screenwriters had omitted, including, it seems to me, the heart and the meaning of the book. I see why: the book is elliptical, fine-grained and lacking in narrative thrust. But the effect of my predecessors' emendations would be to make a film like other films. The Fitzgerald note is absent. So what I'm trying to do is to write the screenplay Penelope would have written had she wanted to tell the story as a film (she didn't, and doesn't. When we met, she expressed herself delighted but surprised that anyone should want to make a film of the book). Doing this forces me to contrast the sense I have here of drawing on something – the novel, a knowledge of the author and her other works, and familiarity with the world depicted – with the continuing obfuscation of work on Dušan's film. Clearly I'm desperate for his approval, which is shaming and embarrassing, but I also want the sense that I'm working on the right lines – that I can get on those lines and bowl down them, instead of having to push the fucking engine (me and the film, of equal inertia) from behind all the time.

I find I'm not concentrating. The debate with Dušan rages in my head. So I write letters. I wrote a long one to Peter Ackroyd, whom I've met a couple of times, to tell him how extraordinary I found *Chatterton*. Generally liked, it had had a rather bad review in *The Times*, of which Ackroyd is of course chief book reviewer. By an odd chance, his generous review of my book about Laughton appeared next to the condemnatory review of his. But even the good reviews of his book, it seemed to me, failed to do it justice: they were right for the wrong reasons, just as the one in *The Times* was wrong for the wrong reasons.

Thinking of the Laughton book, far from bathing me in a golden glow of achievement, sets me brooding all over again, keeping me from *At Freddie's*. The book has had generally excellent notices, much better than those for *Being an Actor*, and the literary editors have given the book to much more interesting reviewers – Peter Hall, John Mortimer, and so on. One review, though, a stinker, has stuck in my mind. I know it by heart, and churn it over again and again. It's by the *Observer*'s excellent theatre critic, Michael Ratcliffe. What upset me so much was its tone, as if he really disliked me personally and loathed my writing: 'Very poorly written indeed . . . hideous neologisms.' He attacks me for using French and Latin phrases, for describing Vivien Leigh's face as having 'the quality of a squeezed rose', for alluding to Gary Cooper's 'ravishing androgyny', and quarrels with my metaphor of Laughton pulling himself off his cross, pulling out the nails, and making 'with faltering steps for real life'. In short, he thinks I can't write, and says so in the tone of an aggrieved Manchester Grammar School dominie. Naturally, he strikes where I am most vulnerable. 'Can't write.' Those are the words that I've dreaded to hear since I first dared to fulfil my deepest, earliest, ambition. Remarkably few people have said them, but of course the ones who do are the ones I believe. Nobody can say, 'Can't act', to me. They can say, 'Act better', or 'Act different', but by now I know that there's a certain level below which I won't slip. But writing . . . I'm learning my craft in public. I took a gamble with the Laughton book. I deliberately chose to write it in a heroic, rhetorical vein. It was intended as a celebration, a glorification. The language was accordingly heightened. As for Ratcliffe's review (and it's doubly wounding in that I've had a most cordial acquaintance with the man for some years), he doesn't prove his case. To take one example: my phrase 'ravishing androgyny'. There is a word androgyny. It can presumably be either positive or negative – someone could be said to be revoltingly androgynous. So why should Gary Cooper, whose blend of masculine and feminine qualities is widely acknowledged, not be held to be ravishingly androgynous? And I refuse to apologise for using foreign expressions. The English language has always used them. They express shades of meaning that can't be caught in existing phrases. I am planning my reply: concise, devastating. I imagine Michael quaking as he reads it. It goes: Caro Michael, Non erat demonstrandum, mon vieux. Simon.

But I don't, of course, send it. I pace, before plucking up the stamina to make a call to England. The Hotel

Krim is becoming as penitential as its name suggests. The food is not good, but one can go elsewhere for that – except for breakfast, which stops being served the moment it starts, and is anyway barely food at all – rubber omelettes, jam like glue and bread the colour of a much-washed handkerchief. All these things are endurable. What is not is the telephone system. Essentially Bled's switchboard is the size, age and efficiency of that of a small village. But Bled is a large town. The result is that it is sometimes necessary to dial the number as much as eight times in a row – only, as often as not, to get a wrong number. But even this is not the worst. It is impossible to make a call in one's room. It must be done from the foyer, standing at the reception desk. Thus highly intimate or confidential conversations have to take place at the top of one's voice – the line is intermittent, voices float in and out of the ether, and anyway, Barbra Streisand is in full flood over the hotel's muzak system.

I had one such conversation tonight. Its contents, to the extent that I could hear them at all, were not pleasing, plunged me, in fact, into dark gloom.

Work on *Freddie's* was intermittent, too.

10 October 1987

After a sleepless night I came onto the set this morning in a surprisingly up frame of mind, knowing that I had a couple of long scenes. That is to say what passes in films for long scenes – each one consisting of a page or two of words. Something to get my teeth into. Within seconds my good humour was destroyed by the fact that not a word of English was uttered at any point during the shooting of the scene. When the scenes were over, one just guessed that they had come to an end. One was merely fitted into the scene; it was never explained why anything was happening. The assistant director walked up to me at the last moment and said, 'Now this is what you do,' and that was that. Admittedly all the guys playing my agents are Yugoslavs but *I'm here too*. I became angrier and colder, rather noticeably, rather disgracefully noticeably so, to the extent that one of the sound men, Mark, came up to me and said, 'Why are you so glum?' and I said, 'Well, it's rather a surprise at this point of my career, after fifteen years of acting, to find that I've become an extra, admittedly a highly paid extra, but an extra nonetheless.' That continued to be the form all morning.

So much for the scene of the arrival of the fire engine. It's a beautiful old war-horse of a fire engine, and its appearance in the little square is startling and will, I imagine, be even more so on film: a dream-like apparition – great big red and brass thing. One wants so much to be part of it, to exploit it. I have done nothing but lend my presence. I'm not looking for 'moments' – simply to be engaged.

Next scene, the pulling down of the statue. I invented a couple of little things. Dušan immediately came up and said, 'No, no, no. That's too much. That's too much.' Then he directed me very closely, giving me for the first time specific movements, precise reactions. Again I knew that every single impulse that I have as the character displeases him. So I am absolutely on to the wrong thing. But he never says what the right thing might be because he simply adjusts details and never gives me a grasp of the whole.

We came, after lunch, to the scene with Wango, the photographer, the character that Chris Haywood plays – the character, in fact, that I might have played. Chris is English, but you'd never guess. He's just flown in from Sydney, and makes Paul Hogan look like a Pom. He's been there for ten or so years and is distinguishable from the real thing only by being rather more so. It is hard to see how England could have contained him. Short, balding, eyes glistening, he is all relish, a man of pleasure. He talks without the slightest inhibition about, and with an assumption of common enthusiasm for, the things he loves (they seem to include most human recreations: sex, art, sport, sex, food, wine, sex – above all sex, of which he speaks with a connoisseur's relish, assessing the erotic merits of this race or that race, this section of the anatomy or that). Life is his hobby. He is rather better cast as the satyriastic Wango than I would have been; is indeed the real thing (but perhaps that will make it harder for him to act it). He also has a deeply romantic streak. He described his courtship of his wife-to-be, who will join him a few days from now. A doctor at the Arctic circle, she arrived back in Sydney from a six-month spell in the snow, to a reception devised by Chris which involved raining roses down onto the deck of her ship from a helicopter, each rose chosen for its ability to shed its petals in mid-air. Their wedding, which he has planned to the last detail, will be celebrated in a chapel atop a cliff near Sydney Harbour which faces due West. When the sun hits the horizon, the chapel will be flooded with its rays, at which moment the boys' choir will burst into song with a little-known anthem of Britten's. This is the science of pleasure, of which he appears to be the professor.

He's worked with Dušan before, and gives him a very good press. One can see that he is someone who might have a special gift for having happy accidents in front of the camera. We started to play the scene where Wango accidentally happens on Hunt and his agents trying to tear down the statue of the previous king. Immediately Dušan gave me some contradictory notes. First he said, 'Now. This is a scene of great pressure, so you should play it casually,' then gave a line-reading, something he *never* does. An agent (tall Tom, in fact) says, 'What shall we do with the hole in the horse?' – they've just blown it up – and Hunt says, 'Fill it with flowers.' I elected to play it poetically, a sudden poetic inspiration. And Dušan said, 'No. I don't think so. You should just say it casually, lightly. Nothing more, old boy.' So I sighed with vexation (a noise which, I'm sorry to say, I make increasingly as the years go on, and one which, I'm even more sorry to say, I realise I get from my mother). He said, 'You don't agree with me?' Relations between us are sort of baffled on both sides. His enormous warmth and goodwill towards me seem to have dried up, but that's probably because my enormous goodwill and enthusiasm towards him have dried up. So we are just two rather unhappy people yoked together at the moment. He said again, 'You don't agree with me?'

I said, 'He can be whatever you want him to be.' I started to lose my temper. I said, 'Each line can be said in twenty different ways but only you can tell us what the correct one is. Nothing is correct, or everything is correct: only you can tell us which is the inflection that fulfils your vision. You wrote it, it's in order to fulfil your vision that we are here, that's all.'

Dušan:
When I read a script, even if written by myself, I try to read it as if written by someone else. I laughed at Hunt's lines, but couldn't get rid of the bad feeling that Hunt is

written as a second rate clone of Avanti, too cabaret. I made him as he was because I do not like this kind of person. I got him, in a previous draft, to enter the scene and meet Avanti the second after he stepped in dogshit with his impeccably shining shoes. When the author hates the character, the director should help the character fight back and survive. I needed an excellent actor to defend Hunt, explain him and make him alive. Simon Callow, with his 'the sky is the limit' ambitions, and 'nothing is good enough for me' energy, was the right man for the task.

Later in the film, Simon did Hunt exactly as he described his 'man without qualities'. Hunt became a desperate man, unsure of himself, who by hook or by crook, as a caring tyrant, keeps the world from bursting at all seams.

I then explained my intention – the notion of a sudden access of poetic feeling, something which, it seemed to me, was in accord with the contradictions, the element of the unexpected of which we had spoken at the beginning. He said, 'Well, you see, sometimes it is more poetic if you just throw it away. He is a soldier, a military man in uniform, sometimes in the army people do say poetic things, but they just say them and because they just say them, they become more poetic.' I despair because it seems that I could do nothing which was in accord with his notion of the character. Clearly I had no idea. In fact I just began to get angrier and angrier. He said, 'I think Hunt is very, very angry with my influence disturbing him. Play that. Play the whole text with anger.' He didn't need to ask me twice. I gave in completely to my own personal anger and played the scene with great violence. Of course it thrilled Dušan. And indeed the scene did work in a way that nothing else has worked so far – at the price, I would have said, of playing the character a a really heavy policeman. But as a result of playing that way, first of all I had a quite spontaneous physic impulse, which resulted in a gesture of some power; a secondly, I held the look at the end of the scene, whi because of the passion of what preceded it, was filled v

intensity. It sounds very insignificant in the re-telling, but gestures and looks are of the essence of film performances. Dušan saw the power of that single look and left the camera on it for a long time before shouting 'Cut'. It entirely delighted him for the first fucking time, so I have to count the playing of the scene as something of a breakthrough. He said, 'Marvellous. Marvellous. It's fantastic. Beautiful, what you did.'

All the tension which had bedevilled us the last couple of days disappeared. I said, 'This is the first time that I've felt that I've played the character. At last I understand.' 'No, no,' he said. 'The stuff in the station was very, very good. Marvellous. I'm just trying to find layers.' I said, 'Yes, yes. I also want layers. Of course I want layers. But it's clear to me that my idea of the character has been totally different to yours.' 'No, no,' he said again. 'We agree about everything in the character. It is just that you are very judgmental in the way that you play.' I said, 'I saw Hunt, Dušan, as being rather narcissistic and rather trying to boost himself all the time.' And he said, 'Yeah, yeah. I think so too, but what you must do, like always, is to defend your character's narcissism. You must play narcissism, so it is loveable, the most marvellous quality in the world, not ridiculous.' 'But, Dušan,' I said, 'I find ridiculousness rather loveable.' And he put his hand on his head and said, 'Ah, my God. Now we really are in trouble.'

At least, thank God, I've recorded something that has some conviction in it. I think, honestly, all the rest is very poor. But we'll see.

Random P.S. to the night that Lindsay didn't get away. We sat and guzzled caviar madly laughing. It is very cheap and very good, and we ate it, and nothing else, like kids eating custard.

Sunday 11 October

I was on first today. Although I was there at about 8.15 I wasn't needed till 9.30, and it was a question of getting in and out of the fire engine twice. And that was that. So then I went off to think about other things in the hope that I might perhaps be called to do a scene by about 11.00. And I came back and I wasn't. And then it was 1.30 and lunch-time. And still nothing had happened, and they had just set up the scene before the one that I was to do. So I had lunch. And after having had lunch, while we were around the caravans, Dušan said, 'Can I have a word with you?' I said, 'Yes,' and he said, 'Now, what we were talking about the other day, this misunderstanding between us. What I want to say is that in the scene that we are going to do in an hour or so I think that Hunt is perfect. I think he really does his job brilliantly and beautifully. I want to be able to admire him.' He said, 'There was someone (I can't remember his name) who ran a concentration camp. He was faced with a very, very difficult task of getting rid of fifteen hundred people a day, and he made a bonfire with a thousand people on it, and he discovered that if you threw the fat from the people onto the top of the bonfire that you could get another five hundred people into it and burn them. There is a sort of perfection about that which I somehow admire. I think we should see it in Hunt. I understand your conception of Hunt. I think you see that he has a hollow in the middle of him. That's good and I agree with it, but in this scene I would like to see him dealing so brilliantly and so well with the situation that we don't see the hollow. You understand?'

'Sure.' I said. 'That's absolutely fine. I understand exactly what you're saying. There's a little something I'd like to say to you before we shoot. But anyway, go off.' So off he went and as he turned round he said, 'You know, I am very concerned to create new balances and add a little more here and a little less there. They are all difficult things but then what I have to do is to choreograph my confusion.' I said to him, 'The Choreography of Confusion – A Life in Films by Dušan Makavejev.' And he laughed.

As it happens we never got to the scene. The other scene went on for four hours across a number of different shots. There were problems with sound. There were problems with light. There were problems with the camera. Every conceivable problem. And they never got to my scene. So I came back here to the hotel. I went for a long walk up to the station, brooding about the events of my life and sometimes thinking about my screenplay but almost never thinking about the film we're shooting. I went and had a mackerel in the local café and half a litre of wine and got slightly drunk. I came back to the hotel to get some black coffee and some water and to work on the screenplay. Bojana and Veliko, the designer, were sitting at a table and asked me to join them. Then Dušan suddenly turned up and, almost as if we had an appointment, said, 'The thing you wanted to talk about is this.' What I had wanted to tell him was that I understood exactly what he was saying. I wanted to quote to him the Auden poem 'Epitaph for a Tyrant', which starts with the phrase 'Perfection of a sort is what he was after', which seemed to be the essence of Dušan's comments on the concentration camp. But he launched into something quite different.

'There are in our film some wonderful "new style" actors here, Svetozar, Tanya and so on. They all come from Atelier 212. Now the people who founded Atelier 212 were basically all of them Russian-trained. Stanislavski-trained, Eisenstein-trained. They were very interested in gloves, in details, in physical details, glasses and all the rest of it, but only in order to find a whole life to the character. Then when they opened up to the west they started to do plays by Arthur Miller, by Ionesco and so on, and there was a terrific clash of cultures which proved to be very fruitful because they played beautifully, whimsically, madly, politically, radically. They were very avant-garde in technique, they'd suddenly quote, on stage, in the middle of the play, from reports in the local press or something like that. These things that they did, these curious steppings out of the character, were all spontaneous and amusing.

'There are such different approaches from different actors. Stanislavski actors look for the central core, and they play it, and they play strictly within the confines of the reality that they've created. English actors see something outside and call it the character, and they think, "Fine, I understand it, now I shall perform it". Brechtian actors always want to tell you, "Look. It's a play. Now you should think very seriously about the principal point because the miners are struggling, etc". What these guys did was different. They were always engaged in something playful. When they stepped out of the character it was not in order to say, "The real serious point is this or that or the other", but "Isn't art playful? Isn't life playful?" This is something that I love. It's something that I don't completely understand but I love it very much and I think it's what we should be trying for.'

I was very excited by what he said. It was so close to my own position. Here in the restaurant, the stalemate of our work on the film dissolved. We were talking again. I said, 'May I throw in five or six things in reply to what you have said? About English acting, or the understanding of English acting. I believe that one of the great contributions of the English to world culture is nonsense. A great deal of English work, English attitudes, English humour is based on nonsense. Nonsense which is sometimes surreal, sometimes poetic, sometimes fantastic, sometimes just nonsense. But it goes across English culture from Laurence Sterne, to Blake, Lewis Carroll, through Oscar Wilde, N.F. Simpson, Ronald Firbank, Joe Orton', and he put in, 'Right through to Monty Python,' and I said, 'Exactly, the Goons before them, and almost all the music-hall comedians of the past, and many of the present, and it may come from, who knows what, some kind of emotional immaturity, a return to childhood, an evasion of reality, but it is a deep response to the tyranny of logic. It contains a deep anarchy, and a genuine poetry of its own.'

'Yes, yes,' he said, eagerly, thrilled and delighted by all this. I said, 'It's a world view, a distinct way of looking at things, and it's deeply rooted in our traditions, both of writing and of acting. So when I read, "Mr. Hunt, Chief of Police," and I see the comic pitch of the screenplay, I immediately plug into the long tradition of English policemen who are ludicrous, rather touching figures. Sometimes they are also magic figures who do solve the crimes,' (I was thinking of Priestley's *An Inspector Calls*). And he put in, 'By accident', so I said, 'Yes, kind of.' He said, 'Yes. Yes, yes, yes. Yes I see. I see. The theory is beautiful. It's lovely. Yes, yes, yes. We can have this.' 'No, we can't,' I said, 'because the entire cultural background is different. I understand that for you the word "police" means something quite different to what it means to us in England.' And I told him my story about the policeman in Belgrade who, when Joint Stock were doing *The Speakers* there, tried to stop one of the actors from lighting a cigarette. The actor – in character, of course – told the policeman to fuck off, and there was a murmur of the deepest approval from the audience. The actor had said something that everyone had been want-ing to say for a very long time. This is not to say that the police are exactly folk-heroes in England, but, despite a radical transformation in the image of the police over the last twenty, thirty, years, from *Dixon of Dock Green*, shall we say, to *Law and Order*, and beyond, there still remains a strong residual tradition of the policeman as harmless buffoon. 'Now,' I carried on, 'I'm not going to simplify your script and say that it's a parable of the political situation in your country, but there is a certain reality behind it. To me the most important thing that you've said, though I'm ashamed to say that I haven't been able to do anything about it yet as an actor, is that what you missed from the reading Fred gave that day in the hotel in Zagreb was the sense of panic that you experience in the presence of real life. I have only slowly begun to understand that Hunt must be based on the reality that policemen are powerful figures. In any analysis of Hunt if you'd asked me about the character I would never in a million years have used the word "power". Now you've used it I begin to understand much more about him.'

I then explained to him, what I have said many times before, the problem of the way in which every time that Hunt speaks he is put down by the other characters. Nobody ever says, 'My God. Mr Hunt, the Chief of Police,' and jumps to. He is always obliged to assert himself and that immediately makes him weaker, makes him over-assertive. Bojana said, 'Yes, that's a very good point. That's absolutely true. Why didn't you say that before.' I said, 'Well, actually I did mention it before.' 'Yes,' said Dušan, 'he did mention it before, and of course it is one of the faults of the writing, it's bad. But that is one of the tasks of making a film. The actors and the director should club up against the writer and correct his mistakes.'

'Ho, ho,' I said, and told him that when David Hare directs his own work, he uses phrases like, 'I think what the writer intends here is . . .' and that when David Storey, who doesn't direct his own work, is asked a question about one of his lines, he replies, 'How can we tell?' Dušan murmured his approval of this remark. 'But we'll never know,' I said to Dušan, 'unless you tell us. We can't work it out for ourselves. The script doesn't give enough clues. In a play you read the words, the words give you the rhythm, they give you the texture, the sense and all the rest of it. Now here we have something which is fragments of words, and maybe sometimes you use a word with a particular colour, thinking it means something completely different.' 'Yes,' he said. 'Yes. It's a big problem.' 'The same script could be filmed in completely different ways by different film-makers,' I went on. In that sense a screenplay is like an opera libretto. The film-maker, like the composer, decides what value the elements of the verbal text shall have. Mozart chose to sound the depths that Lorenzo da Ponte barely suggested in his libretto for *Così fan tutte*, the music sometimes taking very lightly what seems serious in the text, sometimes underpinning frivolity with a terrible gravity. But imagine if Rossini had set the same libretto! 'We simply won't know unless you tell us,' I said. 'It can be played twenty-three different ways. At least. There is, for instance, one very valid way of making your film in which it is a sort of operetta without music.' 'Yes, yes,' he said. 'Operetta. Operetta.' And he clung on to that. And he agreed and he said, 'You know, I like your acting very much indeed, and I like it because you're really intelligent, thinking all the time, and it's great to have you around. As long as we understand each other.'

'Yes,' I said, 'we do understand each other perfectly, and I want you to be able to say to me at any time, "No that's not right", and not worry about me being temperamental. I want to be your collaborator, you know. That's the idea. But we can't collaborate unless we communicate. That's quite impossible.' Then I led on to the question over which Fred had exploded rather impotently today against the assistant director, Dejan, which was that one simply doesn't know when a scene has ended, one doesn't know what's going on, whether anybody likes it or not because they are all talking Serbo-Croatian.

'It's true,' he said, 'we have this problem that in our language we don't have "please" and we don't have "thank you" used in the same sense in which they are used in English. It's just that those words don't really exist in the same way. There's also a cultural difference here, you know. Americans sometimes seem to me to have been very nice, in fact they've been very rude. English people seem to me to have been very rude, in fact they've been very nice.' Bojana said, 'Yes, but that's not what he's talking about. He's talking about response.' 'Exactly,' I cried. 'The very word. It's not merely approval one wants, it's a response to something that has happened. It wouldn't matter if you came up to us at the end of the scene and said how much you'd liked it in Croatian because at least we would know that something had gone on, that you had seen our work. You know, we actors are in a position, having given a scene, of having had an orgasm, and at the end of it you can't expect us to say to you, "How was it?" You have to say to us, "How was it?".' He seemed to recognise that and said, 'Yes. It's difficult.' 'Of course,' said Bojana, 'he's terribly worried about the camera and the sound and the light and all that which is such a nightmare. It's so difficult. And Škofja Loka is a problem in itself.' I said, 'God, yes. I do understand. But let me *help*. Let us all help. But we must be able to work together on it, though.'

Altogether I hope it was clearer. We seemed to understand each other. But who knows? No doubt tomorrow the next scene will prove yet another thing that I really don't understand. I went back to the example of the flowers, and filling the hole, and I said, 'You see, Dušan, my idea was that it was a moment of absolute poetry, that there is an unexpected side to the man. He has a vision of flowers.' 'Ah,' he said, 'but you didn't really show me that. I didn't see it.' 'No. Of course I do a little bit of a shorthand the first run-through but you know, if we had been rehearsing for two weeks, I would have expanded it.' And as I spoke, I knew I was talking nonsense, self-justifying nonsense. I obviously didn't do it clearly; or more likely I did it much too clearly, so instead of a moment of real poetry, it was a heavy-handed touch of sentimentality. I felt ashamed to be talking like this to this brilliant man, for whom I feel such warmth. I feel my objections are paltry, narrow, literal-minded. I wish I could wind the clock back, and we could go back to that little station and start all over again. Oh well, oh well.

13 October 87

Today is scheduled to be rather a big day. For some reason I was given a call at 7.30 instead of 7.00, which meant I was completely confused, overslept and arrived on the set with, of course, plenty of time. We actually started shooting at about 11.30. It was the scene with Wango (Chris Haywood), and I feel very, very much more comfortable with the character. I have a centre to him, I know what I'm doing. Now things can start to happen of their own accord. We played the scene. It was quite complicated but I was able, at last, to suggest certain things which delighted Dušan. For example, Hunt has to have a look at some photographs of himself which Wango has taken, and the script says he is supposed to flick through them. I suggested to Dušan that Hunt might put them in his hat and then put them on his head and he was absolutely delighted with that idea. We did it and he was even more delighted. There were a lot of adjustments to the scene to try to accommodate the lens. Pinter, the cameraman, was very helpful with suggestions for moving a little bit more here and a little bit more there, and because I now know who I am, I can take any adjustment of any kind, it just doesn't matter. He can say, 'Faster', and I play it twice the speed, or he can say 'Slower', and I halve it. He can say, 'Move here, move there', and all of that is perfectly easy. I know who I am, I have some self-respect, I can get on with it.

At the end of the rehearsal Dušan said, 'It's marvellous. It's great.' We shot it, and it really was very satisfactory. So there is little to report except that there is now in Hunt a sense of power and focus, which by some paradoxical means, looking as I do and given the situations and drift of the text, is both powerful and funny, and this is obviously what Dušan had in mind from the beginning. Well, I have learnt something. It didn't occur to me for a minute that it could be like that. I didn't want it to be like that. When Dušan said to me that I should avoid playing the comic I was angry but of course that is essentially what I was trying to do: play a comic style.

We broke for lunch. After, we did close-ups. The experience of doing a close-up is quite different to that of doing a medium shot or a long shot. You are aware of the camera eating up the pores of your skin, of it recording every flicker. Every intention is exposed. Any self-consciousness or inhibition is immediately revealed. It requires deep relaxation, a relaxed 'thereness'. You absolutely have to be there, at that moment. One becomes terribly, terribly aware of one's eyes, of them being open, of moving strongly and freely about in their sockets. The fact that I can think about this at all, that I sense it, that I am now aware of this technical refinement, is a symptom of the great breakthrough that I have had. Two days ago I couldn't possibly have thought of any of those things. They would have been meaningless. You could have said to me, 'Move your eyes slowly from side to side', and it would have just sat on top of a terrible hollowness. Charles Laughton said the secret of film-acting was to feel it very deeply and then let it dribble out through the eyes – that there's a direct connection between one's guts and one's eyes. There's a flow, which is a real, physical thing, and which the camera records, and now, at last, it's flowing through me.

When the close-ups were over, we were free, Chris and I. I went off for a two-hour walk and came back long before time for the last scene, which they had suddenly decided to do – the scene in the post office, the scene which we had worked on a few days before when it had been pouring with rain and where I had been completely baffled and where Dušan and I had talked and talked and talked and reached no place at all. But now I feel no anxiety whatever about it. Before I went onto the set I spent a little time in the caravan, and Fred told a joke about actors. A psychiatrist wants to investigate the idea that dogs become like their owners, so he assembles a group of dogs, and one is the dog of an architect, another is the dog of a mathematician, and the third is the dog of an actor. The architect's dog is placed in front of a pile of biscuits and bit by bit he pushes them together until they make a little house, and the psychiatrist is delighted. Then the mathematician's dog lays them out and counts the biscuits and woofs the number of biscuits and the psychiatrist is thrilled by that too. Finally the actor's dog is brought on; it eats all the biscuits, fucks the other two dogs and asks for the afternoon off.

That's us, alright.

Went on to the set a little later to find that Fred, who had been called before me, was terribly unhappy. He had had a row with Dušan. Dušan had said one thing, Dejan, the assistant director, had said another, and Fred had confronted Dušan. Who should he listen to? Fred takes it upon himself to some extent to speak for the tribe and to articulate the frustration we all feel over the lack of communication. Yesterday he had made quite a big scene with Dejan, who hadn't indicated to the actors that it was the end of the scene or what the next scene would be. Confronted by Fred, he had accepted, without any great remorse, that it had been his fault. As he had moved away Fred had turned to us and said to Chris and me, referring to his outburst, 'The twenty-five yard sprint, was that? Was that acceptable?' He'd done it quite deliberately. I fear it hadn't made a tremendous impact. Now here he was, very, very unhappy again. He'd received all these conflicting instructions and had raged at Dušan, telling him that communication was needed, and so on. And Dušan apparently had said nothing at all – had just walked away. They had gone on to the second set-up. Fred by now felt that nothing he did mattered, nobody cared, *he* didn't care: he didn't care if it was a good film or a bad film, he didn't care if his was a good performance or a bad performance. He just wanted to go away as soon as possible.

I agreed with everything he said and tried to share in his mood of depression, but it was no good, cheerfulness kept breaking in. I felt very buoyant, I had had my long walk, and I feel I've done some acting which I'm satisfied with. I am elated and jolly and trying very hard to keep that in check so that Fred doesn't feel too angered by the spectacle of my elation. David Hare says of rehearsing a play: there's a kind of wheel of fortune on which some of the actors go sailing up as others glide down. Today I'm up, Fred's down. But it'll be the other way round tomorrow. I went straight into the scene. Eric and I ran through it between ourselves. Dušan passed by and said, 'I thought it was very, very good, very excellent. Perfect,' and clearly thought, 'Now I've got no more worries with Callow', and then went off and gave a note to Eric and a note to Tanya, and rather elaborately avoided Fred. We then played the scene. Dušan made a suggestion. It's the scene with the postman, the scene which has caused so much trouble. I will now play it very light, very quick, quite sinister, quite strong. He asked me if I could just put my arm on Eric's shoulder because that would create a certain feeling between us. I said, 'Absolutely fine.' There was no problem. Honestly he could have asked me to play the scene hanging from the ceiling and whistling dixie, it wouldn't have mattered. I knew what I was doing now and started to make little inventions. How would it be, I asked, if Hunt, saying hello to Christopher, suddenly spotted the portrait of the king and bowed to it as if the king were there himself. And Dušan said, 'Well, of course for him he is.' I said, 'Exactly, exactly'. So we committed it to celluloid, and it seemed satisfactory. He seems very pleased with what I'm doing. I sense that there's a new move to get a lot more work done. Everybody is worried that we are getting very badly behind. So maybe he's being less critical. But no, I think I sense that there was genuine pleasure in what he saw me do. I went back to the caravan, and there were Tanya and Dušan and apparently they had been having a terrible emotional work-out. Tanya was unhappy, Fred was sitting rather quietly in the corner. His unhappiness had been outbid by her greater unhappiness. When Dušan left she turned to Fred and said, 'Forgive me for the great emotion', and Fred said, 'No, no. I'm sorry for interrupting you.' All is not well, but I'm afraid that, for entirely solipsistic reasons, I'm very jolly. I was in a funster mood and cheered people up in a slightly manic way.

When we're all struggling along in this crazed situation, the sound men, Drew and Mark, get a terrible lash from everybody else because they sometimes have to ask us to do the scene again. They never create really big trouble. If they ask for another take, or perhaps for us to wait for an aeroplane to pass overhead, that's absolutely all they ask. In the end it saves everybody a tremendous amount of work; the scene is never as good re-dubbed as it is on the set. How can you re-create what you were feeling in a square in the middle of Slovenia six months later in a studio off Wardour Street? Thank God for their persistence, but it does make them terribly unpopular, which is very unfair, because they are the nicest guys in the world. Scholarly, amusing in an almost academic way, quizzical kind of guys. Both of them are always reading books, and you have a rather wittier joke with them than you can with most people. (It was Drew who pointed out the other day that Bojana, who has been wearing a bright red mac, appears to have been designed by Maurice Sendak, which is brilliantly accurate.) Both are very handsome in different ways, Mark, with straight, silky hair and large grey eyes, is from Minnesota and dreams of fishing. He is given to long solitary treks; Drew Kunin (as in Ba Kunin? I wanted to know) has a noble, Levantine face, swarthy, dark-eyed, with crinkly golden brown hair. He is nominally the boss – though they always work together and seem to have no hierarchy. Drew has a droll image for film-making. It's as if, he says, an entire factory was created in order to produce one Ford car. In this case I'm not absolutely sure whether the car is being produced. I suppose bits and pieces of it are, but I don't know whether the whole thing is coming along terribly well at all.

Dušan is extraordinary, though, in having maintained his good humour despite all kinds of difficulties – like me, for example. He still finds time to pop off and just chat to people. He'll talk to the costume designer, he'll talk to the make-up woman, or an actor or something, and really talk, and really listen until he's called back onto the set by the assistant director. Sometimes he has to be told, as he was today for example, when to say, 'Action'. He has no instincts for command. In a sense one could rather cruelly say that he was an amateur, playing with this teriffic box of toys that he's been given. More kindly, and more accurately, one could say that he was like a scientist interested in an experiment. He certainly isn't like any film-maker that I've ever met. He isn't ruthlessly pursuing his vision, as most of them are. He isn't as goal-directed – not as concerned with the final product somehow, although he is certainly concerned to shape it, to influence it. He obviously trusts Pinter, who has, from what people have said about the rushes, worked out some wonderful angles and compositions. What, finally, is the director's degree of authorship? Pinter has obviously devised a great deal of the look of the film personally, there and then. It's fascinating the degree to which he allows him actually to devise what he calls the choreography. It doesn't worry Dušan at all. He has no sense of pride, false or otherwise, about these things.

There's a chap on the crew with a hearing aid, a very nice man, very sweet guy, whose life's work it is to give me a chair to sit on. As it happens I prefer to stand when I'm watching the film being made, but I have no idea how to communicate this preference to him. First of all I don't speak Slovenian, secondly he's so deaf even if I did speak Slovenian he probably wouldn't understand. He is determined that I should have a seat. So wherever I go there is a little prodding at the back of my knee and I realise that a chair has been placed behind me. So I smile and say, 'Thank you', and keep standing. And I move perhaps ten yards to see the scene from a little closer, and there's the prodding again, and another chair comes. Sometimes about ten or twelve chairs can be standing around me. It's like Ionesco. Alarming.

We did an extended shoot which could have gone on till 10.00 but in fact only went on till 8.00 because everything went well and smoothly. That means that food is served on the set, and it becomes a sort of soup kitchen. It's like war-time somehow, clutching cups of hot coffee and snatching bits of buns and so on. It's rather heart-warming.

Then off to supper with the gang.

14 October 87

I wasn't used at all today, which is just as well, since I was violently sick last night. Crawling ashen to breakfast, I bumped into Bojana who wrote down on a piece of paper what I have to get from the pharmacy. It worked brilliantly, so from now on she is Dr Bojana. But what caused it? Obviously it was something I ate, but what? Not the very good fish, presumably? I simply can't work it out. I never have food poisoning. Other people have it; or at least they say they do. I have dark suspicions that there is no such thing as food poisoning. It's just malingering, I always feel. Except for what I've just had. Now that *was* food poisoning. Feeling better, I began to write some of the screenplay, sitting at the window of my room at the Krim (the phrase 'my room at the Krim' has a certain ring to it, I feel). Odd to be writing a screenplay while acting in one. The two things seem completely separate. I try to imagine what Dušan might have gone through, except that in his case it all comes out of his head. He isn't drawing on something that's already in existence.

Dušan:
Main inspiration for Manifesto *was a dark expressionistic play,* Events in the Town of Goga, *written in the late twenties by Slovenian, Slavko Grum. He took a plot from Émile Zola's story, written about 100 years ago,* Pour une nuit d'amour. *Zola, in his turn, found the plot in Casanova's memoirs. Several versions of Zola's story appeared on film, the last one very cruel and feminist, by*

Spain's Pilar Miro, the woman who became the Spanish Minister for Cinema after Franco. Mine was the first sweet one and the first comedy.

But the process, the translation of images, ideas, words into film form must be the same. In my case, the problem is to remain loyal to the writer without necessarily being loyal to her book. Having read dozens of screenplays over the years, I am aware for the first time of their elements. Time, place, a kind of journey through the story. So very different in feeling from a play, where the action is entirely revealed through the characters' inter-relations. The dialogue, all-important in a play, seems to need a lot of space around it in a film. It looks terribly bare on the page, seeming to hang in the air. This, I conclude, is because it's only one element in a film; the others – the composition of the frame, the actors' faces, the background, even perhaps the music – being at least equally significant. That, certainly, is the experience of acting in one. Words are secondary. The action can be furthered more by the flick of an eye, or by a dog running rapidly across the street, than by the most eloquent speech.

This evening I went to have supper with Chris and Gillian, his wife-to-be. This is not as simple as it sounds. He determined, on arrival, not to stay in a hotel (how heartily we Krim-dwellers envy him), so he hired a small house on the other side of the lake. I decided to hoof it there, not by the relatively straightforward route through the town, but around the lake. I know the lake very well. I have walked round it again and again, wreathed, mostly, in melancholy, and lately I've taken to walking round it at night. Parts of it are lit, and some of the pathway is in good repair. For the rest, it's a Stygian obstacle course. You're likely at any moment to fall down a hole or get your face whipped by brambles. For some reason I find all this, and the sheer terror of hearing a sudden sharp noise behind one, or the pad-pad-pad of a nocturnal jogger, or a dog's sudden bark, exhilarating, sexually exhilarating, to be precise, pitting oneself against one's fears. I feel very alive after these forays, and sleep well. Aesthetically, it's ravishing. The church on the island in the middle of the lake is floodlit, and bathed in yellow light, and could be Debussy's submerged cathedral, just risen from under the waves. Confused birds sing lonely tunes. Peace, beauty, fear.

In this heightened state I arrived at Chris's house, a glorified bed-sit, really, crammed to the rafters with delights accrued on his travels. Coffee from Vienna, jam from Belgrade, fish from the market just up the road, crystallised fruit from Ljubljana, booze from everywhere and anywhere, cheese from – yes! – the Isle of Pag. He and Gillian have been travelling in a caravan and have disgorged its contents into this place. He was presiding over the stove, while Kodály played on the C.D. machine, and Gillian opened bottles. She's a very pretty young woman – fifteen years younger than Chris – with no nonsense about her, and it's hard to imagine her response to her fiancé's grand romantic gestures. It is both sexist and ageist of me not to be able to imagine her as a doctor, but I can't. She, like many young Australians, has quite enjoyed Europe, but only quite. She tells me about her six-month tours as the medical officer at the North Pole. Her description of the frozen desert, the unending vistas of snow, and the deep, deep silence, make it quite understandable that from a certain viewpoint, the delights of Vienna, Baden-Baden, and Paris, might seem paltry.

Chris's pasta is perfectly *al dente*, a triumph. Conversation lingers on many succulent topics, including his portable word-processor, of whose qualities he is as amorous as his wife-to-be's body, and a sauce he once had in Henley. We finally talk about the film, which is merely one thread in the rich weave of sensations of which his life consists. Even he, benevolent to the point of indifference, has noticed that our assistant director is not all he might be. We talked about how absolutely crucial the assistant director is on a film, especially if the director is not an authoritarian or a leader. The assistant director is really the man who creates the rhythm of the shoot, much more so generally, than the director. His job is to take up the slack whenever it appears. The director on this production actually creates slack. So the assistant director needs to work twice as hard to counteract it, and he doesn't. The pulse on the shoot is appallingly sluggish and it seems that we frequently go into drift, nobody knowing what they're doing, much less why, and it affects the whole unit. Yesterday was a day of great achievement because Dušan was in a tremendously dynamic mood, whereas today, apparently, was far from great in its achievements.

Chris was interested in, and interesting about, these matters, but, ultimately, he was here to have a good time, and he would. I left feeling rather feeble in my inability to dwell in the moment the way he does. When I'm working, I always feel as if my whole life is on the line, as if there is terrible shame in not getting it right. Then I feel ashamed about feeling shame. Brimming over with cognac (discovered by Chris in a delightful little delicatessen in Schleswig-Holstein), I wove a perilous path back round the other side of the lake, down by the ornamental gardens and across the boathouses, discerning through the mist a couple of lonely figures, middle-aged men walking aimlessly about, peering into the dark this way and that. I take them to be the local gay community; at least that's what the gay guide book suggested ('*Cruising:* At your own peril').

15 October 87

I got to the set at 10.30, started shooting at 4.00. I arrived
in a fire engine, opened the door for Avanti, got in and
sped off. And that was that. One noteworthy thing. A
couple of days ago, I'd suggested to Dušan that, as I can't
drive, instead of getting a stand-in and shooting in long-
shot he should have one of the other agents actually drive
the engine, while I stood on the running board. I had an
image of Hunt as a ship's figurehead. Dušan was
unimpressed by the idea at the time. Today, because I'm
golden boy at the moment, my appearances in the last
three days' rushes having been 'very, very good' (I've
sensed approval on all sides), he said, 'Yes, yes. Try it.'
And when I tried it they were absolutely thrilled and
thought it was wonderful. Bojana came up to me and
said, 'You are in too many good scenes in this film'; and
I said, 'Sorry'. We laughed.

A remark of Fred's, attributed to Jim Goddard, a
brilliant remark, I think: 'Films are always the host,
television is always the guest.' Namely, television comes
into the house, whereas one has to leave home to see a
film. It marks a crucial difference in the attitude to
filming, going some way to explaining the quite different
prevailing atmosphere. Even in this chaos, we feel
engaged on something big and expansive.

I finish work at about four. The idea of going back to
Bled fills me with no enthusiasm. The little room, the
repetitive meals, the sandy coffee, the treacherous tele-
phones do not represent an enticing prospect. Round the
corner from the square is a bus depot. Only three minutes

away from the eighteenth-century disneyland in which we've been filming, the scene is totally different: energetic, urban, industrialised. People are fighting each other for places on the buses. I decide impulsively to go to Ljubljana. My first experience of it was totally in the dark, and I saw nothing other than the motorway and the back of the studio theatre where we saw *Bludnje* (no one – and I have asked everybody I could get hold of – can translate the word for me. When asked, they simply smile, as if it was something we all know but don't like to talk about). I had no great hopes of Ljubljana, but at least it wasn't Bled. I finally negotiated a ticket on the bus, was duly shovelled onto it, and was amazed, an hour later, to find myself in a small Austro-Hungarian city of the greatest charm. Nineteenth-century rococo seemed to be the prevailing style. There was a river running through the centre of the city, and the walk along its banks was quite Parisian in its romantic feeling. There was a baroque church (seventeenth-century), in which elderly women in black were raising their trembling, wobbling voices in prayer and song; and there was what appeared to be a student quarter, appropriately on the left bank of the river. I popped into a bar or two. The liveliness was exhilarating by contrast with Bled's nay-saying sedateness. Eventually, I found a splendid restaurant which, unimaginably, took Mastercard. I daintily despatched some pungent venison and a plate of fresh vegetables which shamed both Bled and our caterers, bless them, it's not their fault. And then I went for a stroll. 'Hrad,' a sign said, and – remembering the identical Czech word – I set off for the castle. Up, up, up I went, lit by the watery lamplight. The road went on and on. One could see the castle, but the light was getting murky and finally stopped. I found myself in some bushes, almost a forest. Ljubljana was below, the castle was above, and here I was, in the middle, lost and a little frightened. Suddenly someone lit a cigarette; and then another. 'I see,' I thought to myself, and, feeling it to be rather late, started to make my descent, illuminated by increasing numbers of cigarette tips, glowing on and off

174

like fireflies. It was a sort of vision, the hillside studded with silent smokers, as I stumbled and slithered down the steep escarpment. Once I bumped into a couple, a young man and woman, actually copulating, and murmured some ineffectual apologies. Finally I reached the main square, and took a taxi (which cost about fifty quid) back to Bled, which seemed far further than a cab ride away from the spirit of the Hill of Venus I'd just left.

16th October 1987

I'm just about to go home for a while, I hope. Back to England, that is. Today Dušan said to me that he only wanted a few little pick-up shots because he was so pleased with what he had of Hunt. I was the red thread, he said, running through the film, the only way in which he could see that he had a film. So far he hasn't caught Svetlana and Avanti in action, he says. I said, 'Well, they are rather reactive, aren't they, as they go through the film.' I suddenly realised something, and said, 'The little discussion we had the other day' – row I think would be a more accurate description, but it seems a long time ago – 'changed Hunt from being a passive character into being an active one. I suppose that would account for why he appears to be more purposeful and his story is clearer.' He said that he hadn't thought of it like that at all, but of course it was very clear now. Anyway off I went to London, with the feeling of having escaped from Colditz, though my new ease with the part suggests a more charitable simile: it feels like half-term. And it's bye-bye Bled, Bled which I would have loved had I not been working here, beautiful, unfairly maligned Bled. It's Zagreb's turn next.

I only got out by the skin of my teeth. There was trouble at the airport, the direct flight was cancelled, and I ended up by taking three different planes across Europe. It was nearly midnight before I arrived in London, thoroughly drunk from bottles of wine imbibed first in Zurich and then, even better, in Frankfurt. I went straight to bed and slept deeply, waking briefly in the middle of the night because there seemed to be a rather strong wind. Next morning I set out for Earl's Court station to get to the first of innumerable appointments and was surprised to see a tree lying across Redcliffe Square. I turned the corner to see two more. The streets were strangely empty. It was like *On the Beach*. I got a train – also eerily empty – and finally arrived at my agent Peggy Ramsay's office at eleven to be told about the great hurricane that had devastated Kew Gardens and torn roofs off and actually killed a number of people. The deserted streets of the West End were shocking; it was as if the wind of God had passed through. Later, on the television that night, staff from Kew gardens talked about the loss of trees – some of them hundreds of years old – that they had tended all their lives, and they wept.

ZAGREB
18 October 1987

Back to Zagreb and the Interconti. I negotiated to have
my old room, on a corner: plenty of light and a view over
the still spanking-new Mimara Museum, the square
opposite it and that little opera house, grandiose rather
than Grand. To the other side there's a high-school
playground. These views are ideal, allowing ample
opportunity to speculate on the lives of the singers, the
actors, the curators, the schoolkids, milling around eight
floors below. I have a lot of work to do in this room, still
struggling along with *At Freddie's*, trying to read some of
the pile of new novels I've brought with me, and – oh,
yes – playing Hunt in *For a Night of Love*. I also have to
come to terms with *Die Fledermaus*. I was asked by
Scottish Opera to do a production of it while we were in
Bled. There was only one phone which was really
effective, and it was in the bakery in Škofja Loka, so
negotiations took place in a fine mist of flour. I've always
loathed *Fledermaus* on stage, while adoring the music. It
invariably comes over as some sort of sexless middle-
aged party, a Good Old Days romp, a chance to get into
a lot of Victorian costumes and pretend to drink
champagne. An examination of the libretto – as so often
– reveals it be something quite other, a sharp satire of
yuppie Vienna, 1872. I agreed to do it, thinking that
maybe I could persuade Caryl Churchill to adapt the
libretto. The implications have to be worked out here in
this room. A large portion of that work will be done
gazing out of the window, so the view is important.

I'm fond of hotel rooms, a life away from life. Ideally, I'd have permanently available hotel rooms all over the world. I have never really made a home. People have tried to make homes for me, and very nice too, but I have a basic reluctance to project myself onto walls. It may be an uncertainty of taste, though I think it's deeper than that. Maybe an unwillingness to commit to anything as permanent as wallpaper. Whenever I talk about my ideal room, my ideal space, I notice that it's neutral. I say that I love Japanese style, but what I love is its bareness. If, however, I lived in such a space, I would be terrified of choosing the few items which make a Japanese room what it is: that one flower in that one vase. Which flower? In which vase? Nightmare. So generally I am much happier to live in a place which has been created by somebody else, someone else's house, for instance, where I can stay forever without wishing to move a stick. Or, even better, in a hotel.

Zagreb is in the throes of autumn, which suit it very well. More and more of the day is spent under the sickly light of those 60-watt street lamps. The spectral quality is enhanced by the peeling paint, the empty trams rattling down the high street, the music from restaurants wafting like mist across the city. A funicular railway leads to the upper part of the city, where there are the university, the parks, and the grand bourgeois mansions so different from the apartment blocks of downtown. Up there, too, there's a wonderful restaurant, with a kind of student clientele, though not student prices, so I'm not quite sure who these people are. But the place is always on a roar with laughter and debate.

20th October, having done a day's filming

We weren't needed, yesterday, Monday, so Lindsay, Fred and I took ourselves on a little outing, to a tiny town nearby which proved as pretty as Škofja Loka, though more tourist-conscious, and therefore slightly less charming. They too have a square; they too have a castle, ruined in this case, and we clambered over it like children, photographing each other in silly poses. We ate in a restaurant where there was no menu: one simply asked for what one wanted, and if it was humanly possible, they made it. We had a local dish of some kind, a sort of bouillabaisse, which was the best thing any of us had had in Yugoslavia. To eat, that is. Unable to get a taxi, we bussed it back to town, which took a very long time, squashed up against the rush-hour hordes, but it did at least feel as if we were actually living in Zagreb.

Today we had two scenes in the forest, in the role of which they have cast the great park just outside the city centre, in the suburbs. The scenes were very simple. There was one on the fire engine. Dušan and Bojana both warmly praised me for standing on the running board of the fire engine. The next scene was one in which, according to the script, Hunt has to arrange the agents in the bushes and then whistle to them when they're all hidden. I went up to Dušan, feeling myself to be very much the golden boy still, and suggested 'Would it be interesting if I lined them all up and sent them off one by one?' and he said 'No, it would be rather better if we avoided anything obvious like that.' 'I see,' I said. My golden period has clearly come to an end. He told us

181

exactly what to do, which we did. It involved me being seen running. The whole scene seemed to be one of tremendous action, so I did indeed rush wildly about the place, and everybody laughed a great deal when he shouted, 'Cut'. Not him, though. You always know when he's amused because he always laughs when he says, 'Cut'. But he sat there deep in thought and with the limitless quantities of paranoia at my disposal I naturally assumed that he was appalled. I sometimes catch an expression in his eyes as if to say, 'Well, that's just hopelessly vulgar and obvious and ordinary but what can be done'. I can see that it might have tumbled over into Keystone Kops, but that was exactly what I had in mind, I must confess. We'll see what he has to say after the rushes, and whether the scene is in the completed film.

I was off then for about five or six hours. At about 4.00 we attempted to shoot a scene in the forest itself. These other scenes have been in the open air. As ever it does make one marvel at who exactly it is that is in charge of devising the schedule because they might possibly have guessed, a child of seven years of age might possibly have guessed, that the light inside the forest would be rather less than it was outside and that maybe it would be advisable to shoot such scenes when there was lots of light, but that had not occurred. The result was that after about half an hour we ran out of light. Played a very, very brief scene with Lindsay. Dušan came up and said, 'No. It's too strong. You must play it quicker and lighter. He's on his way to do other things, and he just happens to see the teacher,' which certainly doesn't appear to be the way it's written. It's written with some considerable underlinings and exclamation marks. It's very curious, the way in which he gives the notes, as if he was saying, 'No, no, not the black one, the white one' – as if there were two bags sitting on the floor and you could equally have chosen one or the other. It doesn't occur to him that you had actually chosen to do what you did, and that you might be slightly attached to it, and that you might like a reason for doing something else. He just speaks as if it's perfectly obvious. No anger, as with Milos – just total neutral dismissal of what you have done.

So the day came to a rather unfulfilling end but was given a lift by the arrival of Tom Luddy, the executive producer on the film, who is the head of Francis Coppola's now somewhat slimmed down Zoetrope Studios. He seems to be the only man from the side of the production who actually knows what he is doing. Cannon would only pay him for three days' work in London, which he duly did and which apparently were the best three days' work done on the organising of the film. And here he is again. When I asked Nada, the voluptuous, witty red-haired woman who is in charge of continuity and is also Makavejev's personal assistant, how long Tom was staying she said she thought just two days; he'd just come to say 'Hello' to Dušan because he likes him very much. Nobody seemed to think that was sad, disappointing or distressing.

21 October 87

Called at 7.00. Actually came to the set at 1.00. Sat with
Lindsay in the caravan, which is parked in the middle of
a leafy glade. I stayed there because I'm reading, reading,
reading. I've just finished the book about the making of
Citizen Kane, an interesting, clear, well-researched book
which challenges the notion that Orson Welles was
personally responsible for the entire glory of the film.
Pauline Kael started the work with her (now thoroughly
rebutted) insistence on Herman Mankiewicz's sole
authorship of the script. Robert L. Carringer, in this
book, goes one step further. He carefully analyses the
contribution of all the various creative collaborators on
the film. He is very keen on the word 'collaboration' as
applied to this film or perhaps any film. He doesn't
entirely make his case because he seems to be under the
impression that the greatness of the film lies in its
innovations, but its innovations would mean nothing if
they didn't express what Welles wanted them to, and he
doesn't analyse that at all. Moreover, Welles encouraged
these innovations – inspired many of them, and created
the atmosphere in which people were moved to challenge
the limits of their abilities. The book is nonetheless
informative, absorbing and thorough. But there is one
extraordinary lacuna. His analysis covers the cinemato-
graphy, the sound, the editing, the light, the set design,
the script, and he's very scrupulous about unravelling all
these individual contributions, and others by people who
have hitherto been completely unknown, the people who
did the storyboards, for example, the woman who put

Mankiewicz's first script into some kind of filmable shape, many more. Not once, however, does he mention the contribution of the actors. Never, not a line, not a thought, not a gesture, not a contribution towards a characterisation, not once anywhere are any of these things mentioned. Evidently Mr Carringer has never been on a film-set during filming. In our film there's rarely a phrase that any of us has said as it's written, mainly because it's not grammatical, and it doesn't really seem to have any great rhythm to it. This is very often the case. It's not just Dušan's foreignness that is responsible for that. Actors almost always make adjustments to the text of a screenplay, but often also suggest or invent visual notions that become part of the film. Mr Carringer knows nothing of that. Somehow his book seemed a very fitting one to be reading while trapped in this caravan waiting to go out to film some other tiny sliver of the work of Makavejev.

(Having inventive actors is both a blessing and a curse for the director. Every invention has somehow to take its place in the sequence of images that is what the film, in the final analysis, is. I remember on *Amadeus* suggesting a certain visual moment to Milos. In the scene where Mozart, Schikaneder and the three girls fool around at the piano, shrieking, wailing and howling fragments of *The Magic Flute*, I as Schikaneder found myself playing with the skull that I'd asked the designer, Patrizia von Brandenstein, to place on the set – Schikaneder was a famous Hamlet in Vienna in the 1780s. I said to Milos, 'Could I bring the skull close up to Mozart's head and make it sing?' I knew that it would have a certain impact; Mozart was very ill at this point in the film, and the juxtaposition of the death's head and his ailing features might be very powerful. Milos listened to me with fierce concentration. I had the impression that he was mentally reviewing everything that he'd shot so far. After a minute or two of this intense silence he said, 'OK. We'll try it.' He liked it, and it's in the film. It didn't make quite the impact I'd imagined because of the angle from which he shot it, and the fact that it was a medium shot rather than a close-up. He probably decided that any larger would have made it altogether too significant. And I'm sure he was right.)

When I started after 1.00 it was to do yet another shot on the fire engine. Before the shot, I stood on various parts of it being photographed by the local press. This image of me on the outside of the fire engine now obviously delights Dušan. It is a part of the film. Next there's a shot of me in the bushes, as the king and Avanti pass by on horses. He had a notion that I should be just sitting there very quietly, on the fire engine, of course, maybe on the bonnet in a nice relaxed way. 'He's done his job.' It occurs to me, and I tell him, that Hunt is never really relaxed. He's always thinking about what he's done or what he might be about to do. Dušan thinks that's true, and that's fine. And I find a sort of posture of, not anxiety, but of absent-minded review of things, which seemed to please him very much. The king passes by on the horse, I leap up, I take my hat off, I sit down. Avanti comes by, I leap up again and make a little gesture to indicate that all is well. This seems fine the first couple of times, the master shot, and then there's a shot of just me from Avanti's point of view, looking straight into the camera and making the sign to say everything's OK. I do this but he isn't pleased – I look too frightened, too anxious. What he wants to see is strength, content-ment, happiness. The simple movement on top of the fire engine – I don't know the king is coming, the king passes by, I leap up, I take my hat off, I sit down, I see that Avanti is there too so I leap up again – that gesture of leaping up again almost inevitably dictates a sort of sense of having been caught out sitting down. But Dušan is absolutely right when he says, 'No, no. He's happy when he sees Avanti and he can tell him that everything's going well'. That is perfectly right. I play that and that's good, that's fine, though I can't pretend I really know why. It remains difficult to grasp the whole of Dušan's view of the character.

The king and his court were very impressive as they rode by on horseback. The king is played by a very pleasant Albanian actor, Enver Petrovci. Albanian/ Yugoslavian, that is. Born in Yugoslavia, though un-Yugoslavian by name and by looks: dark-haired and swarthy. He is apparently one of the great stars of the Belgrade stage, playing Macbeth at the moment. The court are simply extras. They have all been kitted up with moustaches and beards, and they look, particularly on their horses and in their uniforms, infinitely severe and serious men. Once again one is completely amazed at how one endows people with qualities according to their appearance. In fact the men turned out to be rather silly, giggly chaps, one of them slightly camp. But with their noble noses (they had of course been chosen for their profiles) and the goatee beards and resplendent moustaches which have been stuck onto them, they rather inspired one, made one a little nervous and respectful of them as they rode past. Fred, too, in his début as an equestrian, acquired even greater insolent authority. He should play a Velasquez Hapsburg after this.

Next: restaging the scene with the children that we tried to do last night (of which the rushes, as predicted, were completely hopeless, dark and unusable). Dušan has a problem with Lindsay, who is not amused by children. She is playing a teacher, and she is very happy simply to act her part with great feeling and conviction. Dušan instead wants her to form a relationship with the children, to play with them, to become their favourite auntie. Not the character, Lindsay herself. She does not see this as part of her job. *Impasse*. Then Dušan has what is really, I think, an inspiration. He sets the whole scene on the side of a hill so that the children have to run up it, and they can't quite make it, and they fall over and all the rest of it, and it makes Lindsay very vigorous, shouting and trying to control them and that all works beautifully. I have to come in on the fire engine and leap off and say, 'Hello' at which the children swarm all over the fire engine, on top of which are baskets containing the king's rabbits, for him to shoot. I have to try to haul the kids off. It's all rather sweet and rather charming. Lindsay's character and mine are having a conversation

while all this is going on about the king, and how he will
arrive at 'exactly about 4 o'clock' (whatever that means,
it's a wonderfully incongruous line, so I preserve it
exactly as it stands).

Shooting the scene, royal rabbits, kids swarming all
over the fire engine and all, one of the children attempted
to get into the cabin, reached up to the handle and
unexpectedly pulled it off. In the middle of the shot she
rather shyly came up and handed it to me – quite mad,
in the dramatic context. Conscious that the cameras were
still rolling, I stayed in character, looked at it for a
second, and then, just like in the silent movies, I threw it
away, then pulled the children off the fire engine. Great
laugh when Dušan called 'Cut.' It was surreal, beautiful,
but there was something wrong with the shot, so we
couldn't use it. Just as we were about to shoot again, we
discovered that one of the rabbits had died. It's not
surprising, they've been bounced and jolted up and down
on top of the fire engine, and one of the kids tore a box
off, and the rabbit and its box fell on the floor. It looked
alright but is, apparently, dead. The scene goes on
regardless. Dušan says, 'The trouble is you are dealing
with the children realistically.' I said, 'You know, if you
are going to chase after children who have been told
simply to run up to the fire engine and then run away
from it, how else can you deal with them but realistically,
moment to moment?' I bite my tongue. One doesn't want
to get into arguments. What is the point of arguing? So
one just says, 'What would you like? What would be
best?' And he, weary, too, of the unending debate, says,
'Let's just shoot again,' so we do that, but this time
certain children find they are frightened on top of the fire
engine, so one has very gingerly to take them down, able
to offer only limited reassurance because one doesn't
speak their language, by which time of course the shot's
fucked. But eventually we got something.

Sound had a problem today. An unusual problem. A
James Thurberish problem. They had to cope with the
sound of seals barking in the nearby zoo. When the seals
seemed finally to have died down a mysterious female

singing began to fill the air. It moved around through the bushes. It was operatic, but wordless: a vocalise. Clearly a diva doing her exercises, for whatever reason, in the bushes. Secretly preparing to astonish Zagreb with her Norma? Perhaps her husband has banned her and her vocalising from the house. Or perhaps she's a Method Diva, and she's researching the wood-bird in *Siegfried*. The trilling persisted. A search was mounted, but we never tracked her down. Eventually the sound faded, and died. As if these two were not enough the final surreal problem for the sound department was that the children became delighted with the word 'Action', and whenever Dušan cried, 'Action', forty Yugoslavian tots would struggle up the hill shrieking, 'Eksion. Eksion. Eksion. Eksion.'

I begin to believe that Makavejev's temperament creates spontaneous Makavejevian happenings. Yesterday, for example, while we were shooting one of the scenes in which I place the agents – this apparently wildly exaggerated scene of the seven agents dressed exactly like each other and like me, hiding in the bushes with their bikes – at that precise moment seven members of the Zagreb Forestry Commission walked solemnly by, all in identical green costumes not dissimilar to ours, and each of them with an identical dog in a muzzle. They could have stepped straight out of, or straight into, the film. I am amazed that Dušan didn't turn a camera onto them, but he seemed delighted just to watch. It seems that the whole universe is falling apart and mad images are proliferating and he's happy.

22 October 1987

Yesterday I saw rushes (the dailies, as they're generally called) for the first time. Some directors are very strict about not allowing the actors to see what they've done, others are quite keen. Some actors, likewise, absolutely refuse to see themselves, whereas with others it's positively contractual that they do so. I'm not quite sure, personally. One probably only learns by seeing the results of one's work, but while still doing it . . .? It's all too easy to become self-conscious. On the other hand, it's often the simplest possible way to see what one's doing wrong. I'm really not sure. We had gathered together in one of the hotel rooms commandeered by the film – the make-up artists, costume people, the boys from sound, the cameraman, the assistant director and Dušan, all fiercely assessing their own work. Well, on their own terms the rushes are very good, very clean and full of striking images. It's a considerable challenge for the imagination, though. For one thing you see them over and over again, and secondly they are all just raw material. But they were good. Fred was riding his horse splendidly, and I think what I did was good, except that it was definitely operetta-ish. I don't quite know what else I could have done in the scene, though I sense that the accent was playing me, rather than the other way round. There is a certain amount of face pulling and so on which stems directly from the effect the accent has. It's a bit extreme. The rushes are shown on a small screen. It will be eight times that size in the cinemas. I'm not sure whether that's going to be a plus or a minus, it's hard to tell. When it was all over, absolutely nothing, as is traditional, was said at all. Then I remembered that the reason I don't go to rushes is because the silence afterwards is unbearable.

Going to the restaurant, I found big Tom Gotovač sitting alone, so I joined him. I had heard earlier from Bojana that his mother had died the previous day. He is about fifty, so she can't have been awfully young, but he was clearly very upset. I offered some words of condolence, and he started to cry, noiselessly. After a second he said, 'My poor little mother. I will be strong man. My poor mummy.' Tom Luddy joined us, and Tom G left shortly. Tom L is a genial man, a creature of limitless enthusiasm, wandering the world in search of film ancient and modern. His long, balding hair and sparkling spectacles give him an appearance at once monkish and naughty. He has known and worked with Dušan for many years, and told me that Dušan was the first person to be offered the direction of *Apocalypse Now*. We went over to speak to him. Tom said, 'I've just told Simon about *Apocalypse Now*.' Dušan said, 'Yes, yes. Of course then it was just this little story about four guys in a boat going up the river and being shot at by the natives. The problem was that I was on the side of the guys in the bushes. So I don't think it would have worked out.' Luddy also told me a story about Abel Gance, at the age of ninety-four, having more or less lost his reason, being brought to the film festival which Luddy runs in Telluride, Colorado. They showed *The Charm of Dynamite*, a documentary by Kevin Brownlow about the making of the Napoleon film. It was to be followed by a showing of the whole of the reconstructed *Napoléon* as it then stood. All this was explained very carefully to Gance. He sat down and watched *The Charm of Dynamite* with the rest of the audience. At the end of the documentary, he was in tears. 'They have massacred my film,' he said. 'This is a travesty. This is not my *Napoléon*. It is not my *Napoléon*.' He thought that that was it, that that was all there was. Brownlow knew nothing of all this. He came up on stage, made a speech about the greatness of Abel Gance, and what an honour it was to be able to have done this work for the film. Onstage tottered Gance, raving – in French – at the audience, telling them that he. had been betrayed, that it was a scandal, that they must not believe that what they saw was his film. Brownlow doesn't speak any French, so he got the French Ambassador to try to explain the situation to Gance, but Gance was implacable, couldn't be comforted at all, and went away. The next day his brain cleared, and he realised the absurdity of what he had said, what he'd done, his ingratitude to Brownlow and all the rest of it. He was absolutely mortified and said to them, 'I am too old. Please help me to die. I shouldn't have lived so long. It's pathetic to be as old as this. You should pity me, pity me.'

When Gance finally did see the reconstruction (he never saw the absolutely final one that we saw in London and New York), there were whole sections Brownlow had discovered that Gance said were out-takes and should never have been put back. He had only filmed those sequences – the ones with the sentimental woman who praises Napoleon's picture – because the actress was the girlfriend of the Russian backer, who had insisted that some kind of a part be found for her. Gance was mortified to see the sequences back in the film. Brownlow being essentially an academic, a reconstructor, insisted that they be in the film, but Luddy respected Gance. In the Radio City Music Hall screenings (financed by Coppola) those sections weren't in the film. Quite a little lesson for those of us who try to do 'the original version'. Maybe the composer or the writer was only too glad to get rid of what we are so lovingly restoring. (Now that Gance is dead, Brownlow insists on re-restoring the scenes.)

This attitude of Brownlow's is a minor fault compared to his glorious achievement in restoring the film to the world. Who that was there will ever forget the first showing of the complete film in London, to an audience (including Kurosawa and Satyajit Ray) which, weeping, stood and cheered the absent film-maker, as Brownlow held up a telephone for him, on the other end of the line in Paris, to hear how his masterpiece had at last received its due. He wept, Brownlow wept, we all wept, but worse was to follow. His voice barely under control, Brownlow told us that Gance was in desperate straits, that he was frail and penniless, living in a tiny, cold apartment, and that if we really liked to show our appreciation, we should send money to him c/o the London Film Festival; alternatively we could put it in the buckets that ushers were holding as we left the cinema. The overflow of five, ten, and twenty pound notes littered the floor of the Empire Leicester Square like autumn leaves.

He died shortly after, and I have no idea whether he knew how tangibly he was appreciated by hundreds of anonymous English people.

25 October 1987

Bruno arrives from London, bearing his model of the set for *Shirley Valentine*. We apportion the room, one desk each. His desk, covered in bits of cardboard, razors, erasers, newly sharpened pencils, dominates. The room has become a studio.

26 October 1987

A confrontation. Yesterday Fred phoned at about 6 p.m.
to say that Tom had suggested it might be a good idea
if he, Fred, Lindsay and I were to sit down and talk to
Dušan and Bojana and explain some of the difficulties we
are having with the production. Fred said, did I want to
come? He thought it might be worthwhile. I said to him
that I thought I had already expressed to Dušan's face all
my opinions about the way he deals (or doesn't deal) with
the actors, and about the non-communication, and so on,
and I didn't really want to turn it into a confrontation or
want to kick him when he was down in any sense,
because he must know all of this already. However, I
would come and see how it turned out. So I joined them,
in the Huntsmen's Bar on the ground floor. This is a big
hunting region. Dušan, Lindsay, Tom and Bojana were
sitting in the corner, with the heads of stuffed animals
looking gravely on.

Uninhibited by the sad, noble beasts hovering above
them, all were merry with humorous reminiscence about
this and that. Then Tom pulled the meeting together and
said we should really talk about what was going wrong
with the film. Fred started, making a passionate speech
about the lack of communication. This is the key phrase:
'Lack of communication'. There is a big communication
problem, says Fred. We all agreed entirely. He said that
he had already lost his temper three times, and he had
never ever done so on any film that he'd worked on before
and almost never in the theatre. He hated doing it. But
even then nothing had improved. Dušan said that he had

taken great note that Fred had lost his temper, and that Fred had used a word which had absolutely paralysed him. 'You talked about "manners",' he said. 'I was completely amazed and didn't know how to respond because I have no manners. I know nothing about manners. I don't know how to behave, I don't know what to say or how to say it. I can't go to good restaurants, I don't associate with classy people; because I just don't know how to handle myself. I know nothing about manners. But also,' he said, 'it struck me as so peculiar to be using the word in this context. Manners has nothing to do with filming. Filming is entirely to do with the job of getting something done.'

Fred said, 'Yes, yes. You misunderstand me. I am not talking about the way you hold your fork, I'm talking about simply respecting other people that exist, that are there, and need to be spoken to. It's like a kitchen. We are all there trying to make the meal but somehow nobody tells anybody what is going on.' Dušan said, 'Oh, I am delighted you mentioned kitchens, because that's exactly how I see film-making. It's like a kitchen. But you know, the fascinating thing about kitchens is that nobody ever talks to anybody. Everybody knows what is being done, and so it's up to you to get on with it. The same with filming. If we have to shoot something again, if we have to do a scene with a different lens for example, you should be able to look over and see that the lens is being changed, and you work it out for yourself. You look at each other's work. We should all be looking at each other and seeing how we are doing and what's going on. We should be aware of the production.' 'But in a kitchen,' I said, 'people do say "saucepan", "herbs", "spatula", and know what all these things mean. Here, because those simple key words are in a language we don't understand, there's no chance of us being able to pick up the clues. We can't tell why a shot is being done again and nobody lets us know.' Dušan said, 'Clearly the problem seems to reside with Dejan [the assistant director].'

Then we had a long discussion about Dejan. Dejan,

handsome, cool and flip, has become a focus of discontent. I said that the job of an assistant director seems to be two-fold: one, the ability to be the master of everything that's happening on the set and to take appropriate decisions; secondly, to have authority. Dejan is totally deficient in both these aspects. Apparently he can't seem to keep track of everything that's going on, nor make decisions, nor convey the reasons for delays; and he completely lacks authority. He shouts in order to try to impose himself, and it only makes people more hostile. Bojana agreed with this.

I said, becoming altogether more involved in the discussion than I had intended, 'Quite apart from Dejan himself, the chain of command, which is so absolutely crucial between the assistant directors, doesn't exist at all.' 'That's true,' said Bojana; 'Dejan isn't talking to Sasha. He doesn't like her, and he doesn't like Dubi either.' 'What is this?' I said. 'A temperamental assistant director is the worst catastrophe imaginable. His job is to ease tension, not to create it.' Then we all weighed in and said that Dubi, little wide-eyed Dubi, was delightful, intelligent, effective, admirable. Somebody suggested that maybe Dubi could be elevated into the position yet to be created of someone who translates all that's said in Serbo-Croatian and who communicates the decisions and so on to the Anglophones. I said that it seemed to me incomprehensible that the assistant director should be allowed to adopt positions whereby 'he wasn't talking' to his fellow assistant directors nor indeed, apparently, to the camera crew. The grips and all the rest won't talk to him, they don't like him, they find subtle ways of not telling him what's going on. He's a completely isolated man. Bojana and Dušan agreed with what we said. The weird thing is that neither of them seemed to think that this indicated in any way that he should be removed or changed. Lindsay spoke very eloquently about the contribution that we want to make, that it would really be so much better if we were all working towards the same thing. If all the obstacles were removed, the contribution would be at its greatest. Lots of noddings, agreements from Dušan.

Dušan:

Now, we are into the letter H, as they would say on 'Sesame Street'. Hysteria. Hypocrisy. Histrionics. And worst of all: Humorlessness.

My Merck Manual, Thirteenth Edition, 2165 pages, covers every sickness you can imagine (including Pancake kidney, Palindromic rheumatism and Münchhausen's syndrome). It says that 'a hysterical syndrome arises at a definable point in time, nearly always in response to stressful life events. The anxiety is relieved by converting the conflict into a somatic symptom'.

'1. Hysterical (histrionic) personality: Hysterical personalities are conspicuously egocentric, and since the conquest of the esteem and admiration of others is very important to them, attention-seeking theatrical behaviour tends to be characteristic. Their emotional immaturity is manifested in an exaggerated childish emotional response to any wounding of their vanity. Inconsistencies in behaviour arise from the fact that the hysterical personality can adopt whatever pattern of conduct will place him in a favorable light or boost his self-esteem.

A hysteric's lively manner lends itself to easily established superficial relationships. They may combine provactiveness or sexualisation of non-sexual relationships with sexual dysfunction or fears. Their relationships are affected by a seemingly insatiable need for affection, and behind their sexually seductive behaviour lies a childlike wish for non-sexual affection and protection; i.e., they tend to be dependent. The crises that arise from these relationships are managed with manipulative behaviour that may include suicidal threats and shrewd exploitation of the other's emotional susceptibilities.'

Treatment is described as 'tedious and prolonged', the patient's self-esteem must be supported while his maladaptive modes of behaviour are confronted' etc. What a disappointment Merck!

This discussion was becoming stranger and stranger. The whole event is an unimaginable one to occur on a film. That is to say, a discussion with the director, the executive producer and three of the leading actors as to the way the film is being run. I simply can't imagine it on any film I've been involved in.

Dušan always takes what you might describe as a very humble attitude, a very modest attitude, but in fact it's probably more correctly defined as an irresponsible attitude, or, to be even more precise, an attitude that avoids responsibility. He talks about the situation with humorous despair, as if to say, what can one do? At the same time there's something in it bordering on relish. It is as if he rather enjoyed the idea of everybody being completely confused and disturbed. He kept on advancing elaborate theories. For example I said, 'One day, we sat in a caravan for six hours and never knew what was going on at all.' And he said, 'Well, you see, here we are dealing with the cultural difference, because we come from a culture where people don't expect to be told things. They would expect to get up and find out about it.' I said, 'But I cannot believe that's true, Dušan. Boris, the man from Jadran Films, is savagely critical of the organisation and particularly critical of the communication, and he is from Zagreb, he is a Croatian, and he is a man who works in Croatian films. So I don't buy this business of the cultural problem.'

Dušan kind of accepted this. Tom Luddy kept on backing us up. He was being an honest and fair broker, chairing the meeting very sensibly. He was pushing Dušan a lot, saying, 'It's not satisfactory, Dusan. I can't see any reason why these things should be. Surely it would be better . . .' Dušan was agreeing, but in a wildly frivolous way.

The discussion was circular. It smacked of democracy. We became a little talking-shop. There we were, airing our opinions. We would, each of us, build up a head of steam and suddenly make a little passionate outburst. Fred sank into terrible depressions and then would rise up again and speak very strongly and clearly about what he thought should be the way of dealing. Dušan began to treat the phrase 'lack of communication', which kept on coming up again deadeningly, thuddingly, boringly, in a sort of satirical spirit. He would say, 'Lack of communication. Yes. Lack of communication. Ha. Communication is so much my problem,' with a peculiar twinkle in his eyes. Most odd and quite aggressive, I thought. Then he spoke about the rushes, how satisfied he was and how he'd spoken to the editor and the editor had said to him how good it all was. And Dušan had said to him. 'Now you can say anything at all you like. Is there any comment at all?' And the editor, Tony Lawson, had said, 'Perhaps the British actors are too reverential towards the text.'

I found myself tightening and hardening and I said to him, 'What do you think, Dušan?' 'Yes, I think, maybe you are too reverential towards the text. Very good.' 'So what do you want?' 'Well, you should be less reverential, of course.' 'That's an absurd proposition,' I said. 'It is a useless remark, something you can't say to an actor if you want to get any kind of result. It's something a critic might say. It isn't anything which has any practical application. Would you like us to change every third word, for example? Would you like us to make up our own words?'

Dušan often expresses himself as despising the work of the writer. Of course this is a joke because he is the writer as well as the director, but it does cut right to the heart of our problem as actors. The relationship between the actor and the writer is a natural alliance, and the work of the director must always be some kind of intervention. It may be a brilliant and useful and revealing and rewarding and triumphantly important intervention, but it is always an intervention because the words of the writer are all that the actor can work from. If the words don't matter then there is no law, anything goes, because then we are dependent on the director's inspiration. In this film one has always had the sense that there is nothing to which one could appeal, there is no constitution, no bill of rights, no body of law. There was only the inspiration of the inspired man. Great for him, rotten for us.

'No,' said Dušan, 'what I'm always working for is something more casual.' 'That casualness comes from the sense of the character,' I said, 'and if you want us just to use the text in any old way then you have to be clear about who the characters are.' I mentioned my experience on *Amadeus* (the play) of finally getting hold of the character of Mozart and how it had transformed the way I handled the text. I used the text, instead of serving the text, but that couldn't happen until I had got the sense of the character. Lindsay pointed out that it takes five years of work, five months, at the very least five weeks of actual rehearsal with the characters and their world to reach that kind of security. Dušan, a little surprised, I think, at what he had unleashed, said, 'Yes, yes, yes,' and then explained that he had many problems with the cameraman. This was more or less what we knew already, but he said it very openly and expanded on it at great length: how Pinter is a wonderful photographer and is very interested in certain framings, and so on, but it worries Dušan very much that it is too perfect, too finished, too polished. He can't bear anything perfect, he says, it disturbs him, it upsets him, he wants to undo it, to spoil it, and he thought that maybe our acting was too good. And he turned to me and said, 'I'm less worried about you because you do all kinds of funny strange movements, and you help to break up the perfection of Pinter's frame, but nonetheless I feel of all you English actors, that you are all very talented, very skilful, but I feel I'm not demanding enough from you. Because of all these problems, I haven't been able to work properly with you yet. I want to get into a position where I'm not worried about the light, I'm not worried about the weather, I'm not worried about getting the shot in the minimum amount of time, but where I can just start to demand more and more of you.'

I said, 'Right at the beginning you said you had to have your kind of actors. Actors that you could throw in at the deep end, to whom you can suddenly say, it will be like this, like that, and they won't be fazed. But we're all like that, all of us sitting round the table. The company that you have assembled can do anything you like. We can stand on our heads for you, we can roll with the punches without any difficulty at all. We want to do it, we really do. You just have to *tell* us. We have to be in communication with you. You have to talk to us.' 'Yes, yes, yes,' he said. Twinkle, twinkle, twinkle. The whole thing was really over by then. Tom had done what he thought had to be done: he had brought the matter out into the open; he had aired it, everybody knew what everybody felt. Surely only good could result. We started to move off to go to supper. Just as we were going, Bojana said, 'One thing you should know. This film is the most organised film that Makavejev has ever made. Every other film has been an absolute living nightmare.'

When we went off for the meal, Fred felt that he had completely wasted his time, and Lindsay and I both felt the sterile emptiness of that kind of discussion, the pointlessness, the meaninglessness of it. There was only the very limited satisfaction of listening to one's own voice. Dušan is not a film-maker like other film-makers, not, indeed, a man like other men. There is something deep in him which is opposed to the idea of anything worked-on – polished isn't quite the right word – structured, shaped, and so on. He doesn't want to know about it. Over supper Fred and I recounted our dreams from the night before. Mine was that I had seen a film starring Alec Guinness and Margaret Rutherford, who were in the audience as well. I turned round to them at the end of it and said how marvellous it was and then attempted to give them notes on their performances, to say in which ways I thought they could be improved. Alec very gravely and very courteously reminded me that it was too late. Too late is very much what I feel about my work in our film: half of the character has already been committed to celluloid, and that's it . . . Fred had a more extreme dream. He dreamt that he had died. Auditions were held to find his replacement on the film. He began to work out who were his friends and who weren't. There were the ones who refused to play the part because his memory should be sacred, the ones who took a little time before accepting, and the ones who eagerly jumped at it. Finally somebody was cast and the filming resumed. But the most extraordinary image he had was of Dejan speaking into his walkie-talkie and just saying 'Fred is dead, Fred is dead'. Terrible dream.

Dušan:
During the actual work, not only was I not 'properly explaining' my intentions and desires, I was also absolutely unaware what my attitude against 'acting' could produce in someone who had written a book on Being an Actor. *Reading Simon's diary I found some relief in discovering that he had had similar problems with Milos Forman, who also did not care about 'acting'. Towards the end of our work in Zagreb, the 'problem with the British actors' crystallised. We had in the crew Eric Stoltz, a Method actor who mixed easily with others, actors, sets, props, weather and crew, Chris Haywood, as Australian as you can get (mixing easily with nature, trees, animals, absolutely indivisible from anything that surrounds him, things or people), Rade Serbedzija and Svetozar Cvetkovic, trained both in Method and Brecht, both brilliant on stage, both aware that film is something else, aware that they are with us just for the shoot – a few days or weeks – and we are with a film for a year or two, knowing exactly what they are needed for and making themselves available body and soul. They know always when they don't have to look like actors and when their acting skills are called for. Camilla Søeberg was the only star on the set and, not being the star in real life, she filled her part in her natural way with liveliness, innocence, freshness. Whenever she was wrong, the material was useless. When she was right, it was absolutely right. Her talent was obvious, it was good for the camera, for the other actors and for me.*

The next morning I was supposed to go on the set at 10.00 but got a call from Dejan at 7.00 in the morning to say that because of the rain it was not possible to do the scenes that were scheduled, that instead, we would be doing the scenes in the sanitorium, and that we'd be leaving at 8.00. So I stumbled down for a meal, we left at 8.00. and Fred and I sat in the bus together. He was again in despair because he had had breakfast with Dušan and had said to him, 'I'm terribly glad we had that discussion, even though I suppose it didn't really make any difference, but I'm terribly glad we had it so now we all know what we think.' And Dušan of course agreed enthusiastically and said that he had been asking around Jadran Films a little bit to find out about these differences in culture. What were the different film-makers like? What were the Italians like? The Italians apparently cheat and lie and steal and will do anything at all and are completely without morals. The French are very efficient and analytical. The British are very arrogant and very demanding. The Americans are very dramatic and shout and rave a lot. And he said, 'You see, there's something that's worrying me about British acting. I just don't think I understand British acting, basically. Because, you see, the Australian actors and the American actors bring things, they bring business, they bring suggestions, it's marvellous. But unfortunately the English actors, who are terribly good and skilful, expect me to tell them what to do. How can I tell them if I don't know?

Dušan:
Fred's recollection of my words from our breakfast talk, re-told to Simon on a morning bus, recollected by Simon late at night and dictated into his oral diary, appear here as my words within quotes. Unauthorized. I'll never sign them.

Fred told me that he had said to Dušan, 'Why do you use British actors then if you know this about them?' 'Oh, no,' he said. 'They are all wonderful. It's marvellous. It's just this strange lack of bringing things to the film.' Fred said that this made him feel unimaginative, uncreative, ungenerous and made him despair, made him hate the film and hate himself. I completely understood. I felt entirely similar things. I said to him, 'You know, the only way to get through this is to say, "Fuck him". Get angry.

204

You have to find and maybe even artificially create an anger in yourself and get on with doing what you want to do and what you know you can do. And that's all there is to it.' 'You're right,' he said. 'I know you're absolutely right. But I have no heart for it at the moment.' And I perfectly understood.

Dušan has the most extraordinary genius for unsettling one. As Fred amusingly said, he is charming and witty and curious and original and everything one would hope from an Eastern European intellectual, but, underneath it, he gets to you. There is a peculiar sense of reproach, a sense of disappointment, a sense of dissatisfaction that emanates from him which is terribly unnerving. What he somehow manages to imply is that one is some kind of a rep hack. I noticed him on the set today when Fred and I were laughing and joking, and I saw him looking at us out of the corner of his eye and resenting it, disliking it and feeling that it was typical of our approach, that we could be making these jokes and then suddenly snap into giving a performance.

English actors laugh all the time. We all laugh. It's our natural instinct, our natural impulse to laugh or to make someone laugh. England is a humorous nation. The rarity of this quality only becomes apparent when you step across the waters that surround our island, that is to America, to Europe, in general. They all have their ways of laughing, but England has, it seems to me, a uniquely pure way of laughing which I associate with the great tradition of nonsense. It may, as I said before, be a product of emotional immaturity. Certainly it is innocent, emotionally, politically, intellectually. It is a humour beyond meaning, a humour which actually attacks meaning. It is a Wittgensteinian humour, if such a thing can be. It suspends the laws of language, turns social relationships upside down, destroys pomposity. Perhaps it's simply an escape from the awful cage of the English temperament, uptight, organised, sensible, domestic. It may of course have something to do with this central fact of not having been occupied by a foreign power for nearly a thousand years. It is not the humour of resistance.

Now Dušan is often playful, and many of the Yugoslavian people one has met are playful, but behind the playfulness is a kind of terrible seriousness. Behind English playfulness, what we call English humour, is a terrible unseriousness. There is an ultimate sense of absurdity among us that not many other nations possess. It may embody a kind of hopelessness, it may be the only possible escape from an enormously successful and established body politic, it may be an inability to face things as they really are; but there is, in the whole of English literature and the whole of English life, this strand which underlines everything we do. Somehow on this movie that sense of humour is out of place, and its absence has soured things for us; and when we have supplied it, it seems to have caused offence, to have been perceived as merely frivolous and, as such, resented. I wonder what he expects, what an inspired Yugoslavian actor, or an inspired Australian, or an inspired American, would be doing in between takes. Would they be In Character? Or would they perhaps just be Being Original, dwelling in Originality? He obviously thinks that we are cerebral in the least interesting way, that is to say that we plan, control and programme our performances, which is a bit of a joke, in my case.

He keeps on saying how much he admires English acting. American producers and directors say the same thing. Everybody says it, it's an automatic remark: English actors are the best in the world. But if they think

Dušan:
English playwrights are the best in the world as well, English cars, English football . . . How about pudding?

that then why don't they trust us to use our own methods? Why don't they trust us to use the methods that created this wonderful acting? Why do they want to impose their method of work on us? They want the same result, but they want their method to be used to get it. It is very peculiar: as if it couldn't quite be authentic unless you had gone through the process that they believe in.

27 October

Today filming was in an extraordinary 1773 building which is now a home for retarded children. Again it seemed as if Makavejev had somehow created a Makavejevian world all around him. Here was this place swarming with sweet little children in various degrees of deformity, but who clearly weren't a danger to themselves or to anybody else. They were romping around and talking, some of them talking rather cleverly in English, so it seemed, and yet apparently all mentally retarded. At some point the electricity failed, and there we were, in this huge eighteenth-century house full of tiny mad children, sitting in the dark without any heating or food, and that somehow seemed entirely Makavejevian.

First there were a couple of shots of the famous fire engine, then of Fred and me meeting Doctor Lombrosov. Lombrosov, the crazed director of the asylum, is played by Patrick Godfrey, the latest to join our little band of English actors, the Zagreb Raj. Paddy was in both *A Room with a View* and *Maurice*, in which he gave a startlingly malevolent performance, especially startling since in life he is the gentlest, mildest of men. When roused, however – to anger or to laughter – he betrays huge emotions only a millimetre or so beneath the surface. How will he respond to Makavejeveianism? 'Welcome to the madhouse,' we said.

The next scene is actually in the asylum, just walking down the corridor. I made a little joke to Bojana. Two characters in straitjackets were being pushed by on a trolley. I said, ' The original actors who played Hunt and

Avanti, I presume.' We shot what were basically very simple scenes, in which I didn't have any dialogue, so at least I couldn't display an over-reverential attitude towards the text. In the scene in which Lily Sacher is carried out screaming, Dušan had one of his curious conversations with Lindsay in which he said how 'marrvelloose, marrvelloose' it was, but somehow it was too real: 'But I can't see how it can be comic in any way. I don't know where the comedy would be. How can we make it lighter? How can we make it more amusing?' He is very odd. Is he just a very bad director? That may be the simple fact that is staring one in the face. One of the most elementary rules of directing is to go for the cause and not the effect. Dušan says, 'The effect that I want is that it should be a bit dangerous but also a bit funny,' and so on. The first thing you think of as a director is, 'What would make it like that?' and then you suggest that to the actor. To ask the actor to, as it were, act the reviews is impossible and frustrating.

They tried it once more. Lindsay played the scene down. Dušan rushed up and said that Pinter had come up to him and said, 'But it's got no intensity. It's no good. Go back to doing the original.' So Lindsay went back to doing the original but a little less impassioned. We are in the area of fine tuning – up a little bit, no, no, down a bit, *that's it* – which is OK if you're building on something that already exists, but which is merely puppetry if not. So what? you may well ask. After all, this is film, you only have to get it right once. Well, of course I can't prove it, but I swear that a performance which comes from inside the actor, which is actually flowing through him, must be better and more interesting – but once the flow is going, then you can dam it up or let it surge. Billy Wilder said to me, apropos of Charles Laughton: 'I can contain a fire, but I can't get one going.' But Dušan only seems interested in *adjusting the faggots* – a sort of structuralist approach. Or is he? Fred had pointed out that Dušan had only seemed at all satisfied after the couple of times he had lost his temper and, still fuelled by anger, had done a take – my own experience exactly, of course. I said to Fred, 'We do have to face the fact that he is a genuinely dialectical, Marxist-trained thinker, like Brecht' (whom he might, it suddenly occurs to me, rather resemble, for all I know). What is anathema to him is a bourgeois approach to creating character: the attempt to produce anything finished, anything which has a completed quality about it, that has solved the character or, to use the classical Brechtian formulation, suggests that the character can't change. What I do and what I suppose Fred does is, by these criteria, essentially bourgeois and therefore basically dead, however accomplished, polished or forceful it might be.

To me he says nothing. Nothing at all.

O.K., I'm paranoid, but Makavejev is a man who creates paranoia. I don't know whether he dislikes me, no doubt that's too strong, but I feel that the respect, or at least the enthusiasm, that he originally had for me has become very diluted or reduced. I sense that he probably thinks of me as a man without solidity, as all talk. I get from him a response that I have had from only a couple of directors, and when I have had it has absolutely killed me. One was Milos Forman and the other was Bill Gaskill. A feeling that I was a lightweight, a rather ridiculous person who didn't think through what he did, who was lazy, who was unimaginative, who lacked poetry, who was just a show-off of a rather shallow kind. What other people find buoyant, optimistic and energetic in me, he obviously finds merely bumptious. What other people find amusing in me, he finds either calculated or frivolous. There is a hopeless and unbridgeable gap between us and in such situations one should normally get out quick but of course here you can't. There are contracts, there are commitments, there is responsibility (his dreaded word). Obviously this feeling is so powerful in me because I feel that there is some truth in it. I feel found out, seen through, rumbled. In other words, I feel that the very essence of myself as a person and as a performer is rejected, and I cannot see how one can possibly do good work on that basis. The film is therefore

completely unenjoyable for me and I am learning nothing
and I wish I hadn't done it.

Dušan:
*The director's indecisiveness is notorious. In some genres
there are easy ways out. In action movies when they don't
know what to do, they get actors to run through dark
corridors and shoot each other. Fellini gets everybody
dancing. Tarkovsky would stretch the shot and let it last
until the least perceptive viewer starts feeling guilty and
thinks of God. What am I going to do when we have to
get the whole old train (rented and paid for dearly) to enter
the station and disperse two dozen chickens among a few
actors, if suddenly, one of these actors expresses an urgent
need to discuss his character and ways of saying a few
trivial lines, and it happens to be the very first day of his
working with me? Obviously, whatever I did, out of my
respect for him, was wrong. All my worries about other
things he, inexperienced in films as he was, could not read
but as related to him. When it gets later forgotten, as it
mostly does, no harm. But if the actor is an ambitious
writer as well and has a contract for a book about his
experiences as a film star, how to get him to understand
that there are scenes (or there were) in which the chickens
were carrying more weight and meaning than the other
actors in the shot? (Could I even convey that everything
that acts in the shot plays the role of the actor, or is the
actor?)*

*The first draft of Simon's diary was an endless tapestry
of sighs, whines, complaints and criticisms. Next drafts
moved on to 'whining and dining', and were easier to read,
but still difficult for me.*

*Several drafts later there is a funny book full of stories
from the shoot and around, still with long whining
chapters. It seems I am asked retro-actively to nurse and
attend wounds that still bleed. At the same time, I am
getting a note from London: the publisher is urging me 'not
to fight with one arm behind your back'.*

*I would like then, instead of 'fighting back' to quote from
a diary almost three hundred years old:*

October 14 1699. *The king was purged nine ti.nes with his usual physic. The stools were big, boiling, and of wateriness both oily and smarting.*

June 29, 1701. *Nine stools full of green peas.*

June 16, 1702. *Nine stools full of fish.*

February 4, 1704. *Between one and two in the afternoon, after the deer hunt, he went quickly to the closet and produced a stool, watery and undigested. After dinner, about one hour after his first stool, he produced a second one as loose and no less rotten. At 5.30, upon his returning home from a stroll, he produced a third of the same quality, but a little smaller, followed by a fourth which was similar, immediately after supper.*

December 23, 1707. *Dead worm found in stool. Doctors theorized that it caused the vapours which were afflicting the king.*

August 9, 1710. *At eight and ten o'clock he produced two stools, undigested and smelly, while visiting his mistress, Madame de Maintenon.*

(From 'The Journal of the King's Health', a log kept by the physicians of Louis XIV as reproduced in "End Product" by Dan Sabbath & Mandel Hall.)

28 October

Yesterday, 27th, was a major, an enormous day of filming. In the first shot there were 96 extras, 4 musicians, and 40 children. Or rather, there would have been 40 children, but this is a film called *For a Night of Love* and it is being produced by Cannon Films, so someone has omitted to notify the children. That meant that we couldn't do the first shot first, filling in the time instead with close-ups, while children were kidnapped from every available source and crammed into costumes. They eventually arrived at about one o'clock. Naturally a scene of that enormity was slow to set up and slow to shoot. It was a question of single lines here or there. One had very little communication with Dušan, not that one ever has very much. One fulfilled one's part in the overall scheme as best one could, and I'm sure it will be very beautiful. The master-shot was a long tracking-shot with horses and all the rest of it. It started with a scene in which I instruct the agents where to stand to throw their bunches of flowers. This scene confirmed, if ever confirmation were needed, the degree to which one is totally dependent on the reaction of one's fellow actors. To put it more particularly, if you say something and the other actor doesn't understand what you are saying and therefore does nothing, you are likely to say it more strenuously and louder. Of course the agents don't understand me when I say, 'Move over there,' 'Get over there,' 'Come here,' 'Come there,' so I start getting pop-eyed and bulging, and Dušan can't understand why it's so strenuous and weak. Why don't I just give my commands? I have power. Just tell them! and so on. He doesn't understand that I can only do that if they obey me. The source of my power is in their obedience, not in my inherent strength. There is a line: 'Throw the flowers.' The agents all threw their flowers before I said the line, so of course the line is redundant. Wouldn't it have been better if they had thrown them on a command from me? But no, he couldn't see that, it didn't really mean anything to him and we went on to some other major philosophical discussion.

Dušan:
Being allergic to horses, and obsessed with the 'proper timing' of his lines (in the huge crowd and noise) Simon stayed oblivious to the fact that the horses carrying the king and his entourage were – in several rehearsals – frightened of the flowers thrown at them. They would stop in the middle of the shot, go left and right, or backwards. The problem was (amongst all the crowd, cheering children, musicians and our actors, hunters, agents, photographer etc) to get the flower throwers to throw their flowers in such a way that the camera perceived them as thrown at the king, while they crossed the horses' path actually before, so's not to frighten the animals. What was happening would be obvious to anyone who, with a corner of his eye, checked what the camera saw (it was a wide shot for the movement). Simon's lines were, a few months later during dubbing, properly recorded and edited where they belong.

He has the most peculiar way of laughing when one suggests something to him different to what he has just suggested. It is the fascinated chuckle of someone given a glimpse of a world-view, totally alien and indeed risible, but in its own way intriguing. As if one had said, for example, 'When the sun sinks I am frightened, because how do I know it will ever rise again.' At such a remark Dušan will perhaps chuckle as if to say, 'Yes I see. That is quite interesting. It is quite poetic. It is quite fascinating. But it is also wrong and incomprehensible.'
In our dealings, there is a new note of impatience. I

think that in Dušan I have struck one of the people I have met from time to time in my career, who find me personally antipathetic. I irritate Dušan at a quite deep level. So he feels obliged to tamper with whatever I do all the time, picking at me just for the sake of it. I, for my part, talk back to him, trying to justify what I'm doing, which is not only ludicrous, it's impossible, and petty. 'I was over there because I thought that you said . . .' 'But you just said that you were doing such and such . . .' 'Oh, but I thought we were all supposed to be . . .' 'Oh, I see. Well, that's that . . .' It's undignified for both of us, nagging and snapping away like an old married couple.

●●●●●●●●●●●●●●●●●●●

Dušan as Zen Master (Aside)

A more elevated interpretation of his attitude: it is as if he were playing Zen games. The classic Zen manoeuvre of the master asking a question in the form of a riddle, the purpose of which is not to get an answer, but to bring the student to the point at which he gives up the absurd quest for meaning, loses his self-consciousness and preparedness, and thus allows himself a moment which is entirely alive and entirely spontaneous – which has an 'is-ness'. And this is Enlightenment, Satori. Alan Watts maintains (perhaps rather mischievously) that this is the underlying mechanism of psychoanalysis: the patient is presented with an unsolveable riddle. The attempt to make sense of it finally breaks down, the patient abandons the attempt to find meaning in his life, and this releases him to actually live it. There seem to me to be parallels with the Makavejev method.

For example, as soon as you appear to have worked out what he wants, he doesn't want it any more. He doesn't want what he wants. He wants what he might get, but if he gets it, he doesn't want it again. What he wanted wasn't really what he wanted, he was just using that as a means of getting something else from you, namely, spontaneity, reality. This is an R.D. Laing world of circular, mad reasoning. It may give him something absolutely unique. But it is a nightmare for a professional actor. It makes a mockery of acting as a craft. I think he's terrified that whatever one is doing is actorish, therefore cerebral in some way, whereas all he wants is a visual reality to appear on the screen in front of him. Actually, the reality that will appear on the screen is frustration and anger.

As it happens, I had a spontaneous experience of reality of my own yesterday, which delighted him: I am allergic to horses – they make me sneeze – and there were forty horses there. No there weren't, there were no more than eight, but it was enough to send me into paroxysms of sneezing and reduce me to a state of abject exhaustion, as if I'd been beaten about the face with a lettuce. He was enchanted by it, and said, 'How wonderful if Avanti is sneezing and perhaps Hunt sneezes as well to please his master,' but I am afraid I wasn't actually able to arrange that on camera, so again more disappointment, no doubt. I remembered today that he had said, again with a kind of mad relish, when we were discussing the difficulties of working in Yugoslavia, 'Of course the alternative was to work in Budapest, where nobody understands the language at all, nobody speaks a word of English, nobody speaks a word of Serbo-Croat, nobody speaks any language except Hungarian.' It was clear that the total confusion of such a situation was not without its charm for him; chaos is his medium.

● ● ● ● ● ● ● ● ● ● ● ● ● ● ● ● ● ● ● ●

Drew (the sound man, butt of many dear old jokes, such as 'a sound man is hard to find,' and that's about the best) was saying that he doesn't know where we're shooting next because nobody ever, ever tells him. He and Mark have worked out by the placement of the director's and the cameraman's chairs where the next set-up is going to be. It's an infallible sign. But that is the only way that they know. Of course it is perfectly simple, not, actually, a bad way of finding out, but there isn't any other film in the world that doesn't think it's important let alone courteous to let the sound man know where the next fucking scene is going to take place. It's extraordinary.

Back to the hotel, where Bruno has been slaving over a hot model for *Shirley Valentine*. We have worked out our scheme. Act One takes place in Shirley's kitchen. Act Two on a Greek island. We want to find the maximum contrast, obviously. Act One will be all straight lines and sharp angles and synthetic materials; Act Two as real and natural as can be contrived (I'm choosing my words carefully here). Act Two is basically a rock, and sky. Bruno will make the model rock in London; it's the kitchen we're concerned with now. The first problem we face is the usual one posed by a naturalistic play set in one room: whose kitchen is the size of a West End stage? How do you limit the space without only using half your stage? We discussed this at great length in London. I had been talking to John Gielgud about Kommisarjevsky a few days before, and he'd said that one of Kommis' innovations had been to angle sets: instead of being square on, a room would have its corner centre stage. I wondered if we could use that? Bruno pointed out that it'd have the huge advantage of bringing Pauline (Collins, our Shirley) closer to the audience. Great, I said; perhaps the opposite corner, the lip, as it were, of the stage, could jut out into the auditorium. We could put the play, and Shirley, right into the audience's lap. This is what Bruno has been working on, and it looks as if it might well work. It's still rather large for a kitchen, and there remains the problem of the height of the proscenium arch (we don't actually know where we're playing but no West End theatre is less than a certain height). We discuss all this further, in preference to talking about the film.

It's such a joy to work on something that seems soluble.

29 October 87

Another big day on this very large picnic scene. Horses and children, a blind accordionist and a few trailing extras, but basically we are doing Lindsay's close-ups in the scene where Lily Sacher begins to go a little crazy because she has been denied by Avanti. There were several rather striking moments in this. In her very first close-up, on the horse, she says, 'We have a prisoner waiting here for justice.' Dušan said, 'Yeah. Very good. Very good. Marrvelloose. Very good. Except I have the feeling that you are a void, a complete void. There is nothing happening inside you at all. Of course it's very early in the morning and it's hard to do this without being a void but you mustn't be a void. So, do it again with some life and intensity.' And he says these things in a very casual, off-hand way, as if it couldn't possibly be offensive. Anyway, Lindsay did it again, with intensity. And life.

Later she has a scene in which she makes a speech to the king and Dušan said, 'It was too fast. It was as if you were playing on 16mm, just quickly going by, and I had the impression perhaps it was because it was cold, that the weather is very bad, so don't do that.' To say to an actor you are playing it as if it was on a 16mm film is about as bizarre a piece of direction as I think I have ever heard in my life. So Lindsay said, 'You want it to be slower, so OK I'll play it slower.' So she played it slower and that seemed to suit him particularly well.

Later, Bruno strolled by to say hello and to watch filming. He saw an old woman – nothing to do with the film, just walking in the park – go up to the counter where there was a sort of running buffet, pile a large amount of food onto a plate, scoff it ravenously, then sit down – in the chair marked 'Director' – to watch the filming, as if this was what she did every day, as if the whole thing had been laid on as a little diversion for her. She watched for ten minutes or so, then suddenly and spectacularly vomited. Nurses rushed around, she was taken to a caravan where she lay down for an hour or so, then off she went on her way. A pleasant way of spending the morning, no doubt.

There is a frisson on the set when we first glimpse Fred, wrapped up in a sheet, bandaged and bleeding, with flowers woven into his hair and beard: an extraordinary image, entirely Dušan's and wonderful (I had overheard Fred say 'this symbolic moment' and Dušan had said 'vaguely symbolic'. It's as naked and open a symbol as can possibly be, a Christ figure even down to the crown of thorns. But Dušan won't be pinned down. It's not necessarily a symbol, but it's also not necessarily not a symbol: it could be all kinds of things simultaneously). Fred asked Dušan a simple question: 'Shouldn't I try to conceal myself a bit? It seems to me that Avanti wouldn't want to face the king openly looking like this. He would want to hide himself a bit.' And Dušan wiped his face with his hands in his usual way, anti-clockwise, up over his cheek, over his brow and down the other side, and started to talk about Beria.

Beria, Stalin's Chief of Police, was, he said, a terrible man, who killed all these people. He was absolutely the most feared man in Russia, but he was a kind of court jester to Stalin. He made him laugh. He was an absurd figure, made to do absurd and laughable things, while nonetheless terrorising millions. In the same way, Dušan said, Avanti, although he has killed people for the king, can nevertheless be an absurd figure in the king's eyes. When Dušan finished speaking, there was a complete silence. What possible response could there be to such an enormous statement? What he said was fascinating, but why have we never heard a word of it before? He had spoken reluctantly, wearily, almost, as if we children who had got stuck with a quiz, and he, the bored parent, had finally allowed us to turn to the back page, where the answer was to be found, printed upside-down. 'Oh well, if you don't want to play any more . . .'

The remark about Beria is a brilliant illumination, a revelation of what Dušan has left out of the script, but is at its heart. It transforms one's understanding of the part and the scene. Not that one would play the symbolism, not even add a subtext, but it would give significance, focus – reality. It makes perfect sense, of course. Avanti is the king's security supremo, and therefore, as this is an intensely repressive kingdom in Dušan's vision, he does fulfil the same sort of function for him as Beria did for Stalin. As far as the text actually reads, though, we have nothing but a series of operetta situations. It is possible, of course, that Dušan himself wasn't aware of the resonance when he wrote it, is only now aware of it, now that he sees it before his very eyes. Semiotically speaking, of course, everything signifies something beyond itself and inevitably refers to other realities, which includes other films, other works of art, history itself, regardless of the conscious intentions of the author. I have no difficulty in believing that this complex and sophisticated man writes his films in a state of innocence, the images dictated by his unconscious.

But, not being him, we need these things to be elucidated. If this script had been a play and we English actors had been doing it, we would have sat down and considered its origins, namely that it had been written by a Yugoslavian who had been expelled from his country fifteen years ago, who is a political-sexual revolutionary and who has been brought up in and lived through a communistic, socialistic upbringing, during the late Stalinist era. All of those resonances would be in the back of his mind, we would have assumed, and we would have viewed the play in the light of them. We would have looked at the history of the Austro-Hungarian Empire, we would have looked at Yugoslav naive art, we would have examined the rest of Dušan's oeuvre. And I think, curiously enough, we might have come up in the end with something very Makavejevian. All of this makes clear, if it needed to be made clearer, the difference between making a film and doing a play. Everything is instant, you must produce the character instantly and it's gone instantly. If you haven't got it right then that's it, and what I find so frustrating is that you can have a breakthrough on one scene but you can't sustain it the next day nor can you re-do previous scenes in the light of the new discovery. There is never any sense of getting the whole thing right.

● ● ● ● ● ● ● ● ● ● ● ● ● ● ● ● ● ● ●

Reflections on Character (Aside)

The Beria anecdote is a pure example of Dušan's 'both/and' theory of character. In the end, all acting embodies a theory of human nature, and I think that is what is at the heart of the whole conflict. Dušan's materialism – in the philosophical sense – means that he sees a human being as an assemblage of impulses, galloping madly off (as Stephen Leacock would say) in all directions. I don't know if you can dignify my view of life with the term Idealism, but certainly – perhaps this is a religious impulse – I am always looking for some sense in a person's behaviour, some matrix which accounts for their actions. I conceive of a human personality as an organism, which has a ruling principle, like any other organism. It may be hugely complicated but it *is* a structure, and when you've discovered what that is, it has certain repeated patterns of behaviour. This is, I realise, exactly what Brecht reviles as the bourgeois conception of character. I must say, however, that the evidence of most writers, including that of Brecht himself, is that their characters take over, acquire a life of their own, surprising their creators by conforming to some law of which the writer is wholly ignorant. It is in my opinion the actor's duty to get in touch with that law. He doesn't need to spell it out, or even *know* it, any more than the writer does; but he does need to submit to it.

So often, the actor's understanding of the character will come about by accident or intuition. A word, a gesture will strike the right note, and then everything falls into place. It's awesome when this happens, because hitting this centre can cause the instant realignment of the whole of a lengthy part. It works exactly like the computer to which Gurdjieff compared the human psyche. I was lucky enough to go to a drama school which taught a theory of character (a synthesis of Rudolf Laban's analysis of movement and Jung's Psychological Types), but I've explored many strange paths looking for more precise ways of understanding its mechanisms. Astrology, properly conceived (which Jung described as a complete theory of human nature), bio-types, and the curious system of William Gerhardie and Prince Loewenstein (*Know Yourself as You Really Are*), de La Bruyère's *Characters* and the morphs (meso-, endo- and ecto-); the Enneagram, with its nine personality types; and Reich's *Character Analysis*; and I don't believe that there's a character ever been created that wouldn't yield some of its secrets to analysis by any of the above systems.

Now the curious thing is that I'm sure Dušan would be fascinated by all of this, because he really is interested in everything. But as we don't share a common feeling about what human beings are, what acting is, and what the purpose of making a film might be, we keep kicking each other's shins. We could *talk* about it happily, unendingly; but *doing* something, actually trying to create something together, requires agreement at a fundamental level.

• • • • • • • • • • • • • • • • • • • •

Dušan:
Any beautiful and meaningful 'agreement at a fundamental level' among the cast and crew, in advance, gets tested by wind or rain, an unexpected baby's cry from the neighbourhood, or a single member's indisposition or drunkenness. Great football or basketball games, remembered for some magical victorious momentum when the whole team victoriously 'seized the moment' and won, tell us that mysterious 'agreement' arrives as if coming from nowhere. I speak of great collective moments when every player acts intelligently and harmoniously according (or 'as if according') to a divine plan.

America was 'discovered' on a trip to India, as all great discoveries happen. The fact that the discoverer did not know in advance that he would strike gold and change history does not minimize the importance (and depth) of his luck.

No anxiety is ever sorted out and dispersed by 'intelligent talk'. Only blind confidence can properly light the road.

It's impossible. It seems, I'm afraid, to be one of those projects where one has to say, 'Well it might have been marvellous if only one had known'. I know I have personally failed to do what he wants, and I realise also that he realises that and he's cutting me out of more and more of the film. He is using me as a sort of extra, just as an amusing silent figure somewhere around the edges. He said to me when it came to taking off the gag from Avanti's mouth, 'You use the knife for that.' 'Knife?' I said. 'Yes, your knife. You are going to have a wonderful big knife'. 'But I haven't had a knife up till now.' 'No, no. It's over here. We'll show it to you.' 'But why haven't I been allowed to see it?' 'Well, it didn't matter. We didn't need it until now. Just use it. You produce this wonderful big knife and then you cut the gag with it.' So they brought me the knife, which was sharp enough to carve the Sunday joint. I demanded sellotape to cover the blade, much to everybody's surprise. They thought it was rather boring of me and said, 'We'll sellotape it later, but use it as it is for rehearsal.' 'You've missed the point. The point,' I said, 'is that Fred only has two eyes, I only have ten fingers and there are small children all around. No, I won't use it until it is sellotaped.' So then the sellotape came out. Yet again I am an arsehole. 'Action!' says the assistant director. I flourished the knife. 'Cut!,' cries Dušan, 'No, no, what you're doing with the knife. . . .' 'You'd make more of it?' I said. 'No, no. Make less. Make less. I want it to be very matter-of-fact. You realise that this is the scene of Lindsay, of Lily Sacher, I think it is important that she is in the centre of the scene. This is just a detail at the edge of the frame.' There was an unmistakeable subtext to his remarks which said, 'You are trying to make moments for yourself. You are trying to do some vulgar piece of business to distract from the other actor in the scene.' So one just has enough of that.

One dies off inside totally. And I have just died off inside totally towards this film. I am indifferent to it. I couldn't care less. I will do anything for a quiet life now.

The only delight comes from the humour around the set. Something really amusing happened today. It turns out that Enver, the excellent Albanian actor who plays the king, pronounces English perfectly, but clearly can't speak it at all. The other day he came into the make-up van and said, 'Good morning.' 'Good morning,' said Fred. 'How are you?' 'Very well,' said Enver. Fred said, 'I'm Fred.' 'Me too,' said Enver. Today he came to me and said, 'Excuse me. I would like to . . . what is the word . . . to . . . *ask* . . . you something. It is . . . about your . . . your . . . *book*.' 'Yes?' I said, eagerly. 'I would like to . . . to ah! what is the word? . . . to . . . to . . . *translate* it.'

But also there are large temperaments. Mary Hillman, the make-up woman, had a real raging row. She stormed onto the set saying that she'd never worked on such a badly organised film, a fairly uncontroversial remark. Bojana came over to her and said, 'You mustn't talk like this, shouting in front of everybody.' 'Why not? Why not? It's true.' And Dušan went and consoled her, comforted her, hugged her. It was a major outburst. But in the end you realise there is no point in it. It makes no difference whatever. These people (by whom I suppose I mean the entire Serbo-Croat race) seem to be able to take an unlimited amount of complaint, rage, and reproach with perfect equanimity.

The only thing that could make any difference would be if one were to walk. Actually to walk out. Yesterday I conceived my master plan. This is now the only hold I have over anyone on the film; they couldn't care less, couldn't give a fuck about me one way or the other, except that I have filmed half my role and the only way, short of killing myself (messy) or walking out (unprofessional), in which I could really upset them would be if I cut off my moustache. They couldn't possibly make a moustache that fitted me in anything less than three days. They would have to send it over from England, four days, at least. If I chose the moment really cleverly it could completely fuck the film up. I would say that I had had an accident shaving and they could say nothing to prove otherwise; they could do nothing about it. This of course is lunacy, fatuous, pathetic, the fantasies of impotence, but there we are, that's the way it is. That's what's happened, that's the outcome of things on this film.

Linda Marlowe, big-eyed, smoky-voiced, passionate and ever so slightly pixilated without having touched a drop all day, has now joined us. She, Bruno, Fred, Lindsay and I – still trying to penetrate the mystery – gathered in Svetozar's room to watch tapes he's brought with him of two of Dušan's earlier films. *Montenegro* and *W.R.*, which I now finally caught up with, but only in a bowdlerized version taped from BBC Television. It's unfair to judge it on this basis, but its techniques seem a little passé. The footage of Reich himself made my heart beat faster, though, and the film's cheekiness is undiluted by time. It must have been quite astonishing for contemporary Yugoslavs in 1970 – the playfulness – playing with the idea of revolution. The sex, by contrast, is rather dull, almost meaningless now (though the most famous scene, where the woman takes a plaster cast of the man's erect penis, has been filleted out by Auntie BBC). Reich is not dealt with in any depth but the assault on Stalin, and the satire, the wicked parody of the Soviet system, and by extension the whole Eastern European system, is still fresh. The basic subversiveness of the film is not so much in its content, though, as in its form. As the Russian film-maker Yosselliani observed, surrealism and indeed any abandonment of strict realism is a challenge to the whole idea of order which becomes directly political.

Seeing the two movies together, it was striking that every film of Dušan's contains, and indeed culminates in, a death which is somehow associated with love. That is true of *Montenegro*, it is true of *Tragedy of a Switchboard Operator*, true of *W.R.*, and certainly true of the film we are filming at the moment. It struck me, too, that *W.R.*, was the dry thesis of which *Montenegro* was the rich proof. Sveto's swarthy, sexy performance is more remarkable even than before. Seeing him sitting here in the room, so pure, so Nordic, staring intently at his transformed image flickering away on the television screen, is a little uncanny. It is as if he were gazing into a crystal ball, receiving a vision of another self, past or future. Actors: artists in mutiphrenia. There are wonderful, rich things elsewhere in the film, too. The ostensible story line is the least remarkable thing: the American woman's discovery of her wilder self, the release of her id, or at least the triumph of her Dionysiac self over her Apollonian self, something to that effect. That is the central notion of the film, but the richness of it is the fantastic succession of surrounding events. Dušan's quirky fantasy, and his visual imagination, are no less in evidence, it must be said, on *For a Night of Love*. Perhaps it was hell for *Montenegro*'s actors, too. Sveto is irritatingly loyal on the matter, refusing to be drawn, pretending not to know what we're talking about. I made a joke, one not, perhaps, without some truth. One of the very first shots in the film is of an ape in a cage, a gorilla. I said, 'Dušan's perfect actor.' The animal exactly fulfils my earlier description of Dušan's ideal. The ape is a very interesting creature indeed to whom happy accidents constantly occur in front of the camera.

Thursday was the first night of night-shooting. I was very briefly involved in it. We're filming in a beautiful 1870's house in a genteel suburb of the city. It's filled with photographs and paintings of the occupants; or are they? One simply can't be sure on a film. The set decorators may have imported all this. But it's a splendid house, with its wooden panels and corridors and winding staircases. Who lives in such a house in socialist Zagreb? Someone suggests that the occupants have done some sort of deal with the government. Quite curious. At a certain point, Dušan and I found ourselves alone on the verandah of the house. After a little awkwardness, which I broke by mentioning the two films we'd all just seen, we managed to have a long and quite absorbing conversation. He told me that he had never expected to be thrown out of Yugoslavia for making *W.R.* It seemed at the time that there were no constraints, no official constraints, and he was amazed at the reaction. He talked about the cycle of Stalin films (of which there are ironically intercut excerpts in *W.R.*) and about the guy who played Stalin, who had learned every single detail of his deportment, how one arm was longer than the other, and so on. We had a lovely chat. As we talked, all my fondness for him and admiration of his work returned. The scene we're about to do is a beautiful one, a party which the king arrives at and says hello to Avanti, after which Hunt, reassured, goes off. The king has his entourage including a cardinal and adjutants and so on. There were lots of young people, twenty-five year olds, extraordinarily handsome Yugoslavian men and women dancing together. There are, too (of course!), nuns, not actually dancing, just part of the throng. I have almost nothing to say in the scene, but I was quite happy to be a little touch of colour: it's such a lovely scene – the band playing, these beautiful young people, a real sense of occasion. This is partly to do with the chill in the air which has a stimulant effect on everyone. Huggy in his sweet way keeps slipping me cups of black coffee, upon which I subsist almost exclusively. I'm cheerful partly because Bruno and I are off tomorrow to the coast. Hols. It only amused me that in the take that Dušan asked to be printed one of the extras, the old gentleman playing the cardinal, was so confused and uncertain about climbing up the steps, that he stood exactly slap in front of me, so I assume I am not in the shot at all. There was a great, it seemed to me, festivity in the air that night, partly because it was a party, partly because it was the first night-shoot, but also because we seemed to have passed the halfway point in the film and the end is in sight, which means that the madness is now extrovert instead of introverted. A great relief.

A breather. The *Shirley Valentine* model is built. We started to think in terms of projections, to flesh out

Shirley's domestic world: projections down the side of the proscenium arch, the whole kitchen framed by an impressionistic collage of her inner landscape. I worry a little about this. First of all, I'm not quite sure how much visual competition a solo performer can take (Lily Tomlin works on a virtually bare stage); secondly, I note an increasing tendency in my productions to aspire to the condition of film. Slides, projections *needn't* be filmic – Piscator's use of them was evidently intensely theatrical – but I think here I may be trying to reproduce the enclosing ambience of cinema, its gift of sucking you in. And Willy's play is nothing if not theatrical, a sort of operatic scena cum music hall monologue, and that must be respected.

I have a few days free, so we take off for Dubrovnik. Everybody recommends it warmly, and the air fare is ludicrously cheap – about half what it costs to go to Birmingham from London. There is a travel agency in the hotel, from which I got my ticket to Vienna (that was uncommonly cheap, too). It is run by a witty, sexy woman who chain-smokes in a rather suggestive manner. Bruno and I go to see her and feel rather sheepish, like schoolboys with the sexy French teacher. This impression is heightened when we pick up one of the magazines from the pile on her desk. It turns out to be hard-core pornography. In England it would have been *The Lady*. On one of the pages, a young woman is fellating a gorilla. Our friend behind the desk sees our expression and shrugs. 'Flying makes some people nervous,' she says. 'I should think this would make them even more nervous,' I say, but she doesn't follow. This stuff is available on every newstand, at every tobacconist's kiosk. What's the problem? Finally her computer comes through, we get the tickets, and are on our way to the airport.

DUBROVNIK
October 30

Dubrovnik. Bill Gaskill once did a production of *Oedipus Rex* here. I remember him saying that he'd been haunted by the Serbo-Croatian words for the play's phrase 'grim death' – 'smrn-smrt' – and for some reason they pop into my head now, ten years after he first told me: 'smrn smrt'. There is, in fact, nothing remotely smrn (or is it smrt?) about Dubrovnik, its golden bricks made more dazzling by the fierce sun. The tiny city is fortified with walls and ramparts, and it's on them that the plays are staged, every summer. As one drives in from the airport, it's an impossible vision, a Renaissance painting brought to life by some eccentric businessman trying to create a quattrocento Epcot. It seems brand new, but I'm sure this is exactly the sight that greeted fifteenth-century visitors to Ragusa (its name until it was Balkanised in the last century). In aspect it has nothing whatever to do with the Austro-Hungarian world we've just come from, is in fact more like the city-states with which it competed, Venice, Trieste, Naples.

We're not staying in the city itself, and have taken a room, just outside the walls, in the unexpectedly named Hotel Argentina. We took the room on the best possible recommendation – from Dubi the third assistant director, who comes from the city and is indeed named for it, an ideal son of Dubrovnik: small, perfectly-formed, gentle, nothing to do with the twentieth century (apart from his walkie-talkie, which has become an extension of his arm). Nothing here is far from anywhere else: the city is

229

within sight, ten minutes' walk away. The hotel is oddly laid out: a cramped little foyer, full of German and Italian tourists, a large ugly dining room, furnishings in the 'contemporary' manner (i.e. the style epitomised in Coventry Cathedral: etiolated abstract). It's hard to find the lift, and when you finally get into it, it judders ominously. The corridors are hideous, filled with the naïve art whose charm, like naïveté itself, is attractive only in very small doses. Oh Dubi, Dubi, why hast thou forsaken us? But once in the room, everything is wonderful. The room itself is utterly simple, which is fine: but the view's the thing. It makes everything else insignificant. The room juts out over the sea; there is only sea to see. A little to the left, if you stand on the balcony, is an island, green and silent. To the right, castellated Dubrovnik; otherwise, nothing but the black deep, and the brain starts to clear.

November 1

We've spent two days just wandering about – though in truth you can wander about the entire place in an hour and a half. There can have been no more than five or six hundred citizens of Ragusa at its height, but it was a rich and culturally complex society, entirely contained within its walls. As in fourth century Athens, but on a much smaller scale, the entire community came together at public events, such as theatrical performances. Here there was a flourishing school of playwrights, and the first great play to be written in Yugoslavia, the cornerstone, in fact, of the repertory, was written here. The constitution was original and effective. The Doge was elected annually, and for the whole of his period of office he was separated from his wife and family, the better to concentrate on his duties, a rather sensible arrangement, it seems.

Now, of course, tourism is the staple of the city, but it offers very little in the way of gaudy enticements. There are restaurants, there are shops specialising in local craft work, there are many boutiques (some in converted chapels, of which there were an astonishing quantity). There are several little patisseries. We were sitting in one of these, quite late one night, when a youngish man, mid-twenties, came up to us – he was very drunk – and offered us sex. To be precise, he offered Bruno sex, but as it was being offered on a strictly financial basis, I probably would have done just as well. Bruno declined, only to be violently abused as homosexual filth. The boy lurched off, but not before throwing up on the steps of the patisserie, whose patron regarded his vomiting with the same indifference she had extended to the entire encounter – conducted, incidentally, in heavily accented German. Speculation about the boy and his life proved to be inconclusive and depressing. It's the first overt sign of gay life (and was it even that? Gay, I mean, let alone life) that I've observed in all my time in Yugoslavia. In that respect, Czechoslovakia was quite different. In the centre of Prague, in Wenceslas Square, there is an attractively preserved *salon de thé*, with chandeliers and silver service, which has an entirely gay clientele – apart, that is, from the police, of whom there is one for every gay, and whose relationship with the regulars seems very friendly. Flirtatious might be a better word. The lights are very bright, but that seems to suit everybody – the atmosphere is frivolous, with much table-hopping and anxious checking of coiffure. The reigning divinity is not so much Sex, as Gossip. Elsewhere in the city, there are other establishments, of varying degrees of loucheness, though nothing to compare with the West Berlin or the New York of yesteryear. But it is all official, and the name of everybody who attends the clubs is registered with the police.

No such thing in Zagreb, not detectable to the naked eye, at any rate; and certainly nothing like it in Dubrovnik. I suppose the boy in the patisserie had discovered a way of making a few bob with the tourists. After our little encounter, we padded down an alleyway where some shops were still open, including an art gallery. There was a small exhibition of drawings and oils by a painter called Veličkovic, mad, angry pictures, swarming with rats, painted in thick bold blacks and reds and an entire sequence based on Muybridge's walking man. This man is one of the great Yugoslavian painters, apparently. He now lives in Paris. Worried about packing and transporting a painting back to Zagreb and then on, I didn't buy one, but I couldn't refrain from getting a little thing by someone else, a small terracotta piece of a man hugging his head in foetal withdrawal from the world. It was untitled, but I suggested a possible name for it: FILM ACTOR.

Next day, our last, we spend on the green silent island which we see from our hotel room: Lokrum. There are boats at two-hourly intervals, and we roam all over the wild rocks and woodlands, up to the peak from which there is a panorama of the Adriatic coast, dominated by the great fortress of Dubrovnik. We find inland pools and, on the south of the island, beaches, where, there being no one around, we strip off and swim and sunbathe, noting that it is November 1st. After several failures to be at the jetty in time for the ferry's departure, we finally get the last one back – astonishing sunset, miraculous views, etc, etc. A final flip around the town, under the gaze of Sveti Vlaho (Saint Blasius to us), who holds before him a model of the city – the patron saint of designers, I tell Bruno, who is only slightly amused – a last look at the reliquary crammed with silver limbs (world famous in its time, it even gets a mention in *Twelfth Night*), a last meal in the restaurant in whose courtyard there is a vast well supported by a glorious frieze, and then to bed, the window open to the sea and Lokrum faintly discernible in the black, starless, moonless emptiness.

ZAGREB
3 November 87

Just back from Dubrovnik, with deep relief. We'd booked to come back on the night flight, seven o'clock. There was fog in Zagreb, the plane was cancelled, so terrible hysteria ensued on my part, enhanced by the obstinacy and mendacity of the airport staff. 'Will we be able to get a place on the first flight in the morning?' 'Yes, yes, of course,' they snapped back, offended at the very idea that the question needed to be asked.

We were put up in a hotel near the airport, much bigger than the Argentina, and ate a very good meal, in so far as I could concentrate on it at all. I'd reported the disaster to the production manager, but the dread was that the fog wouldn't have cleared even by tomorrow, and I'd be stuck here for another day – or perhaps indefinitely. There is a train, but it takes a day or two to traverse Yugoslavia. Any actor experiences primitive anxiety at the prospect of not showing up on time – for a show, or for shooting. It's not just the professional disgrace (which can be considerable: once, filming in Munich, I left my passport at home, and had to return to get it; I finally arrived four hours late, and even though the scene I was due to shoot had been deferred anyway, there were official and outraged protests to my agent from both the film company and the casting director). Stronger still is the basic, deeply ingrained feeling of the importance of the event. 'It's only a show', 'it's only a film', are blasphemous phrases for most actors – often uttered, but only out of a bravado which reinforces the contrary. So

235

I was a fitful supper companion. The next morning we left so early there was no breakfast, and we stole a few rolls and slivers of ham from underneath the crisp white linen laid over it the night before.

When we got to the airport, there was, needless to say, no place for us on the plane. I ran from person to person, on the verge of tears, begging, cajoling, blabbing pathetically about the film, the film, with the result that we were finally thrust onto a plane and arrived back this morning well in time, with four hours to spare before I filmed, but not without having gone through agonies of anticipated guilt and shame and fear of professional disgrace, none of which came to pass.

All the soothing effects of Dubrovnik were negated at the airport. Apart from the nightmare of getting a seat, I had an encounter with the Health Service. Bruno had a foul migraine. I said I'd go the airport shop and buy some aspirin, but there was none to be had; souvenirs and novelties aplenty, but a strict ban on anything useful. I went and asked at the information desk for the first-aid post. The receptionist said that there was no first-aid post. 'We have an ambulance.' 'That seems rather extreme,' I said. 'Yes. I will send for ambulance,' insisted the receptionist. There was a long delay as I watched Bruno on the other side of the airport, white with pain. Finally the ambulance arrived and she said, 'Now it's here.' I went to find it but there was no driver. 'Where's the driver?' I said. 'Oh, he's just gone to the shop to buy a few things.' Ten minutes later, he arrived and invited me into his ambulance, not in the front seat, with him, but at the back. Feeling rather fraudulent I perched on the stretcher, as he drove me round the corner to the nurse. I said to her, 'I'd like some aspirins for my friend who has a headache.' She said, 'Where is he? He must come here and sign for them.' 'No. His headache is too bad.' She said, 'I can't give them to you.' There was an impasse. 'I'm sorry,' I said, 'I've made a mistake. It's I who has the headache.' 'You have a headache?' she said. 'Yes, I have a very bad headache. Can I have some aspirin?' 'If you have a very bad headache I think perhaps you should

236

have an injection,' she said, reaching for a syringe. 'No, thank you,' I said, 'just the aspirin will do.' I snatched them from the other nurse who had brought them over, and managed to escape with them, walking back in about three minutes, instead of the ten it had taken the ambulance, finally reaching a Bruno not only riddled with migraine, but extremely worried by my disappearance.

By hook or by crook, I'm here. By now it seems to me that we are mopping up on my part. I had to film a scene of running through the corridor to see that the king was arriving satisfactorily and checking everything. I realised today that some serenity has descended on me. I realised today how to work well with Dušan: I must do just whatever comes into my head. Not work anything out. Not try to think of what could be effective, or original, or interesting, just do whatever comes into my head, because he will infallibly ask me to do the opposite. I haven't the heart to try to calculate what he wants me to do, then do the opposite, so that he will then ask me to do the opposite of that, bringing us back to where I want to be. No, now I just do whatever comes into my head. So in this scene I went down the corridor and, there being two people in the way, I moved them out of the way with great courtesy. I knew perfectly well as I did it that he would ask me to do it brusquely. Then I pushed a couple of people roughly to one side and I knew that he would ask me in that case to do it more gracefully. And he did, in both cases; and there was an odd satisfaction in it. I can't crack the character of Hunt, but I've sure as fuck solved Makavejev. He is the king of contrariness. He wants the professionals to somehow be more amateur, but equally he reproaches the amateurs for not being professional enough. I must at all costs keep my discovery to myself. If he finds out that I know, he will anticipate my strategy and will accept what I do first time, which, as he knows, will throw me completely. I am dealing with a cunning opponent.

I wander around talking to the Yugoslavian actors who

speak English. I want to know about the Yugoslavian theatre. Who are their playwrights? Are they translated into English? They don't know. The other day, I went to the British Council's reading room. Very little translated from Serbo-Croat, some Danilo Kiš, that's about it. There was a scholarly text, rather longer than you might have thought possible, about Shakespearean references to Dubrovnik, which I borrowed. It was strange to be in a room full of English books and English papers, all some weeks or even months old. There were about fifteen people browsing among the books. I had the impression of a group of hardy Anglophiles getting their weekly, or maybe daily, fix of English culture. I'm trying to track down the Yugoslavian soul, but it's eluding me. One of the most magnificent glimpses of it, though, was the sculpture of Meštrovič. I had heard of him before, seen photographs of his work, but I'd no idea of the scale on which he operated. There are paintings, busts, heroic groups. His house here in Zagreb has become a museum (it's up in the student quarter). The curator shows one round personally. In a sense, of course, Meštrovič is a very cosmopolitan Yugoslav. He travelled the world, and his work is on display everywhere, New York especially. There is a romanticism, a yearning quality in his work which marks him apart from Rodin, to whom without apology he can certainly be compared in point of quality. So seeing his work, and the background to it, sketches, maquettes, was an overwhelming experience. But I'm still not quite in communion with the Serbo-Croat soul. I've seen no native plays, heard no native music. Who are the composers of classical music in this country? I've tried looking for their works, but so far drawn a blank. I haven't, alas, made any Yugoslavian friends. So I feel I'm circling round the great mansion of Serbo-Croatian culture, stealing a glimpse through the windows, watching people come in and out, but never gaining admission. We're about to shoot a scene in which Drew has been cast as a crooner. Everyone makes a tremendous fuss of him, make-up, wardrobe, he's been shaved, his hair pomaded, a costume devised for him. The actors look on with displeasure. We all love the man, he is the most engaging companion, his relationship with Marit is one of those liaisons that strikes everyone with its perfect rightness, he has, shaming all the rest of us, mastered basic Serbo-Croat. The guy is a honey. But something comes over us actors as we watch him being prepared for the scene. Rising feelings of demarcation are in the air. It's not just fun and games, you know, we feel; it's a job, a craft, a skill; sometimes, just now and then, it's even an art. We say nothing because we will seem like killjoys. But here's Dušan again, busily eroding the barriers between the amateur and the professional. We take it personally. Anyway, Drew sang the song, very charmingly. Hunt appears in the scene, and I had an idea that it might be rather nice if Hunt found the song attractive and wanted to sing along with it. Actually Dušan got in with that suggestion first (has he *rumbled* me?), so I didn't have to have it rejected, which was fine. I did it, at the same time trying to suggest suspicion of the violinists accompanying Drew's song. But if you're not actually working in collaboration with the director, it's impossible for you to carry your ideas through. Done properly, the sequence I suggested is quite an elaborate one. As it happens I think the camera picked up none of it. I just appear in the shot, whereas it might have been something memorable, funny, accurate. I realised a while ago and now accept with complete equanimity the fact that the character I play, or the way I have been playing the character, is tipping over the comic balance of the film. It's too much, one colour too strong within the framework of the film, and Dušan is now busily trying to keep me out of as many shots as possible. When I am in them, he's trying to contain the damage, to make me have as little impact as possible. He feels I have used up all my impact for this film, I have as it were spent all my primary colours and now I am only allowed pastels. I have used up all my light and now I can only be seen in shadow. Well, that's fine by me. And actually the sane, non-paranoid part of me understands his predicament, is sympathetic. I don't know what I'd do in the same situation, if I were directing.

It would be hard to underestimate the degree of despair that Fred feels. Fred told me that while I was away they did the fucking scene with Linda (Avanti has to make love to Svetlana's mother). The scene went on too long, each take went on far too long. Dušan said he was only going to use ten seconds, but they went on and on and on. Fred kept on pretending to have cramp. There were all kinds of deficiencies to do with the props and the special effects, so the special effects man, Max (whom I and, I think, everyone rather liked, a gracious and funny man, and as far as one could tell, an efficient one) has been sacked. No one seems to be in charge of special effects now. There was a point on one of the takes when an effect wasn't working, so everybody in the whole crew merrily threw stones onto the set to try to make it work. It became a great joke. That enraged Fred terribly. Dušan pulled him to one side and said, 'I'm angry with you. I'm not angry with you for losing your temper, I'm really angry with you on principle, because you have to understand that in Yugoslavia, if there is a problem everybody helps out, it's never just one person's responsibility, everybody helps out.' Perhaps that goes some way to explain our confusion on the film. It was certainly my experience in the airport that everybody was indeed prepared to help out, anybody at all would offer you an assurance or a positive statement about something, regardless of whether they had any authority to do so or knew anything about it. I was promised a seat on the aeroplane by dozens of people, eager to make me feel better. It was only when I actually had to get on the plane that the trouble started. This procedure was exactly replicated on the film. Promises, promises, they poured out like milk and honey; but they had no bearing whatever on the reality of the situation. At the airport I learnt again the lesson I had learnt so well on the film, that you can shout and shout and shout, you can try to plan in advance, but nothing you can do in the end will avail against the inherent slothfulness and capriciousness of the people who are running a country or a film. It brings a certain calm to realise that there is now no longer any point in shouting, because nothing will happen, or if it does, it will only be to make things worse.

A couple of nights ago, Thursday night, was quite extraordinary. We had all been called at 4.45 p.m. for a 6.00 start on the set. Then we were all informed that we were in fact asked to be there half an hour early, 4.15. So we all duly turned up, and it was quite literally three hours before anything happened at all, even despite there having been a huge explosion the night before when everybody had agreed that the organisation on the film was catastrophic. The reason we waited so long turned out to be because none of the extras had been called in time, and there was no one to assist the make-up artists. Mary Hillman was at that moment anyway stating absolutely firmly that, if they took away her make-up van as they had threatened, she would go straight back to London. In the end she kept her van.

5 November 87

Yesterday, the 4th, was a day of extreme frustration and anger. I wasn't called until about 3.00 in the afternoon and had managed to do quite a lot of work in clearing up the hotel room in preparation for going back to England and was in a very, very good mood and very clear of mind. Went to the studio, sat around for about three hours but even that didn't really annoy me too much. Eventually I went to the set and did a scene straight away. It was the one in which Hunt bursts into Svetlana's room, says, 'Oh, excuse me. Where is the balcony?' then goes to the balcony windows, finds puppies creeping all over the floor, says 'Get these creatures out of here', and then goes to get the king. I stood on my mark for Pinter. He had decided to frame me in such a way that I stood in front of the head of a dead animal, a deer or something like that, so that its horns appeared to be coming out of the top of my hat – the very thing that most photographers would try to avoid. That delighted Dušan of course, and Pinter obviously liked it too. And of course I like it too, although it is nothing to me as an actor. I am delighted that they are framing me interestingly, but that is one of the passive elements of being an actor in a film. You can give rise to extraordinary images which are absolutely nothing to do with you. You don't really know what the image you're part of is like. You can't see it. You can't suggest interesting pictures either because you don't know what the whole sequence is, or you don't know what the lens on the camera is, and so on. It really does mean that you become completely passive. All you can be is, in Radu Penciulescu's famous phrase, *disponible*. You must simply offer yourself up, and it's very, very unfulfilling, personally speaking. I suppose it is what Von Sternberg admired so much in Marlene Dietrich. He told her what to do and she did it, filling it from within automatically, unthinkingly. It requires a very special and peculiar temperament to be able to do that. You have to become living furniture.

However, that is the nature of filming, all filming, not just this one, and I am quite prepared to do it, so I found the mark and then said to Camilla, 'Ah, excuse me. Where is the balcony?' as simply and as straightforwardly as I possibly could. I know by now that projection or any attempt to create relationship or to isolate a moment in any way, to give it any kind of pressure, is pointless with Dušan. He doesn't want it, he'll only attack it, so I said it very simply, almost perfunctorily, 'Ah, excuse me. Where is the balcony?' and he stopped me and said, 'I want to say to you. Just be efficient, and less comedic skills. The situation's already funny, I'm surrounded with funny things, I don't need comedic skills.' Something right inside of me blew. Any creative ambitions, any career ambitions, any intellectual ambitions all just died. A combination of anger and, if this makes any sense, violent indifference to the whole thing consumed me. I was longing for him to say something to me, to challenge me, or to approach me in some way, but of course he didn't at all. What I wanted to say to him was, 'You've got the wrong actor and I have got the wrong director, so we have a complete impasse. We have wasted each other's time totally, and I'm infinitely saddened and angered by it, but there is now nothing I can do about it, because the conditions don't exist in which I can contribute what I could contribute to your film. I am merely a body in this film, that is all, a face in a costume.' When I got home and told this to Bruno, I found I was nearly on the point of tears. If what I instinctively want to do is forbidden and he is unable to say what else he wants me to do, there is a void and I am in limbo and that's where I have been for the last seven weeks and it's not an address that I like to find myself at.

> *Dušan:*
> *When Simon fell into the dark well of gloom and isolation, unwantedness and uselessness, often it was triggered by me not wanting him to be more than he is. Actor is actor when he does nothing, and silver nitrate sucks these moments with delight, they glue. The wish to perform, if it is not perfectly disguised, or extremely justified (when a character is lying), does not glue as well. Unnecessary 'performance' makes us less curious and keeps us at an admiring distance, dissuades us from coming closer. The little performer can't hide his wish to be loved, poor Cinderella. So, we punish him: no entrance to the Royal Palace of our hearts. Punishment comes because she was not supposed to sell us her glass slipper. Characters are not supposed to know what will happen to them next. Performers do.*

Mary Hillman told me about a problem earlier in the day with Camilla when I wasn't there. The cameraman had suggested one thing, Dušan had said another, Dejan had said a third and Camilla quite reasonably had said, 'Look I don't know what's going on.' She is very inexperienced. She has very little sense of self-respect as an actor. She had said, 'Who am I to listen to?' and Dušan had replied, 'Now look, you must understand. On a film everybody is fighting for his corner. Pinter is fighting for his corner, I am fighting for my corner, and you must fight for your corner.' First of all, it is in itself an extraordinary, but I suppose typical notion, a sort of dialectical vision of how to get a piece of art together, art as a struggle for ascendancy between collaborators. Secondly, it is completely untrue, because the actor in that situation has no corner to fight for anyway. The cameraman can obviously do what he wants to do, and so can the director, using his influence over cameraman, script and designer, but the actor has no influence, has no power, and has no idea of what he is trying to do.

Finally, what a crushing thing to say to a young, inexperienced actress. In the circumstances, apart from a few tiny bursts of sobbing, like summer showers, she has coped magnificently, and is, I suspect, the stuff of which real stars are made.

I said to Bruno that evening, the sense of disappointment wouldn't have mattered in the least if I had thought, 'This is just some junk for money', or 'Maybe I'm interested, maybe I'm not', but I wanted this so much to be an education. Which I suppose it has been, in some strange kind of way. I constantly reproach myself and think, 'Am I behaving as [a certain actor] behaved with me?' This very brilliant actor is someone I once directed. On the first day of rehearsal I said, 'I'd like us to read the play several times. I have a notion of how it should work, but I'd like to make sure that we all feel the same way about it, and know exactly what we're doing at any one time.' 'Oh God no,' he said, 'just tell me what to do. Tyrone Guthrie was my idol. He never discussed anything. Let's just get on with it.' 'Alright,' I said, and blocked the play from beginning to end. We carried on like this for the first week and into the beginning of the second. Shortly I began to sense that he was unhappy. I phoned him. 'Of course I'm miserable,' he said. 'You've taken away my personality. I'm going to change my name to Sandy Shaw: Puppet on a String. I'm bitterly disillusioned with you. I only took the job because of your book. Well, I'm going round all the bookshops moving your book onto the fiction shelves.' And so on. His tendency as an actor was to fall into comic business borrowed from other actors. When he used *himself*, however, he was brilliantly funny in a most original way, while also being moving; but any attempt of mine to stop him impersonating Wilfrid Lawson or Ralph Richardson (or, more bizarrely, both simultaneously) was greeted with fierce resistance.

Is this me? Have I sketched a self-portrait? Am I being inflexible? Am I insisting on doing a certain kind of work and refusing to share Makavejev's vision? But as absolutely nobody that I have spoken to on the film has the remotest idea what that might be, I don't think I can reproach myself for it.

Bruno and I went for supper up in the student quarter, and the gaiety of the clientele banished my misery. A couple were kissing each other without the slightest inhibition, positively gorging on each other. I said: 'They obviously ordered tongue.' We walked back to the Inter-Continental, down the winding path, across town, with its accustomed ghastly yellow complexion, deathly quiet now. Underfoot was a carpet of dead leaves. We passed the university building, wrapped in Cristo-like plastic during renovations. Wandering in there unchallenged a few days ago, we opened a door to find ourselves in the most resplendent library, with students straining to read under the original light fittings. They wouldn't have cared to be told, but they presented the very image of scholarly diligence, the desire to know incarnate. I really love this city and feel regret that I haven't penetrated it. But I suspect that filming is a very bad way to get to know a place. The unit is such a little universe, and the schedule demands so much of your time. Also, a film crew has the characteristics of an invading army. A film is always a triumph of will over environment, and that informs all our attitudes. The other day, however, I bumped into an old friend of mine, an actor who's appearing in another English-language film here. For him, filming abroad is perfect, a God-given opportunity to follow his romantic inclinations. He feels ill-at-ease and unlovely in England; abroad, he blossoms. His pursuit of sex is all-consuming, but one would hesitate to describe him as promiscuous. For him there is no such thing as casual sex. Each encounter is an overwhelming transcendence: what Holy Communion is to a Catholic, an ecstatic reunion with God. And he seems to have provoked great romantic commitment from his anonymous lovers. He may never see them again, but in the moment they give their all. It is love, of a sort. He always moves me with his stories of trysts and couplings: a time in Morocco when a young man had fallen for him on sight and stood under his window, singing for over an

hour till my friend, jet-lagged and exhausted, nevertheless rose from his bed and joined the stranger for hours of
love; the time in Haiti when as a challenge to him the
brothel-keeper had produced a hunchbacked dwarf as a
potential partner, and how the dwarf had made love
more beautifully than any man he had ever known, and
later, when my friend was leaving, had sought him out
at the dock to bid him goodbye. Here in Zagreb he has
somehow found the centre of sexual activity, a sauna,
and has brought a young man back to his hotel. But the
young man was cold and unloving and didn't give
himself; what's worse, when he left, he had stolen a
radio. And my friend's romantic heart was bruised, not
for the radio, but because the god hadn't descended, and
life is too short to waste a single night, a single hour of
love.

Today one got up very early, and one was slightly
numbed for the very first shots. I had forgotten all about
the previous day's rage and slept and was again cheerful.
No sooner did I walk on to the set, however, to do that
little scene from another angle and to say again, 'Oh,
excuse me. Where is the balcony?' than he stopped me
and said, 'You know, you are acting too much. When
you act, it becomes very dynamic and it's too much.' I
simply said to him, 'Please don't say anything. Please just
don't say anything.' I walked away. I just walked away;
I didn't want to listen to him at all, and that is ludicrous.
I find myself defending every single thing that I do. For
example, it seems to me that it could well be part of
Hunt's character (I had always thought it would be) that
if he bursts into a woman's dressing room and there is
this young girl there *en déshabille* he would be embarrassed, a little bit flustered. He would then quickly move on
to the balcony, because of course that is the more pressing
thing. But anything in the nature of trying to bring out
the dynamics of the scene or to create relationship is
frustrated. Then again, there is the continuing problem
that the agents don't understand what I am saying so
therefore they move at the wrong time. It just goes on

and on and round and round in a little circle. There is no interest in it, finally. It just isn't interesting.

Then I did the lines off-camera for Camilla, whose inexperience makes it difficult for her to do these technical things very simply. The puppies are crawling all over the set, which is wonderful, a wonderful image. These little blind, palpating creatures, furry, floppy little things, groping around their brave new world, are disturbing, funny, beautiful all at once, as they climb and clamber, slipping and sliding all over the dead and bleeding body of Rade. At the end of one scene Dušan said nothing to Camilla, neither good nor bad, and without any apparent intention to put her down said, 'The dogs were very good', as if he were praising the dogs. But the dogs did nothing except just be in front of the camera. Of course they had been good. Anybody who just 'be's' in front of the camera will be marvellous.

Then he rather surprised me by coming up and saying, 'Now, this is the scene where I want to have the thing with the Mozart ball,' which he had mentioned way back, seven weeks before. He found a moment for me to pick up a Mozart ball and look at it. Now he elaborated it slightly, he wanted me actually to eat it and throw the paper away. I did that, ate the sweet, read what was on the paper and threw it away. Drew came up to me and said, 'What is this scene? It's not in the script.' Dušan explained to him that I was the first person to play the part of Mozart in *Amadeus*, that I played it for two hundred performances, and that this moment would be an interesting comment: 'It will undercut the scene.' So that's almost an affectionate gesture towards me, except that really it is nothing to do with me, it is just an idea that he's had. He had it seven weeks ago, it's a good visual image, he wants to subvert the film in that way and so he is doing it. He is using me in the very best possible way, it is just the way he should use me. But he is not inviting me into the process at all. It is the most baffling experience because I can tell clearly that it's going well. There is certainly a proliferation of marvellous images in the film. The man from Cannon said to me today, 'We have a very good film already. It is going to be fantastic when we get to Cannes. It is going to be a big success.' Well, who knows whether that's the case or not, but undoubtedly it will be in all the textbooks. From an imagistic point of view it is an absolute gala. There isn't a scene without some astonishing image in it, and yet it isn't exactly dreamlike, as both Cocteau, and Fellini, who have the same degree of visual fantasy, invariably are. That's quite an achievement. I trust his instincts about everything in the film, but the final thing is: I don't want to be doing it, that's all. So I won't again. But how can one know in advance?

Bruno goes back to London tonight with the *Shirley V* model. He's made something very striking, something which is both a real kitchen and a stage set for the stand-up routine that the play to some extent is. At the same time it presents a concentrated image of her life, her world. We need hydraulics and projections, two special-ised areas that he'll have to investigate. As well as the model, he goes back laden with our discussion on *Fledermaus*. At first, he was far from enthusiastic about doing it. He's already designed it once before and found it a thankless task. Designers and directors the world over roll their eyes heavenward when you mention the piece. The second act is an absolute horror to stage – a very loosely plotted party scene, in which the chorus come on and come off without the slightest motivation, a ragbag of admittedly incomparable numbers, lacking any real dramatic tension. The third act, complete with spoken comic monologue, has only about fifteen minutes of music and culminates in yet another unmotivated appearance of the chorus. None of the great turning points of the plot is musically embodied, being announced in pitifully lame dialogue. So why do it all? Answer: a) the music is enchanting, young, dangerous, sexy; b) it is, if you look at it really closely, about something – sex, drugs and rock 'n' roll, to be precise. The drug is champagne (if you substituted cocaine it would be just about right. I won't, I hasten to say. It's simply that, historically speaking, champagne had swept through the upper and middle classes of 1850's and 60's Vienna just as coke has through ours, and for much the same reasons: gets you high and keeps you high without too many nasty side effects). Sex is sex: is was and ever will be. And the waltz was Vienna's rock 'n' roll: played mostly in huge dance halls crammed to the rafters where people danced through the night until early morning, maddened and possessed by the compulsive rhythm and the music's inherent hedonism. Contemporary denunciations of the waltz bear an uncanny resemblance to the fifties' establishment's wrath against rock 'n' roll.

The implication of all this is that the show (and it is that) needs to be liberated from chintz and chandeliers, which immediately place it in never-never land. What's needed is a shake-up of the kind Jonathan Miller gave *Rigoletto* at the Coliseum. The most obvious thing to do is to change the period; but having said that, what's the point of adding another layer of distance by setting it in, say, the 1890s or the 1920s, as is not infrequently done? When the curtain went up on the first night in 1874 the Viennese public saw themselves on the stage. Shouldn't the Glasgow audience do the same? The parallels, while not absolute, are rather striking: an economically expanding city, short on political power but long on financial activity, a mixed and cosmopolitan populace, a city underneath whose apparent expansion lie darker undercurrents. Perhaps all the expansion is based on rather uncertain foundations. The great and obvious parallel is that both Vienna 1870 and Glasgow (nearly) 1990 are boundlessly self-confident, rejoicing in themselves, and with a young middle-class – a yuppie class, to be precise – dedicated to pleasure. And it is that class to which the characters of the piece belong. That's a bit of luck. Had there been an Opera House in Edinburgh (a likely story!) which had asked me to do *Fledermaus*, I certainly wouldn't have set it *there*. In that case, I would have done my Alternative Production. Whenever one thinks about doing something, it's handy to think about the other way of doing it – just to test it out. My Alternative Production of *Fledermaus* is the Anschluss

Production, but I won't go into that now. No, *MacBat* it is. Of course, I have yet to broach the matter with Scottish Opera. I have a feeling it may prove controversial. *Fledermaus* is the most sacred of sacred cows – especially as it's planned for the Christmas/New Year slot. People are used to seeing *Parsifal* set in a urinal, *Falstaff* in a high-tech parking lot. But *Fledermaus?* Come on! It's a tradition. Well, I draw courage from Mahler's definition: tradition, he said, is 'Schlämperei': slovenliness.

Admittedly, I didn't put it quite like that in *Being an Actor*. I like to think, however, that what I'm providing is not a concept but a context. Erm, does that sound a bit sophistical? (Yes.)

None of this begins to address the design problems, but I'm thrilled (and relieved) that Bruno buys it totally, so we'll sit down and thrash it out. When? Oh God, when? But he's already designed half the costumes in his mind.

We had a lovely supper the other day in Zagreb's only pizza restaurant: a dark, chic place, serving wonderful pasta and better pizzas. It's obviously an exotic rarity here, so it becomes one for us. We ate with Mary Hillman and Linda Marlowe, who's here with her nine-year-old son Charlie. He's been left at home in the hotel, watching Yugoslavian television, which is better than British television in that you can get transmissions from all the countries surrounding Yugoslavia, half of Europe in fact, including some genuinely shocking pornography, from Italy, mostly. I hope he's not watching *that*. Linda, having come over for a fortnight with Charlie and nanny, has had a lovely time, despite any passing irritations on the set. So has Mary Hillman, despite, God knows, plenty of cause for grievance. But she takes it magnificently in her stride, accepting it as part of the conditions of film-making. 'I just have complete confidence that what Dušan wants is right,' she says. So do I, in a funny kind of way, except that I don't seem to be able to provide it. And I am maddeningly fond of Makavejev, as long as I'm not working with him. Under the influence of a very good bottle – several very good bottles – of Barolo, I begin to get sentimental and remorseful. I've behaved badly, paranoiacally, self-regardingly. Fortunately the others disabuse me of this, though doubts linger.

So Bruno's off to London.

Now I am alone. I return to *At Freddie's*. I find myself constantly thinking of Dušan's film and trying to learn from it, but the genres are so different: Dušan's – whatever it is – Dušanesque? *Freddie's* a kind of Ealing comedy. But the book is full of dark meanings, which I'm trying to bring out, and in Freddie, the central character, Penelope has created a massive figure, a Mother Courage, an amoral survivor, whom she hasn't exactly dramatised (and why should she? She was writing a novel). So that's what I have to do. I've invented or expanded a couple of characters, fleshing them out from old-time theatrical figures that I met when I was starting out and whose whole race has since vanished. One of them I'm writing for Alec G – without his permission – but it cheers me up to think of lines and jokes that might make him laugh. The best things I've done, though, seem to me to be silent scenes, reactions. Cuts, above all. I never forget Eisenstein's observation about montage being the art of the cinema. It seems incongruous to think of Eisenstein in conjunction with an Ealing comedy, but there we are. I've been reading a couple of biographies of him during filming. In fact, in our palmier days Dušan took to referring to me as Sergei Mihailovich. On this subject, as indeed on every subject, Dušan is original and curious. I want one day to sit down and have a long conversation with him about it. I want to have a long conversation with him on many subjects, including the making of *For a Night of Love*. One day.

P.S. I discovered that *Die Fledermaus* was Eisenstein's favourite opera. Whenever it was playing, he'd book the front row of the stalls, and when, in the third act, the character called Eisenstein sings his own name, Sergei Mihailovich and his friends would join in, raucously:

'Eis-en-stein! Da dum da dada, Eis-en-stein!' This makes me think of him in an entirely different light.

P.P.S. I've just had a call from Bill Bushnell of the Los Angeles Theatre Centre. I directed Kundera's *Jacques and his Master* for them last year and will do a couple of productions for them next year. He's been roaming the German-speaking countries for the last couple of weeks on a grant from Berlin. He'll be in Vienna; any chance of us meeting? Well, hell, of course. It is literally fifty minutes away by plane, I'm not called for the next couple of days and the thought of all that food and culture and architecture . . . added to which he has tickets for Klaus-Maria Brandauer's *Hamlet*. And of course, it's research. For *Fledermaus*. Except I'm setting it in Glasgow. Well, I'm sure to learn *something*. So I go up to the sexy lady in the travel agency, and she sexily furnishes me, at a laughably low cost, with a ticket for tomorrow. Spirits rise. Great joy.

Friday 6th November, 6pm

I'm back in my room. I got to the airport in plenty of
time to discover that my flight wasn't. It just wasn't. It
had ceased to exist. There was no mention of it on any
of the departure indicators. I went to the desk and at first
they denied its existence. Later, grudgingly – 'Oh, you
mean *that* 3.15 flight to Vienna' – they admitted it had
been cancelled. No reason proffered. As with so much
else in Yugoslavia, it just happened, like rain or a tree
falling down. Too bad. One of those things. This
fatalism is more maddening than any inconvenience
caused by the thing itself. Were there any other flights?
No. Any combination of flights? No. Could I even get to
Vienna tomorrow, when I'm due to meet Bushnell? No,
no and no. Not a trace of regret or sympathy; the
opposite, in fact, a sort of amused contempt for the
absurdity of trying to negotiate with fate. Relax, it's
happened, that's that. Through clenched teeth, sounding
very like my mother on a bad day, I ask for alternatives,
saying that I *must* be in Vienna by tomorrow. Well,
there's always the train. And they look up times, and
there's one at midnight, arriving in Vienna at six thirty
tomorrow morning. Will they book me on it? Sure, they
say, changing tone and wondering why I should think
there would be any problem with a Yugoslavian institu-
tion. And will you pay for it? I ask. Sure, they say, in the
same tone as before, sure, you get the receipt and we'll
refund it. 'Neme probleme.' And the sleeper? Will you
book that too? Sure. So I took a taxi to the station, where
they had, needless to say, no record whatever of any

booking, but yes, I could book, and a sleeper, too. First class, please. Sure. So here I am back at the Inter-Continental, hoping not to bump into anyone from the production, too awful to have to explain all this, and taking out my rage on *At Freddie's*, which doesn't respond very well to such an approach.

9 November 1987

I never believed I'd hear myself say this, but I'm returning to this room with relief. I have just lived through a nightmare of unparalleled dimensions. The only thing which gives me the slightest consolation is the utter consistency of the experience. It has been unmitigated, systematic disaster without a ray of hope. I have passed through tears and rage and prayer and am now simply mad. Insane. I truly believe I have lost my reason, not to mention my last vestige of faith in humankind of any nationality.

I got the train. I searched in vain for the first class carriage: there was none, for the good reason that there is no first class on Yugoslavian trains. Eventually I found the sleeper. But where were the beds? I was trying to puzzle this out when the other occupants arrived: a young married couple, and their three year old child in floods of petulant tears. Understandably: it was midnight. His parents, obviously veterans of this journey, set to work converting the carriage. This meant unfolding the seats, one on either side. The problem was, they didn't join up. There was a gap of about twelve inches in between the two sides. Like my fellow passengers, I put my legs up, and, like them, I found that my bottom fell through the gap. The kid was OK, he lay the length of the seats. The parents, being prepared for all this, had brought a couple of blankets. I had none, so arranged my overcoat around my deformed body, sagging in the middle. I tried to stand to attention, as it were, horizontally, but it was excruciating, so I sagged. My companions put the lights off,

saying good night to me in Serbo–Croatian. 'Dobru noc,'
I replied, and fell asleep surprisingly quickly (not so
surprising, in fact, since I had in my rage downed the
entire contents of the mini-bar in my room at the Inter-
Continental – another reason, perhaps, why the work on
Freddie's was less than coherent. Looking at the work I
did, I find that a number of speeches start DF*nm00$).
This sleep lasted perhaps eight minutes. The door was
flung open, the lights were switched on and the guard
demanded our tickets. This done, sleep resumed. Not for
long. The air was pierced with the sound of the child's
screaming in mid-nightmare. The lights went on, comfort was dispensed, lullabies were crooned, the child slept,
the lights went out. A sort of half-sleep descended, then
bang! the doors flew open, the lights were on again.
Passport control. We were evidently passing through one
of many borders – inter-Yugoslavian borders, from
Serbia into Croatia. Or was it Dalmatia? Or Macedonia?
Whichever it was, the border guards of the ones it wasn't
broke in every hour or so to check our papers. The couple
never evinced the slightest irritation, and I too, on
the third or fourth intervention, succumbed to Balkan
fatalism. And so the night passed. Twice more, the child
screamed – lights on, comfort, lullaby, sleep, lights off –
and once I drifted awake to a gently rhythmic sound
which was somehow different from the rhythm of the
train: my God! the couple were making another baby.
Anon, and noiselessly, they stopped. I fell asleep. The
next morning, as we pulled into Vienna and they drew
back the blinds, they looked at me rather sheepishly. I
don't know why. If I'd been able to say anything more
than 'Good night' and 'Good morning' in Serbo-
Croatian, I would have offered to be the baby's godfather. Or marxfather. Or whatever was appropriate.

The station in Vienna was hardly functioning at six in
the morning, but I had a plate of excellent ham and eggs
and a beer in the cafeteria. It nearly cleaned me out of
my ready cash. I had just enough to get me into Vienna,
where I would get money on my Mastercard. I arrived
at the dear old Bristol, black-marbled and elegant, and

casually asked the hall porter where was the nearest Bureau de Change. He told me. I'll be able to cash some money with my Mastercard, won't I? I asked. Unfortunately, no, not in Vienna. The Bureaux de Change operate according to banking hours. You can change currency at the weekend, but no cash advances. I went up to my room in a trance. There was little solace in the perfectly preserved fittings, the crisp linen. I had exactly fifty pfennigs. I called down to reception. Can one draw money at the airport at the weekend? Certainly, they said. So I waited for Bushnell to arrive, pouncing on him when he did, borrowing some money and setting off for the airport in a taxi – which cost all of the money he gave me. At the airport there were Bureaux de Change, but, alas, they couldn't advance me money; at the weekend they operated according to the banking laws. But the receptionist had said . . . Ah yes, behind the barriers there were indeed places where one could withdraw money. I went to the barrier. I explained my tragic situation – how I would have been on the plane, had it not been cancelled, and would then, from the other side of the barrier, have drawn money. They were sympathetic, sure something could be done, and directed me to the border control. I started to unfold my story again. Almost immediately, the bearded guard interrupted: Why are you telling me this? I explained. Have you got a ticket. No, I said, but – Then go away, he said. But I – Have you got a ticket? No but – Go away. I – Go away. I put on a display of rage which embarrassed me but had no effect on him whatever. There was nothing I could do. He started to deal with the next person. I stood off, willing him dead, and thinking dark thoughts about the Anschluss. I kept this up for about five minutes and then went to find the bus, for which I had precisely and only the right money. Forty minutes later, it left. As we hit the motorway, I saw that there was a jam which stretched literally all the way back to Vienna. Something had broken down. One hour and fifty minutes later, I arrived back in Vienna, sustained only by the thought of the huge meal and many flagons of wine Bushnell and I would down, paid for on my Mastercard. He greeted me – somewhat hungrily; it was now twenty to three. I went to the desk. Can you recommend a wonderful restaurant where I can pay by Mastercard? Unfortunately, he said, on Saturdays in Vienna, the restaurants have their last orders at two o'clock. Two o'clock! Vienna, I thought to myself, is not a great city at all. It's a bloody village. So we can't eat at all, is that it? Oh no, you see over there, by the sign Bierkeller, there you can eat. And pay by Mastercard? But of course.

And so we had sausages and kartoffeln and two pints of beer (both drunk by me; Bush is not of the drinking persuasion) and thought of the meal we might have had. And spoke of the productions in L.A., which cheered us up. My plan is to do two plays, cross cast. I was frustrated last year to have reached a point of communication and understanding with the cast by the time the play opened, only to take the next plane out. Just when I knew them and they knew me, we had to say goodbye. It had the feel of a holiday romance. I was especially keen to draw on the variety of actors that can be found in Los Angeles: black, Chinese, Hispanic. We'd used people from each of these groups in *Jacques*, and it was not simply 'perfectly alright', it was a positive advantage. Bush and his co-producer, Diane White, have created a unique theatre in the most desperate section of downtown L.A., four auditoria in a converted bank, showing a continuous and wide-ranging programme of outstanding theatre. Their great originality has been to import provocative European directors and to encourage daring experiment in design. Many theatres in the same situation would have commissioned new plays, made old ones 'relevant'; Diane and Bush have gambled on art. Diane is a special close friend of mine; Bush I know less well, but, sitting with him here, I missed the feisty audacity of L.A.T.C., which he in his nobullshit way embodies. 'The spunkiest kid on the block,' Charles Marowitz called him, and it's an exact description: red-haired, grizzle-bearded, strident-voiced, ready to take on all-comers to get what he thinks his theatre needs.

It was late afternoon by now; Bush went to the hotel to sleep. I wandered around with the hundred and fifty dollars Bush had lent me (*his* last) in my pocket, now looking for a Bureau de Change that was open. I eventually found one, and went back to meet Bush, to set off for the Burgtheater and *Hamlet*, the thought of which had been sustaining me all day. It was hell. Brandauer strolled insolently through the part, which obviously pleased the Viennese public, because they applauded after every speech, sometimes in the middle. He seemed ill-at-ease with his Gertrude, who was evidently some years younger than him. The set consisted of a revolve of a degree of complexity that I had never before seen: parts of it went up while others went down in the contrary direction, affording a seemingly limitless range of playing surfaces. Notwithstanding this miracle of engineering, it was apparently still necessary for stage-hands, dressed, like stage-hands the world over, in black, to bring on the odd chair for someone to sit on. The climax of the action was when the entire set seemed to break in half, to reveal Brandauer plumply and somewhat unsteadily on top of it. The ghost was a genuine apparition, a huge black giant, his voice distorting around the whole auditorium. And the back-cloth, with lighting patterns of a sometimes undulating, sometimes choppy sea projected onto it, was the most impressive of its kind I've ever seen. The effect of all this design was, however, to dwarf the action. The actors seemed puny in front of it, and most of the play took place on the apron. The court was only impressive numerically. There may have been fifty actors on stage at any one time – among them half a dozen dwarves. Liked the dwarves, I said to Bush at the interval. I've seen ten shows in the last six days, he said, and there were dwarves in eight of them. So. This season in Austria it's dwarves. Our fellow guests – the Austrian diplomat who had arranged Bush's tour, and his wife – informed us that the production had cost the equivalent of $2 million. I felt a pang of nostalgia for the hilarious *Otello* I had seen in the Opera House at Zagreb, where the monumental Desdemona had seemed like the victorious general, her tiny Otello the virgin (and very frightened) bride. The scenery had swayed, the furniture was battered and of the wrong period, and the crowd disported themselves as if posing for the school photograph, eyes riveted to the conductor. But somehow, it had worked. The piece was as moving as it had ever been, and there was something crudely true about it; whereas this *Hamlet* was crushed underneath its own scenery. We left the Burgtheater in a dispirited mood. Even our hosts seemed dampened. They blamed the public. They encourage him, they said of Brandauer, he's their darling. And I have to admit, there was something sexy about him, in a slack sort of way. But it had nothing to do with Hamlet, and little to do with acting.

The diplomat said: We thought maybe you would like for a change to have supper somewhere typically Viennese. There is this bierkeller . . . And so we went down a staircase into a place identical in everything but scale to the restaurant in which we'd had lunch. This one was enormous, filled with waiters running across the floor carrying ten or twelve tankards of ale piled on top of each other, and we duly ordered sausages and kartoffeln, which were, again, very nice. The diplomat, it turns out, apart from his cultural duties, is a nuclear arms negotiator, and had just returned from the last summit. His message was one of utter gloom: nothing would really change. Nobody sincerely wants to reduce; glasnost is cosmetic; the status quo will remain intact forever and forever. And so we crawled back to the Bristol in worse spirits than ever.

Bush went back to Los Angeles at six the next morning, and I faced the delightful prospect of Sunday alone in Vienna. My plane was due to depart at six that evening. Of course, there was the possibility of fog. Zagreb is often subject to fog at this time of year. Perhaps I might change my flight anyway and go back tomorrow, Monday, in which case I could catch the new production of *The Flying Dutchman* at the Opera House, eat some glorious food, and then, tomorrow morning, buy books at one of the many emporia in the centre of town (bookshops all close at one on Saturday in village Vienna, needless to say). I tantalised myself with this glorious vision for a while, deciding that professionalism, etc., etc., demanded that I should at least go the airport in time for the plane, and with any luck, Zagreb would be shrouded in murk, and I could proceed as above. So, wanting at least to see the inside of the Opera House, I bought a ticket for the Sunday morning seminar on the new Gluck production. It was a very thorough affair. I watched it from the celebrated standing section at the back of the stalls, from which many a Musik-direktor and Intendant has been given his marching orders. The place was packed. And very splendid it is, in a monumental sort of way.

I had a slight fracas with an usher at the entrance. She was one of those tiny, black-frocked old women that seem to rule continental state theatres. I wasn't at all sure what she wanted of me at first, but it transpired that she was in the grip of that compulsion I had noticed in restaurants and other public places on my last visit: she wanted to get my overcoat from me. She insisted till she was nearly blue in the face: under no circumstances would I be permitted to enter the auditorium in my coat. Finally – because this scene of ours was threatening to disrupt the entire event – I gave in, resolving that on my next visit, I would turn up naked under my coat.

The form inside was that the Intendant, Herr Gensche, talked, wittily and at some length, about why they were doing the piece, the director said how they were doing it, and Charles Mackerras, conducting, said what it was that they were doing. Some of the singers spoke of their problems. It was very civilised, and the audience – all two thousand of them – were acutely involved, applauding the more telling points, shouting out questions and quarrelling with the answers – behaving, in fact, more like an audience at a political meeting. It obviously mattered to them; it was serious and important. I left after about an hour – barely more than halfway through. My head was beginning to ache with the effort of trying to follow a language in which I have a large vocabulary and virtually no grasp of syntax.

I now made for Schönbrunn, largely for Mozartian reasons. I was duly astonished by the sequence of rooms decorated in radically different styles – a living catalogue of eighteenth-century tastes (Turkish, Chinese, French) and properly awed by the scale and splendour of the gardens. It was easy to understand why court musicians of the time, Maria Theresia's, that is, and her son's, should feel that they had reached the summit of their world when they found a place here. In some odd way, too, the splendour is intact; while the nineteenth-century buildings in the centre of Vienna, no less grand in scale, seem dead – a place from which history has receded; a ghost city, almost.

I returned and ate a far from spectral lunch in a restaurant which looked on to the Votive Cathedral, seemingly a great Gothic pile, but actually, like Cologne's cathedral, entirely nineteenth-century. And then to the airport, hoping against hope for fog. Any fog in Zagreb? I enthusiastically enquired of the man behind the desk. No fog! he said, indignantly. Fog? What's fog? was the implication. For he was an employee of Jadran Airlines, and the notion of anything going wrong was officially impossible – until it did, and then it was all part of the great scheme of things, unnegotiable, inevitable, and probably necessary. I got into the plane, melancholy but resigned, the opening bars of *The Flying Dutchman* splashing around in my brain, and settled in. Halfway through the flight, there was an announcement: 'Due to heavy fog at Zagreb airport . . .' I smashed the side of the compartment in rage. Then I calmed down. We were to be diverted to Split, on the Dalmatian coast. Was there not a great Meštrovič collection there? And it was a town of fabled beauty, second only to Dubrovnik. Perhaps it might be quite interesting.

When we arrived at Split airport, after circling it for nearly an hour, because there was fog there too – was fog, in fact, over virtually the whole of Yugoslavia, and had been all day, a fact that had been unaccountably withheld from the ground crew in Vienna – it took them two hours to organise a bus which took us to the hotel they had provided. The journey took five minutes. The place was pleasant enough. I asked at the reception desk the correct way to walk into the centre of town. They laughed. It was a fifty-minute car drive away. Could I take a taxi? They told me how much it would cost: just about twice what I had in cash. No Mastercards here, thank you very much. I went out into the night, wrapped up in my overcoat and wearing my fedora, determined simply to walk wherever my legs would carry me. I turned a corner, and was suddenly confronted with the ocean: black, moonlit, edged with gently rocking fishing boats. I put my fingers in the water. It was warm. I was seized with a crazy notion of taking my clothes off and swimming in it. I wanted to wash all the frustration away. I'd just got my coat off when a short, drunk, stubbled man appeared from nowhere and started screaming at me. I understood nothing but the repeated refrain of turisticki, turisticki. He was shaking his fist at me, thrusting his face into mine. He was certainly about to hit me when a similar man, equally drunk, equally unshaven, but apparently without the homicidal intentions of his colleague, dragged him away, as he howled more abuse at me, eyes rolling, spitting over his shoulder. Shaken, I put my overcoat and hat back on and made my way through what I suppose was the village. There were taverns and pool-halls. My route back to the hotel seemed to necessitate passing through the surprisingly large number of people who were milling around. As I did I became aware of them murmuring things of an unfriendly nature at me. It became louder and louder, they were laughing mockingly, and shouting incomprehensible jokes at me. What was it? The hat? The coat? Was I the butt of the anti-tourist faction again? I didn't know, but wasn't dawdling to find out. I walked back to the hotel with unnatural speed, determined to eat my way to happiness in the hotel restaurant.

It was closed. But the pizza bar . . . With vague memories of Zagreb's Italian restaurant, I went hopefully to the place indicated, but the first mouthful of cardboard dough was enough to dash them. I ordered a litre of poisonous red wine, determined to drink myself into a stupor, because by now I had become aware that the local pop group had started to tune up in the foyer. Their thudding penetrated the concrete walls of the pizza bar, so I assumed that I could expect a night of rhythm and blues, not necessarily in that order. When I lurched into my room, I was proved right; it would have been quieter if I had tried to sleep in the loudspeakers themselves. I clumsily constructed a pair of papier-mâché earplugs from the toilet roll, and rammed them painfully in, sinking onto the bed, the throbbing from the wine competing with the throbbing of the band. I fell – as from a great height – into sleep, only to be aroused five minutes later with a mighty sneeze, then another, and another. I was allergic to something – but what? It could have been anything: the horsehair blankets, the thin, torn sheets, the curtains, my own nose, life. I finally fell asleep on a chair, having shoved more papier-mâché plugs up my nose. But then – as in a dream – I became aware of talking under my window. The band had ceased playing, but their connoisseurs had gathered to discuss its achievements, which they did until dawn. The airport was a further chapter of nightmare. The fog had persisted. We sat there, hour after hour, having first breakfast, then elevenses, then lunch. Finally, at four o'clock, we set off, arriving here fifty minutes later.

My first action was to go the sexpot in travel and ask for my money back. No, she said, sexily, with a vampish smile, yours was a restricted ticket. You can only take one flight and if you miss it . . . Even if it's *cancelled*? I growled. Sure, she said, with a by now sickeningly familiar that's-life shrug. I tore the ticket up before her eyes with a concentrated energy that would have been excessive had I been tearing up telephone directories, and left absurdly triumphantly.

And now I am utterly exhausted and deeply bitter. And I have a scene to shoot tomorrow.

12 November

Yesterday, we reached the absolute final lap of the film, the hardest part from the set designer's point of view, because they had to construct the mad sanatorium of Doctor Lombrosov for the film's biggest set-piece. Most of us saw it yesterday for the first time, and it is a brilliant piece of work by Veljko Despotović (who, I recently discovered, took over the designing of the film after the original designer had a heart attack or some kind of seizure). He is a fascinating and brilliant man, with a kind of disciplined fantasy which is obviously suited to Dušan. I suppose all his collaborators have to be more disciplined than he is, while at the same time being fully responsive to his fantasy. Veljko is certainly that. One meets him from time to time with a book under his arm: he has found the latest work on Hollywood art deco or fourteenth-century archways or whatever. A lively, funny man as so many are on this film, all very delightful and all properly cynical about the way the film is held together and somehow united – as only the actors have not been – by Makavejev's vision of the film – or rather by their belief in him. That is a simpler and more accurate way of putting it. They feel that they are in the hands of a master, and however irritating it may be from moment to moment it is worth it in the end, as I am sure it is worth it in the end. That is to say it will be a very good film.

There are very few of us left. Eric has gone – to Muswew Iw, as it happens. Linda went a few days ago *en famille*. Rade has gone off to face fresh impossible challenges, to write more poems, sing more songs.

a scene, with Dušan making comments, and then suddenly find ourselves running the whole scene for the cameras, not having rehearsed the remaining two-thirds. Both Fred and I, although we get little bursts of anger from time to time, have succumbed to a terrible passivity, waiting to be told. It is decided to flood the floor with water mainly to make the dry ice more effective. The dry ice is as always magically exciting. As I said to Fred, dry ice is one of the great conjuring tricks of the theatre. It embodies part of its magic. It is the most vivid thing you can do, and it is one of the simplest, immediately introducing poetry and a kind of mythic feeling to a setting, any setting, the more ordinary the better. The moment that smoke starts to creep across the ground and to bubble up out of the retort stands or buckets of water you're in another world. You are in the laboratory of Dr Frankenstein, you are on the battlements of Elsinore, you are in Sleeping Beauty's castle. It is a wonderfully immediate source of magic. And so it is here. Veljko and Dušan have between them created a vision of science gone wrong.

These scenes took extraordinarily long to set up. Fred, Patrick and I spent a great deal of time, as the mist swirled around our ankles, laughing and telling each other jokes, which the mist must have rendered demonic. Patrick's deep, deep-throated laughter spurred us on, and we got into a cycle of what seemed at the time wonderful jokes, though I can't remember a single one of them, even at this distance. The joking, apart from its inherent pleasure, is very important, very practical, because it keeps your adrenalin, your life, your energy, your brain going. We could see that this appeared not to be pleasing Dušan at all. He would look at us through slightly narrowed eyes. He was thinking that we were – which I think he does generally feel about us, the English actors – some sort of reppy core, a gang of old pros who aren't engaged with the work, who aren't imaginatively involved with it and who would prefer to stand round telling each other funny stories.

At a certain point he suddenly asked us to come

Camilla has returned to Denmark. Of the principal actors, only Paddy, Lindsay, Fred and I remain – and Svetozar, indefatigable, pristine, ever-watchful Svetozar.

Sveto is playing Rudi Kugelhof, the imprisoned revolutionary. They have built this huge revolving cage for him, a chilling image based on a black joke: he believes in The Movement, so they give him Movement – perpetual movement, in a cage like a rat's cage, the wheel turning as he runs ever faster to nowhere. It was essentially his and Patrick Godfrey's scene. There was the usual chaos. It took three hours before anybody could even decide which shot we were going to do, and then another hour to work out how the shots were going to be set up. I had nothing at all to say in the scene, I merely had to be at Avanti's side and watch with surprise, amazement, or approval, the goings-on of the sanitorium. The re-writes for the scene had cut the single line exchange that I had with Fred. Movies are for the actor very much an art of reaction, and words are certainly not necessary for reactions. There remains very strongly in my brain the impression that Dušan is trying to cut down on the contributions that I might make. There are all kinds of things that I would like to do, to suggest. A very strong comic idea for me is that Hunt is baffled and mystified and indeed made suspicious by things like retorts and all the mechanical apparatus with which Veljko's set abounds, but Dušan is not amused by my suggestions, so I don't make them any more. One was very aware of him feeling that the scene was too static, that he wanted somehow to involve us, make us become more engaged with it. That is a very hard thing to do when you have nothing to do but to react. There are limits to the numbers of ways in which one can react.

Patrick Godfrey as Doctor Lombrosov has a marvellous physical appearance with his grey and white locks, his flowing gown and his bow tie and that wonderful sharp face of his, accentuated by gold rim glasses. He too is rather baffled by the general confusion which prevails. Nobody really quite understands what is happening, nor even which scene we are shooting. We rehearse a bit of forward (we were standing out of the way because there was by now a great deal of water sloshing around the floor) and said, 'I have the impression that you are not concentrating, that you are not engaged, that you are not sufficiently mobile. You must be more mobile, you must get on with it. I am sorry to use such harsh words, but I have the impression that you are not part of this, that you have separated yourselves.' At which we, and above all me, fell into a trough of depression. None of us said anything. None of us made any answer whatever, just a great silence descended, a sulking obedience. But I was utterly furious. When you consider all the hours and hours that we've waited in complete ignorance. And because we just withdraw a few yards and cheer ourselves up, Dušan is enraged! He feels that we should be engaged and connected with the film at all points, following it closely, practising, thinking, running over what we have to do. But what does that actually mean? You have to wait three hours before a shot is set up, and you have no idea why, what the motives are, what new thing is being tried or aimed for. Most often you don't know, and nobody can tell you, which shot it is. If one isn't involved in the process of creating the film, isn't admitted into the ideas behind it, one will of course slip into something of one's own, which is what we did.

Makavejev simply doesn't think it is any part of the director's job to create a mood, atmosphere, rhythm of work. He is functioning on a completely false premise, which is that we are all collaborators and that we are all equally engaged at all levels and at all times. Now, if we had got together, a group of us and him as, shall we say, students, or let's say we all knew each other and we decided to make a film and we elected him to direct it and all offered our particular skills, then we would indeed be co-creators and we could go ahead on that basis. But if you are the man who has created the film and who has cast everybody and who has in this case written the script, then it is incumbent on you to weld your people into a team. You cannot expect 'teamliness' to happen of its own accord. I feel that he is refusing to take steps to create it on principle, but the principle is an incomprehensible one. If there is a skill of communication and a skill of encouragement which will enable people to do better work than they would otherwise do, surely, principle or no principle, you must learn to acquire that skill. It's sensible, it's practical, it's unavoidable. Refusing to do that, he enters into a kind of sulk with us. Sulk, ours and his, is, I'm afraid, all in all, the word.

The other thing that has been a perpetual stumbling block is that although he uses the word 'rehearsal' a great deal he doesn't rehearse all. He rather sketchily blocks a scene out, runs a tiny bit of it, talks through the next bit of it and then suggests that it should be run. Of course the result is chaotic and you can't really get any grasp on it. It is as if he never would allow you to actually know what the scene was. As if it were a conscious technique to create a mystery as to what was going on. Well, we have all been successfully mystified. But if you are mystified and you are an actor of some experience then what you do is conceal your mystification by doing something very simple and strong but probably quite obvious. So, naturally he doesn't get the strange and fascinating and weird and wonderful thing that he is longing for, gets, in fact, its opposite.

Dušan:
Some time ago, I read in the science section of the New York Times *about a newly discovered star or galaxy, thousands of light years away, with unusual and yet unexplained properties.*

The said star was moving at an incredible speed away from us and , moving at the same time at an incredible speed towards us. Please don't ask me for an explanation. The New York Times *did not know more. Astronomers were obviously certain that they possessed information worth publicizing in spite of their puzzlement and the* New York Times, *as well, thought the news fit to print.*

When I find a piece of news like that, it makes me happy. When driven around Jerusalem, they took me to a piece of road, very famous, leading down the hill. One segment of the road, not very long, is such if you put on it a ball or a marble, it goes up the hill! You don't ask questions in the land of legends. There, in Jerusalem, God's trick against the laws of physics got a smile from me. On the contrary, NYT's piece excited me, enormously. Uneasy feeling. Sort of déjà vu! Slowly, I sorted out my feelings about the fast-moving star. It is the same with the famous case of director's catatonia. Assistants and technicians are tearing their hair: 'He is not saying anything.' Gloom on the set. The director's eyes are out of focus, motionless, seemingly looking at some undefined point in front of him, actually staring inwards into the frightening void, into the huge skies above the Sea of Indecision. This is like that for you, outsiders. Inside, two gigantic interlocked time/spaceships mirroring each other carry him 'at an incredible speed' through his contradictory universe.

You can't easily extract sympathy for a mesmerised director (hated by everyone, progressively), and you can't tell anyone about the pain. Wild astronomical 'inner movement' stays completely unperceived and unrecognised.

● ● ● ● ● ● ● ● ● ● ● ● ● ● ● ● ●

Aside on Orson Welles

The day was redeemed for me by a conversation that I started with Nada, Tomislav Pinter the cameraman's ex-wife. I can't remember how on earth we began to discuss Orson Welles but we did, and she said, 'Of course Tom worked with him for six months.' I said, 'Was he the director of photography on the film about Tesla in which Welles played Westinghouse?' She said, 'No, no. He worked with him as a director.' She then told me about a film of *The Merchant of Venice*, about which I knew absolutely nothing. I must have read about and then forgotten it. He finished over three-quarters of the film, having shot it in Venice, playing Shylock himself. He recruited young English actors who were just passing through and he roped them in to be the Bassanios and the Salerios. Apparently he gave a marvellous performance. He was, Nada said, very, very serious about it. Tom himself then joined us and started to elaborate somewhat. He said that Welles got onto the set every morning at 4.30 to give himself a two-hour make up. Tom said that what was astounding was that Welles knew exactly what every lens would and could do in terms of the frame. He would say, 'Set your camera 18 inches from the ground, use a 30 inch lens, and over there will be the edges of your frame' (pointing to them in physical reality), and Tom said he was never ever wrong, he knew absolutely. He didn't really work out the shots in advance, he wasn't very technical at all, but he knew that. He, Tom, despite twenty-five years of experience, was quite incapable, he said, of such a thing. It recalled many stories about Welles in his later years, when he was mainly a supporting-part actor, acting, for example, in the film *Catch 22* and telling Mike Nichols that he should change the lens and Mike Nichols saying 'but you can't possibly know what lens we've got on, Orson' and Orson saying 'well, do what you like but I think you should change the lens' and Nichols didn't change the lens and when he saw the rushes he realised that Welles was right.

When I was talking to Nada again those words 'Orson Welles, stopped my heart. I cannot ignore them. If anybody mentions Orson Welles I am engaged immediately. I saw *Kane* when I was eighteen, and it swept me away as it has everyone, and particularly every eighteen year old who's ever seen it. Beyond the sheer adrenalin engendered by the film – and it must embody the excitement of its own creation more than any film ever made: you can almost see Welles improvising the shots – two things struck me at the time: the preoccupation with scale and size, with which I identified strongly; and the spectacle of a man become his own older self, becoming, it seemed, his own father, and that too struck a chord. I saw whatever I could of his work, and learned something about his life from the inadequate books about him. It wasn't till I got to Drama School and read John Houseman's *Runthrough* that I felt I had a sense of who he was; and the account in that of the years at the Mercury Theatre gave me an ideal of what theatre might be. I was, I think, obsessed by him for a while. The boy genius, the wunderkind, sweeping everything before him: why wasn't I more like that? One night, while I was still a drama student, I was sitting quietly drinking tea with my dear friend Penny Cherns, silent as only the closest friends can be, and I returned in my mind to him, and Penny screamed, and said: 'Simon, I was just looking at your face, and it suddenly became

Orson Welles's.' Unfortunately it was only his face, and that only briefly, that took me over; but I continued to be fascinated with him and of course with his so-called decline, his alleged self-destruction. He, Charles Laughton and Oscar Wilde were my heroes: three large men, three fat men, indeed, whose careers and lives seemed to have faltered in mid-term. Not very wise models, perhaps, but we don't choose our heroes. I was saddled with them.

• •

13 November

Back, reluctantly, to *For a Night of Love*. The building in which they've built the sanatorium is, quite rightly, hideous. It's an ex-brandy factory. There is no heating in it, there is no lavatory. Fred got very distressed by this and threatened to piss against the wall and everybody said they thought that was a very good idea. On the floor below there are some old showers that people seemed to have decided to use as a lavatory, so each cubicle contained a little pile of shit. Very odd. Very primitive.

Today again one struggled up the stairs to that place. My role now is entirely reactive. Today's scenes are all concerned with the immersion of Rudi in the water on the mediaeval ducking stool that Veljko has devised for him – another startling image. Again Dušan's frustration. He wanted Fred and me to react all the time. Basically he wants us to do something extraordinary and strange, but you can't really do anything extraordinary and strange unless you are put into an extraordinary and strange situation. The moment that Svetozar/Rudi started being dumped into the water, the water splashed all over us, and we *were* in an extraordinary and strange situation. We reacted immediately.

The last few days of this film are like the last few days of the First World War. It feels as if the outcome has been decided, and one is only going through the motions of battle now. I don't engage with Dušan, I don't really talk to him at all, I don't talk to Bojana, which is infinitely sad, we had wonderful conversations – pre-war, as it were. I have had the most curious sensation, a kind of 'out of the body' experience. I feel as though I were hovering above the film. I do what Dušan tells me to do, but I don't feel responsible for it, it isn't me doing it. Fred hasn't quite reached this stage. The guerilla spirit lives in him. He keeps fighting: sometimes he finds some old damp bullets and fires off a feeble volley; now and then he lobs a rusty hand-grenade; occasionally he risks unarmed combat, all to no avail. He keeps trying to make *points*. I don't think any point can be made now. I doubt if it ever could have been. All there is, is to do the film. Unfortunately for me anyway the conviction has become absolute that I should never have done the film and that Dušan should never have cast me.

Saša (the third? or is it fourth? assistant director) is a screenplay writer and a playwright herself. She is also a lover of movies and a great admirer of Makavejev, although she has been badly used on the film and has been very unhappy a lot of the time. She so wants the English actors to have enjoyed the experience. I said to her, 'I'll tell you the simple truth. It is the worst experience I've ever had as an actor. I feel belittled, humiliated, incompetent and non-contributory.' I said, and I believe this to be true, that it would have been a better film if somebody else had played Hunt – somebody who was in tune with Dušan and who could have gone down what are evidently lots of fascinating alleyways. I wasn't able to see them, because he wasn't able to describe them until it was too late. I felt that my notion of the character was completely rejected and that all my impulses have been the wrong ones, and that I was unable either to understand or to put into practice what Dušan envisaged. You can't go on offering up material to have it shot down every time. You withdraw, which is certainly what I have done. It is terrible to think that this has happened because it means that the last eight weeks – eight precious weeks – have been a sulky, negative time, during which I have learned nothing, I have gained nothing, I have given nothing except my face and my body – oh, and, my moustache: I have given freely of my moustache to this film. I said to Saša, 'It was a complete misunderstanding. Dušan and I met each other socially, we seemed to get on terribly well, I was thrilled and flattered by how well we got on. Then we worked together, and the truth came out. We are absolutely different people, we have completely different ideas of the world, completely different ideas of the work. We should not ever try to create anything together.'

It is peculiar. I have had the strange feeling that I had last when I was at school and it was the day on which games were played, and there were a group of boys, the large majority, in fact, who knew exactly what they were doing, they bounced onto the field, they had all the right equipment, sports gear and so on, and they instantly threw themselves into the game, there was no need for any encouragement, in they were, playing like demons, and I sat there on the sidelines, in Bill Gaskill's memorable words, 'like a homosexual aesthete,' wearing the wrong gear, not knowing what to do and dreading being called on to play, because I would be out of place, wrong somehow. That is exactly what I feel in this film, always wrong.

In the afternoon we did a big master shot of a scene in which Fred has a few lines with Svetozar as he is being dumped into the water. Dušan pottered up to him and said, 'We've done the wide master shot and I don't place much store by the master shot, it's just geography really, geography and choreography. But I didn't really see your reactions. I didn't understand your reactions to him, I didn't see the character at all.' Fred of course rose to the bait and said, 'Perhaps you didn't see the character because we didn't rehearse it. There was no chance of us testing it out, so naturally I just walked through it when we filmed it.' Dušan said, 'I am very worried, Fred, by what you say because I feel that you are expecting me to tell you to do something and it's not what I want, it's not how I work, what I hope is that you will offer me things. I was very upset yesterday that you just wandered off the set, the three of you, you just drifted off the set every time you didn't seem to be involved. It is not the way I can make films.'

'Well,' Fred replied, 'if you are very frustrated with me as an actor I am afraid I am very frustrated with you as a director.' 'Ah,' said Dušan, 'I see. Well, we can't argue about this. We have the film to get on with, to make. Just remember that when Svetozar was in *Montenegro* he had ten days off and he could have gone home and I said to him "go home if you like, but why not stay here and work with the workers, find out what it's like to load a lorry". So Svetozar did stay, and he built up his part in the film enormously because he discovered so many things that I couldn't resist putting into the film.' In saying this, which was all basically to Fred, but Patrick and I could overhear it quite clearly, he summoned up, again, the spectre of the creativity of the actor. He implied that we were merely mechanical performers and that people like Svetozar were genuine creative participants. There is a certain truth in that, but somehow Sveto – poor old Sveto, being used as a stick to beat us with – has found a way of pursuing a parallel creativity to Dušan's. He continued to upbraid Fred but more in sorrow than in anger. When Fred tried to argue with him, there was his usual affectation of, 'How interesting it is, your attitude, even though completely wrong, how very, very fascinating'.

Dušan has a curious face, it's sometimes the face of Cézanne, sometimes the face of a thirteenth-century bishop. Drew thinks it is the face of a gremlin or a goblin. I am not sure about that. It's foxy, it is not a very healthy-looking face at the moment. It is rather pasty and white. His eyes have great benevolence about them but you never quite feel that it's personally directed to you, that it comes out of a feeling for you or towards you, it's more like general amusement at the absurdity of the world. It needs to be repeated that Makavejev is very charming in his way. It is a curious kind of charm. It is not warm exactly, it is playful. But it is not exactly humorous either. There is something which could be cruel about it but he's not. I've never heard him be cruel. He sometimes raises his voice, sometimes he shouts. But he isn't destructive. He is certainly very far ahead intellectually and I have the feeling sometimes that he is reining himself back from patronising us intellectually. It amused me to discover that his nickname, what the assistant director calls him anyway, is 'Mache', which is a sort of joke, a variant of Mak (the diminutive of his family name). It means 'pussy'. He is a pussy, claws, purrs and all.

What is very curious, and I suppose in the end commendable, is that there can be terrible rows all day long, but for them it is totally forgotten after a while. The cameraman and the director had a huge row before lunch and other people in the room were throwing their gloves down and raging and storming. It turned out to have been about something really quite trivial and, by the time lunch had been eaten, was a distant memory. But we English people tend to change our whole view of the character of the people we are working with, or indeed ourselves, as a result of an argument or a confrontation. The Yugoslavian way is to have a good shout and then totally forget it. I suppose it is quite healthy. It upsets me physically to have that kind of row, so it can't be healthy for me.

The great help on the thing, Tomislar Pinter, the cameraman, has been an extraordinarily good-natured man and a model of courtesy. It is remarkable how much difference it makes when someone comes up to you and says, 'We're breaking for a little while. It's going to take seven minutes. We are changing the lens. Please have a seat, or perhaps you would like to go back to the caravan.' Sometimes I saw Makavejev looking at Pinter. I felt he was thinking, 'Why is he doing that?' or maybe he was thinking, 'Ah, I know why he is doing that. Just to ingratiate himself with the actors.' But you need a lot of lubrication on an enterprise which requires something like fifty people to create even the simplest scene in the film. You need some kind of flow between them.

We did a scene after lunch. Dušan for once told me what he thought Hunt's possible reaction to Rudi's emotion might be. The scene was very lively and successful. He said, 'Perhaps at this point you could turn round and react' and so on. Suddenly we seemed to be working together as director and actor and it was extraordinary. I don't know what it will look like. But again the feeling at the end of the day was of moving in complete mystery. It would be so interesting if one could get to know the Yugoslav actors well enough to ask them what they truly think about him, because he has such a basic approval of their acting, and they have such a basic approval of his directing, one really does feel oneself to be the odd one out, the one marching out of step. The ugly thing, I should say, is that we have somehow become polarised on national lines, and therefore it has gone beyond ordinary tensions or misunderstandings. Somehow we seem to be sitting there, a little group of the English, feeling bitter against the Yugoslavian nation in general and against Dušan. Although one always experiences irritations, particularly in a country where you can't speak the language and that is as full of bureacratic nonsense and hoplessness as this country is, one loathes a 'Brits abroad' feeling, 'us versus the locals'. It is horrible and leaves a nasty taste in the mouth.

Dušan:
The Brits – Simon Callow, Fred Molina and Lindsay Duncan – felt uneasy on a number of counts. It seems they were irritated with the crew talking a language they didn't understand and 'nobody explaining to them what is happening' (not the case with Eric, Chris or Camilla).
Do they always carry little toilets with them? (In the middle of forest the actress was asking to be driven few miles back to the hotel for a pee; in the trailer in the little town and rain, another Brit would not go on his own to the nearby hotel or restaurant to look for a toilet, but literally freaked out feeling deprived and 'badly treated', letting us know what bothered him only after few hours of private agony.)

It has become a question of our self-respect as actors. The whole British profession is seen by us to be under attack or under suspicion, particularly in terms of our creativity or our lack of it, or our lack of invention or imagination. That also has left a great unpleasantness. The feeling that we, the English actors, just 'do the lines'. He had earlier said to Lindsay (who has almost literally crawled through shit on her hands and knees during some of the scenes) that she had failed to liberate the character. Lily Sacher hadn't had her liberation. 'But there you are,' he said, 'that's film. We can't go back on it. Too bad, what a pity.'

Yesterday evening I went to the bookshop to try to find something on Tesla, the Yugoslav Einstein. I've missed my chance of going to Belgrade, to the museum which contains thousands of photographs, working models and so on – including white gloves, I suppose. My conversation in the shop was curious and characteristic. 'I'm looking for books on Tesla,' I said, 'preferably in English, but definitely illustrated.' 'No books in English,' she said, 'and no pictures. We have only one book on Tesla.' 'May I see it?' I asked. She shrugged. 'Why not?' Five minutes later, it arrived. It was full of pictures, and in English. A little further down the street, I got a wonderful bargain. A jeweller was selling off Russian station masters' fob watches – apparently new – for ten pounds each. I bought four.

● ● ● ● ● ● ● ● ● ● ● ● ● ● ● ● ● ●

Aside about The Times

Last night, too, I found a copy of the London *Times* in the hotel news shop. Their stock of English papers is eccentric and intermittent – one day the *Mail* or the *News of the World*, the next day the *FT* and the European edition of *The Guardian*. Now I know it's pathetic of me, but I have a kind of addiction to *The Times*. It is, I think, a good newspaper, but not specially better than its immediate rivals. I hold no truck with its politics, and although I'm fond of its house writers, it's not because I agree with them, but out of a sort of easy familiarity with them. The paper's better laid out and better printed than its sisters on the street of shame, but it would be an eccentric reader who bought a paper on typographical grounds alone. Pondering the matter, I come to the conclusion that the reason I'm prepared to spend an hour, sometimes two, scouring the streets of any foreign city in which I happen to find myself to find a copy, no matter how many days old, is on account of its fondness for obscure, not to say insane, incidents, which it then reports in an entirely deadpan fashion. *The Guardian,* reporting such incidents, becomes waggish, arch, even, the *Telegraph* holds them at arm's length and the *FT* doesn't report them at all. *The Times* records these preposterous incidents with grave solemnity, exhaustively investigating and documenting them, and never, ever descending to whimsy. As long as I've been reading the paper (twenty-five years), through various proprietors and in whatever format – with advertising on the front page or without, by-lined or sternly anonymous – this has remained a constant factor. It seems to me peculiarly and admirably English, and it's *that* that I'm hooked on.

Today there was a magnificent example of this lunacy. It was in the obituary columns. The gentleman encomiated rejoiced – gloried – in the name of the Wali of Swat.

'Wali Miangul Jahan Zeb, the last Wali of Swat, died on September 14.' Not April 1, which would have explained a lot. 'Swat,' the piece continues, clearly feeling the need to gain some credibility with the reader, 'on the North West Frontier, was envied for many things, but perhaps it was alone in being completely free of practising lawyers. The Wali heard all cases, perhaps as many as eighty a day, and his judgement was final.' It then describes how the old Wali stepped down in his favour. No doubt Wali is pronounced in some characteristically Swattian way – Wa-Lee, perhaps, or Waillee – but I find it impossible to believe that the author of the obituary was unaware of the effect on the ordinary English reader of the constant repetitions of the title. I suspect mischief in the department.

'To the end,' we learn, 'he remained a confirmed and unabashed Anglophile; in dress, deportment and behaviour. His three-course meals were standard English fare, starting with Mulligatawny soup and ending with apple pudding . . . but he never missed one of the five daily prayers of a fast during the month of fasting.' He handed Swat over to Pakistan in 1969. 'The only regret that he was known to have expressed about the handing over, with sorrow in his voice, was the indiscriminate cutting down of the olive trees . . . He had imported them from Italy and had tended them with care.' After this elegiac note, the thunderer thunders in a way rarely heard any longer in the main body of the paper. 'Alas, since its absorption by the state, law and order in Swat has deteriorated, with lootings, kidnappings and murder more common. The world of the twentieth-century is everywhere symbolised by the presence of the video-cassette recorder and a rifle in almost every home.' The twin scourges of modern living unerringly identified. And then, the final glorious flourish. 'In the eyes of his people, in an age of pygmies, a giant has just passed away.' The masterstroke, perhaps, of the whole piece is the omission of the phrase 'we shall not see his like again,' the obvious and longed-for resolution, leaving us, like the people of Swat (Swats?), dissatisfied, waiting for more.

I – heretically – suggested to Fred that the whole thing was an audacious invention of a bored though obviously brilliant journalist, but Fred doubted it. No one, he said, could invent such details, and the next day, with a flourish, he produced *The Guardian* obit of the Wali – facetious as ever, but undoubtedly commemorating a real person. I don't know who it is at Fort Murdoch, valiantly maintaining this steady flow of true madness, but he is keeping a flame of essential Englishness burning, like the monks in Ireland keeping writing alive during the Middle Ages. He belongs to the same tiny fellowship of illuminati who are responsible for the silver service teas on the London-Manchester Inter-City and who produce the sublime irrelevancies of the BBC's Radio Three. 'You have just been listening,' I once tuned in to hear, 'to this evening's talk, "Towards A More Logical Bassoon."' The endeavour is little short of heroic, and they deserve our gratitude.

● ● ● ● ● ● ● ● ● ● ● ● ● ● ● ● ● ● ● ●

15 November

On the 12th we had a rather late start, not planned of course. We were called at 8.00, we finally hit the set at 2.00, but I had serenely anticipated this and had brought my typewriter in so I spent some time working on the screenplay, and it put me onto the set in a much better mood than I think I have been for many days. The set itself is becoming something of a nightmare however because it's awash with water and dry ice, whose magic has begun to wear off since it started invading the bronchi. The antiquated industrial heater (which presumably hasn't been used since they stopped making the brandy) is visibly pumping out carbon monoxide fumes so the moment one walks into the building one feels ill. However Fred seemed to be in a much more buoyant mood and I was in a more buoyant mood and we started to offer various suggestions as to how to play the scenes, which seemed rather to take Dušan by surprise but he accepted most of what we had to say. As the day continued, it seemed to get slower and slower. We were admittedly doing hugely difficult things like the big scene with the hose pipe hosing down the double for Lindsay. But we eventually finished at about 7.00, and it was OK.

On the way back to the hotel, I sat with Elizabeth, whose innate buoyancy has been sadly subdued by the general mood. Gone are the heady days of the beginning when she and Dušan were inventing a new language, when theories were being bandied about and everything seemed possible. Now nothing at all seems possible, and we huddle together like people whose house has been bombed. She has become a tower of strength, actually, supportive and indescribably kind. Her intuition, which I noticed the moment I met her, leads her to say exactly the right thing at the right moment. Now we sit in the bus in total silence, her in front of me, and I suddenly realise that it isn't a wig at all, it's just a very long swatch of hair piled baroquely over her head. I blush to think of the fun I have made of her hair, and indeed of her. I'm too embarrassed even to make a joke of it with her, though she has a lovely sense of humour. I just sit in the back of the bus and blush. Fortunately, though not unusually, the light isn't working so I blush unseen, in the dark.

The next day was the last day of filming and although it was a very bright and pleasant morning, something rather curious was in the air. Last days on films normally have a sense of escape, of end-of-term, of some sort of satisfaction, of merriment and so on, but there was very little of that on this day. Everybody seemed if anything glummer than they had been for some time. It was a most cheerless atmosphere. In the yard where the make-up vans were located, the puppies, their roles in the film over, had been left in an office without any light where they were stumbling blindly about in their own shit. Their trainer had gone, having been engaged only for a couple of days, and nobody seemed to know what to do with the little creatures. A couple of crew members had apparently agreed to take some, but not all, of them. What would happen to the rest? Nobody knew, to the rage of the English crew, who seriously considered smuggling them out of the country. Their whimpering was pitiful, and continued throughout the last day.

I had already spoken my last lines the day before. My contribution, again, was a completely unknown factor. I don't think I was even written into the script. The scene was being shot a different way, there was a critical problem of continuity because Dušan had invented an exit for someone who was still there during the next scene. There was a long, long discussion about how to arrange that. But that is all perfectly legitimate. Anybody can make those kind of mistakes. It seemed to take so long, though, out of all proportion to what was being shot. It was almost as if it would never end. It spun on and on and on. One looked at one's watch – it was only 10.30 – we had started quite early but not that early. Then it was 10.35, then 10.37. Relays of food and things like that kept coming. I got absolutely desperate for food. Having till now scrupulously maintained a diet of black coffee and cheese, I yearned for more exotic oral consolation. I kept on going up to Marit Allen who has no responsibility in this area at all and saying, 'I must have food, Marit', and she, seeing the mad look in my eyes, would go and speak to the caterers and come back with sandwiches or, on one memorable occasion, with a roll filled with chocolate spread, white sugar and butter – something I hadn't eaten since I was seven. I crammed it into my face, eagerly.

Eventually, we did shoot. Enver, the king, is dressed up to look exactly like Peter II of Yugoslavia – moustache, pince-nez, white costume and cap. He looks like, and is playing it like, our idea of a minor Balkan princeling. In the scene in the sanatorium, he goes up to Rudi Kugelhof in his cage and speaks to him. Rudi has a gun concealed in his loaf of bread but for some reason he can't shoot. Instead he says, 'Long live the king,' somewhat aggressively. The king goes away and for a brief moment we see him thinking, 'Did he mean that or not?' Dušan said casually, as an afterthought and not at all in an explanatory way, 'This proves that charisma can overcome opponents. By charisma alone the king stultifies the man who could have killed him. Just like Stalin.' I am still amazed to overhear these little things which suddenly give a glimpse of the film that might have been.

Fred and I knew that our work was over. We weren't in the last scene. Only Lindsay was in that. We both felt very strongly that we wanted to nip off quick, we couldn't bear any emotion of any kind. After we had waited unnecessarily for about an hour, Dušan suddenly announced, 'Fred and Simon are finished today and they

285

are finished on the film. Thank you.' There was a quite long and I think genuinely very affectionate burst of applause from everybody as is common when one has finished one's part in the film. Dušan immediately busied himself on the next scene. Fred went off, but I went round very slowly to everybody saying goodbye and finally came up to Dušan. He said, 'Thank you. Thank you. See you in London, no doubt,' so I said, 'Yes, for the dubbing,' and that was it. It was exactly the right thing for him to have said. It was simple and it was neutral. Perhaps even for him there is a great deal that should be said, but we couldn't, it would take too long, it has gone too deep. It has become curiously sour.

When Fred and I had left the set at about 8.00, rushing off to buy a bag to carry away all the books that we'd bought and all the extra stuff, we walked through the streets both feeling, and I think feeling very acutely, a sense of frustration and maybe guilt. I suddenly felt that I had behaved very badly, rather pettily over the last few weeks, as if I had been demanding certain formalities to be observed, or as if I had insisted on only working to the letter of the law, or as if I had been ungiving and unintelligent and hadn't really committed myself to the project. It is almost impossible if you don't know what you are doing as an actor to give yourself to a project. You become self-obsessed because you desperately want to relieve yourself of the unpleasant sensation of being bad, but it's a deeply horrible feeling. A feeling of 'not rightness', of being out of step. It's different if you think you are doing something absolutely wonderful, but the director doesn't. That's copeable with. You have a strong basis for survival there.

On this film, however, I know that what I've been doing is not very good. Worst of all I have lost faith in my own acting. After this long period of struggling with two professions – directing and writing – at both of which I am a beginner, I had looked forward to doing something that I know how to do really well. Perhaps that was the fatal hubris. I thought I'd swan in, commit a perfect little something to celluloid, and swan out. I should know myself well enough by now. Unless my intuition is engaged, I am incapable of producing anything worthwhile. But even more than that, I'd hoped to learn from Dušan, to push forward the boundaries of what I can do as an actor. I feel I have failed to take advantage of this man and his peculiar genius. I have wasted my time and his. I still don't dislike him. But I do feel rejected by him. I have a feeling that he may deliberately try to reject love from the people with whom he works. Being a director is a role which offers enormous opportunities for provoking love. Directors – I now know from experience – sometimes have quite consciously to stop themselves from making everybody love them. (Some, of course, succeed in this beyond their wildest dreams.) It may be that Dušan doesn't like the potential for adulation, that he can't take it, that it actually disturbs him. The love in question, I should add, is not erotic, not usually anyway; it is father-love. Does he dislike *that*? He doesn't like assuming fatherly responsibilities, for sure, taking decisions, concerning himself with the welfare of his charges. The rejection-of-love theory was given some credibility by Michael Kagan, who, on the journey back, told me that Tom Luddy had told him that every film of Makavejev's ends up in the complete collapse of all human relationships, and that he somehow seems to have brought that on himself. No doubt it is a little too strong to say that he engineers it but I think there might be something in it.

In the end the whole experience has been, minute by minute, one of the most negative experiences of my life. I don't only mean displeasing, unpleasant, uncomfortable, painful – it hasn't especially been any of those things – I mean simply that it has been negative. The spirit has died. I'd rather not have been there.

Dušan:
I discovered with a surprise that the last chapter of Callow's Being an Actor *is entitled* Manifesto. *In it he pleads against directors as colonisers of theatre which*

287

should naturally be a meeting place of actors and writers:

'Instead of being the fons et origo of the entire enterprise, he [the director] would have been chosen – employed, to be blunt – by the actors specifically for his knowledge of the world of the play and its performing traditions. The actors would use him or her to challenge themselves to the utmost flexibility in reaching the play's world and style'.

If only I had read this before our shoot!

When working on a play, of course you start with page one, and it has to grow towards the end, it is linear and safe. Creative work as a voyage through uncharted space is taken under the protective umbrella of a text. If too much fear is aroused while working on a scene you simply can cling to the text-as-written and pretend that truth is to be found in the words. With most of the scenes shot out of order, films do not offer such a protection. In the theatre the actor is always on stage and in the foreground. In film, as soon as the camera moves closer than medium shot, the actor becomes the stage. When a tear rolls down the actor's face, the tear is the actor and his facial skin is the stage, while his face is the background. Anything in the film can act, the tree, the boiling milk, the fly on somebody's nose. It depends on the director's decision.

The printed script is important in films to secure finances in the first place and to establish the starting point. Everything else is a permanent transformation and interaction between the actors and the camera and all kinds of realities around them and within. Everything once recorded has to be edited and re-edited hundreds of times until, after its numerous births and re-births, the unique shape of the new work appears (broken and assembled into and from circa 144,000 separate transparent motionless pictures – 24 times 60 times 100).

When we got back to our rooms, we found very beautiful abstract prints waiting for us, presents from Dušan. That was a little shaming. I had wondered what to give them. In the end I gave them a copy of my Laughton book, which is a present and not a present. I wrote in it: 'To

Dušan. In honour of the beautiful film I know you have made,' which is a compliment and not a compliment. The title of the book – *A Difficult Actor*, might have occasioned a grim thought. Lindsay called to say that they hadn't managed to shoot her scene. She would have to stay another day. Her voice as she reported these things was of a becalmed mad woman – eerie, unnerving. The next morning, Fred and I and Huggy set off for London. Huggy had volunteered to be totally silent if he could sit with us, and he was. We didn't have much more to say than he did. This strange mood of mingled anger, disappointment and shame hung in the air.

As soon as I got home, I wanted to move onto the next thing – had no anecdotes to peddle round the dinner tables of London. I wanted to forget it. Eventually I handed the tapes of this diary to the publisher who'd insisted on commissioning them, eventually I got round to reading the transcripts'. In the middle of doing 'the next thing' – *Shirley Valentine* – I became rather ill. Hiatus hernia was diagnosed, brought on, or at any rate exacerbated, by the gallons and gallons of crude black coffee I drank every week on the set. My throat and sinuses, too, were all but incapacitated by catarrh bred by the pounds and pounds of cheese consumed. In time, both conditions receded, and I started to think more and more about the film. I missed Dušan, and mourned the destruction, as I saw it, of our friendship. I became curious about the film, and I wanted to dissolve the negative feeling with which I had ended my work on it. Since that last day, I have learned more about movie acting. I have come to understand something of what Dušan meant by a casual approach. I have, too, directed more, and understand his resistance to performances which have a clear black line around them. Mostly, I see how funny so much of it all was.

Dušan:
Simon Callow's productivity is immense and I do not know how I feel or what I think about it. (Did he scare me? Make me envious? Did he get me to worry for him? Can we call it 'Toomuchismo'?) While we were shooting, he

was working on a script and a play and another book, and did something like a 'portrait of a hotel' in Vienna for some Sunday magazine. After Shirley Valentine in the West End, he directed Diderot-Kundera [Jacques and his Master] in Los Angeles, then moved Shirley Valentine to Broadway, played in the meantime Faust at the Lyric Hammersmith, an incredible show of seven or nine or eleven hours, and he was 'warming up' for it every day by jogging, sauna and I don't know what else. He was talking about the book on Orson Welles's theatre, and a play on Wilhelm Reich; he wants to direct a film.

When the first transcripts arrived, of the tapes that he had dictated, the quality of it was shockingly poor and seemingly irrelevant. Very soon, the first re-write arrived, and then the next one. In gigantic leaps, random instant notes, some of them dictated self-confessedly in a drunken state, were emerging as fluent and interesting reading, perceptive, self-ironic, intelligent.

Being used to seeing my personal ambitions turning against myself through self-crippling critical and over-critical assessment of my first sketches of projects that would never then materialise, I understood how cleverly he uses his restlessness. I wrote: his drives are more noble than he is. (Or, should the word be: honourable?) He manages, miraculously, to turn his bitching and simply bad moods into something beautiful. What starts as narcissistic whining about waiting useless hours in an unheated trailer turns into witty commentary and acquires, even, some inner dignity.

Now, the difficult part. Slovenian landscapes, the crew, jolly caterers, they all get, deservingly, few sympathetic lines. The director emerges as an incompetent zombie. Of course, I know what he is talking about. After the take he would like to read from my face how good he was. Most of the time I am silent, or talk to extras, or pay attention to the least important corners of the shot. He has no insight into the director's lack of time for reassuring trivialities.

So I am reading about my aloofness and lack of compassion. It boils down to incompetence and arrogance. It is obvious that even the minimal nod, or smile, would be gratefully appreciated. Why was it, then, missing?

I was especially hurt when Simon quotes Tom Luddy, how all my films end with a complete collapse of human relationships. I would like to think that it is not true, but I know that it is true much more than I am ready to confess, or face. It, of course, mystifies me. I, as well, have some proof to the opposite. With so and so, and so and so, we are still very close. Sure we always try to make the film having as many friends around as possible. But, films bring good money and parasites and fake experts creep in from everywhere. Every film is a strange galaxy of characters with a few inevitable borderline psychotics, some suicidal adventurers, depressive loners, jacks-of-all-trades, inventive problem-solvers, gamblers, drifters. A film is an orphanage.

Critical moments, cracks, explosions and catastrophes wait in the wings, and sometimes arrive in clusters. That's why we love films. Two days or two hours are not alike. Film is made in a vortex of mutual uses and abuses, and it is simply wrong for an actor to concentrate on a director as an omnipotent and omni-supporting mirror. Staying obsessed (or concerned) about his 'role' or 'performance', Simon unnecessarily boxed himself between the 'text' and the 'director', as if in a one-way tunnel, instead of seeing himself in a spherical space in which he is both acted upon and being an actor.

LAST WORDS

As I corrected the proofs of *Shooting the Actor*, I was directing my first movie, *The Ballad of the Sad Café*. The more I read, the angrier I became with the self-obsessed, self-indulgent person who had written the bulk of the text. Why couldn't he see what the problems were, and actively apply himself to solving them, instead of childishly sulking? Why was he so wilfully ignorant of the process of film-making? Was it a deep-seated contempt for the whole process, as compared with that of his beloved Theatah? What was it? Whatever it was, it was disgraceful. Didn't he care anything about the film? Or were his own tiny problems the only thing he could see? I had no sympathy with him. With me, that is to say. Because of course, in the throes myself of the very problems that had preoccupied and distracted Dušan, I had been forcibly made aware of the other side of the coin; and till you've experienced it, you never really know it.

In one of many long distance telephone conversations that Dušan and I had over the year or so that it took to create this book, he said to me: 'When I read what you wrote, all I can see is this actor sitting miserably in his caravan, not knowing that the cause of his misery is that he wants to be a director.' And that is probably true. Nonetheless, what I wrote, painful and embarrassing though it now is to read, is a true account of what actors sometimes go through on films. No doubt it will come back to haunt me, just as the stirring words of the Manifesto section of *Being an Actor* have done. But I always say to actors whom I direct: 'Read this. I am as likely to offend against it as anyone else. Just shout at me when I do.' On the first day of shooting *The Ballad of the Sad Café*, after the second take of the very first scene we did, I suddenly caught myself forgetting to say anything to the actors, and then being slightly bewildered when one of them wanted to know why we were going to do another take of the same scene. Didn't he realise? Wasn't it obvious? But of course it wasn't. And again and again I have remembered Dušan's vivid account of the director as catatonic, and understood exactly what he meant.

The experience that the diary records is both typical and unique. There's an element of what we went through in all films, but only Dušan and I could have fallen out the way we did. Our mutual solipsism was a function of who we are — or were, at that particular moment. Reading it over, it seems indescribably distant, and shockingly recent; like last night's drunken outrage recalled through this morning's hangover.

CODA

Manifesto was duly completed but never properly released because of the collapse of the production company, Cannon Films. Symptomatic was the fact that a brief appearance at two or three Cannon cinemas in London in September 1988 was its only showing in the UK. It was nevertheless sold throughout the world and has been screened in most countries in a similarly ad hoc fashion. The video was released by Warners Home Video in 1989.

The most positive response from critics has been in the USA. In Chicago, out of ten critics polled, two put *Manifesto* in their Top Ten films of the year. In Los Angeles the *L.A. Times*' critic, Sheila Benson, wrote: 'Sweetly randy, politically seditious and captivatingly pretty, *Manifesto* is director Dušan Makavejev working at the top of his ironic form. Taking off from an Emile Zola story about a very young and beautiful aristocrat with a spotless image and a taste for sport among her manservants, Makavejev has added his own pungent views on zealots of every stripe, and created a deliciously bawdy fairy tale spun in confectionery colours.' And Henry Sheehan's review in the *Hollywood Reporter* began: 'Located somewhere in the loony no man's land between whimsy and sardonicism, *Manifesto* is a sexy and intellectual romp through the debris of twentieth-century revolutionary failure. Though such a subject hardly sounds fit for comedy, it's merely a shift in focus for Yugoslav wanderer Dušan Makavejev, who had been counselling the bourgeoisie on its failure to heed its sexuality for years. Here he zeroes in on the enemies of the middle and upper classes, and finds that they, too, are just as trapped by old-fashioned repressive notions. More full of smiles than laughs, *Manifesto*'s thoughtful level of accomplishment could bring in comparatively hefty dollars on the art-house circuit if Cannon is willing to nurture this hothouse bloom with special care and attention. The worry is that it will hang around for two weeks and then blow town.'

Manifesto has however been seen extensively on the Film Festival circuit, most notably in Boston, Belgrade, Chicago, Gujon (where it won the Grand Prix), Houston, Montreal, Telluride and Toronto.

MANIFESTO

USA, 1988   Director: Dušan Makavejev

Distributor: Cannon
Production company: Cannon Films, Inc./Cannon International, with
          the co-operation of Jadran Film
Executive producers: Michael J. Kagan, Tom Luddy
Producers: Menahem Golan, Yoram Globus
Associate producer: Bojana Marijan
Production executive: Michael Hartman
Production supervisor: Boris Gregorić
Production co-ordinator: Velinka Fičor
London contact: Julia Robinson
Production managers: Peter Cotton, Gorjan Tozija
Location managers: Marko Vrdoljak, Igor Nola
Post-production supervisor: Stephen Barker
Casting: Bojana Marijan
Assistant Director: Dejan Karaklajić, Saša Vojković, Dubravko Scherr
Script: Dušan Makavejev. Inspired by the story *For a Night of Love* by
          Emile Zola
Photography (in colour): Tomislav Pinter
Special photographic effects: Mio Vesović
Editor: Tony Lawson
Production designer: Veljko Despotović
Art director: Nicola Pajić
Set dresser: Stanislav Dobrina
Draughtsman: Mehmed Muftić
Special effects: Mladen Marković, Peter Živković
Music/music director: Nicola Piovani
Music performed by: Unione Musicisti di Roma
Songs: 'Why Stars Come Out at Night' by Ray Noble, performed by
          Camilla Søeberg; 'I'd give a Million Tomorrows' by Jerry
          Livingston, Milton Berle, performed by Nick Curtis
Costume design: Marit Allen
Wardrobe (master) Franjo Šimek
          (mistress) Gordana Krištof
Make-up: Mary Hillman
Title graphics/animation: Dušan Petričić
Sound editor: Rodney Glenn; (dialogue) Brian Lintern

Sound Recording: Drew Kunin; (music) Sergio Marcotulli, Forum
            Studios
Sound re-recording: Cannon Elstree Studios, Bill Rowe
Production assistant: Hugh Leaver
Stunt co-ordinator: Ivo Krištof
Crowd co-ordinator: Zoran Dragović

CAST:

SVETLANA VARGAS	Camilla Søeberg
AVANTI	Alfred Molina
HUNT	Simon Callow
CHRISTOPHER	Eric Stoltz
LILY SACHER	Lindsay Duncan
EMILE	Rade Šerbedžija
RUDI	Svetozar Cvetković
WANGO	Chris Haywood
DR LOMBROSOW	Patrick Godfrey
STELLA VARGAS	Linda Marlowe
CONDUCTOR	Ronald Lacey
OLYMPIA	Tanja Bošković
TINA	Gabrielle Anwar
THE KING	Enver Petrovci
MARTIN	Željko Duvnjak
BAKER	Danko Ljuština
GRANDMOTHER	Rahela Ferari
OLD MAILMAN	Djani Šegina
1ST AGENT	Tom Gotovac
2ND AGENT	Mirko Boman
ENGINEER	Matko Raguž
STOKER	Branko Blaće
1ST ORDERLY	Ivo Krištof
2ND ORDERLY	Marijan Habazin
SINGER	Drew Kunin
BOY	Alan Antičević
GIRL	Svjetlana Grzelja
MAN IN THE WATER	Siniša Cmrk

8,646 ft. 96 mins.

Hollywood via Kansas

Manifesto was something of an ordeal for me, as the reader who has stayed the course will know by now, all too well. For whatever reason, I did not make another film for four years, which is rather a long time. When I did, it was to work with Jim Ivory and Ismail Merchant again, on an exquisite script by Ruth Prawer Jhabvala drawn from two remarkable interlocked novels (*Mr. Bridge* and *Mrs. Bridge* by the Kansas City Chekhov, Evan Connell). I played the not very significant part of Dr. Emil Sauer, but it meant working with Paul Newman, Joanne Woodward and Blythe Danner, and making the feisty acquaintance of Blythe's wonderfully funny and tomboyish daughter, Gwyneth Paltrow, then 18 years old, and of the remarkable Canadian actress Gale Garnett (now under the name of Zoë Gale Garnett), a distinguished novelist as well. In film—unlike the theatre—it is so often the actors one works with that give the experience its colour, rather than the director, who can often seem a somewhat remote or preoccupied figure; apart from anything else, the actors sit around with each other for long periods of time, whereas the director is always elsewhere. Jim Ivory is different in that sense because we became friends after *A Room With a View* and I have worked with him so regularly that I am, as Ismail likes to say, 'one of the family,' which, like membership of any family, can be something of a mixed blessing for all parties. But the revelation for me on *Mr. & Mrs. Bridge* was Joanne Woodward, firstly because of her superb acting, but also for her comportment on the set. She was the first actor on film I had seen who actually led the whole enterprise, not by dominance or by temperament, but by extraordinary graciousness and good manners. She took the trouble to know everyone's name—my partner was with me and she knew his name and his life story within 10 minutes of his appearing on the set—and it was touching to see her on the set on her morning rounds, asking after everyone. She patiently sat in her place while the lighting cameraman fixed his lights around her. Newman was altogether different, preferring to stay in his caravan or chat to the grips, with whom he seemed most at ease. It's very possible that he was keeping himself aloof for reasons of character; the same reasons, no doubt, that he kept his vocal delivery to a whisper, to the despair of the sound recordists and sometimes even to the confusion of his fellow actors, who were unable to hear what he was saying or indeed whether he had finished speaking. But I had begun to understand that what one saw or heard (or didn't see and didn't hear) in the flesh was not an entirely reliable guide to what appears on the screen. In this instance, Newman's vocal delivery in the film is perfectly normal, if somewhat restrained; it is the perfect foil for Woodward's incomparably affecting performance, which sits at the heart of the film—Jim's masterpiece, in my view. She paints a deeply upsetting portrait of a woman who could so easily have been made happy, but for whom no one she loved would do the easy things she yearned for.

That same year (1990) I went to Hollywood for the first time as an actor, in almost ideal circumstances. I had been called one day in my dressing room at the Queen's Theatre in London, where I was acting in Alan Bennett's play *Single Spies*, by Mike Nichols. I was inclined at first to suspect a practical joke, but the tones so familiar from the Nichols and May LPs on which I had grown up were unmistakeable. He told me without even a hint of persiflage that, having seen my performance in the play the night before, he had made a vow that he would never make another film without me in it. Would I perhaps be interested in starting this life-long relationship by playing the part of the English director Simon who is directing the character played by Meryl Streep in *Postcards from the Edge*? As I was about to direct my own first movie in America (*The Ballad of the Sad Café*), this seemed to me be a highly propitious omen, though frankly I would have acted anything in anything directed by Nichols, a snake-charmer of the highest order, whose brain, talent and astuteness are in perfect equipoise. This inspired chronicler of American life has a curiously European approach which, particularly in Hollywood, is like champagne in the desert.

A month or two after our conversation, I found myself sitting round a large table in the Columbia studios, next to Carrie Fisher, Princess Leah herself, who had written the movie, with my fellow cast members, Miss Streep, Miss Maclaine, Mr Dreyfuss, Mr Quaid, Miss Wickes, Mr Platt, Mr Reiner. Only Mr Hackman couldn't make it. We had all been flown there for two days, from wherever we might have been in the world, just to read the script a couple of times. The first reading was a highly charged event, be-cause—Nichols told me—Meryl had to sing and she was rigid with fear. In fact, she sang her country-and-western number with such fine Partonesque gusto that Shirley Mac-laine was provoked into performing the new version of 'I'm Still Here,' which Sondheim had re-written for her with stadium-shaking bazzaz, leaving her chair, working her way round the table and flashing her legs like a taxi dancer. Carrie (with whom I had friends in common) seized my hand at the beginning of the reading and as it went on dug her fingernails deep into my palms, administering particularly sharp digs when a line got its laugh; as I gazed at my bleeding hands, the fact that all this took place around Easter seemed somehow peculiarly apt. Apart from the inherent entertain-ment of the reading, it was invaluable to read, however briefly, with all, or almost all, of the actors—to get a sense of the whole film, to understand the way in which one scene relates to another. It is increasingly common for films to get a reading, but rare to continue, as we did, discussing the characters and the comedy, to begin to feel a little courage in our performances, and to get the hang of the director's mind.

In the case of Nichols, the most striking aspect of his work as a director is trust, which radiates its way out to the actors, empowering and liberating them. I have seen actors literally grow under its warming influence. A great deal of this is *esprit de corps*; the man is, after all, one of the most brilliant performers in the history of comedy, and his conversation is a form of directing by example, so perfect is his phrasing and timing. He also seems to have very little to prove. Having surrounded himself with the people he wants in every department, he simply lets them do their jobs, rather in the spirit of Sir Thomas Beecham's famous (if disingenuous) remark: 'I just hire the best players and let them play.' As in the case of the great conductor, the secret is in careful preparation, allowing the actual event—the concert or the movie—to live dangerously. When we were actually shooting the film a month or two after the readings, Mike would drop by my trailer for a chat. This is almost unheard-of; directors are normally besieged by unending demands for decisions, but Mike was serenely in command. He explained his method: at the beginning of his career, he said, he used to scream and rant, with very unsatisfactory results. Directing a Hollywood movie, he had concluded, was like being the President of the United States: you're supposed to be at the top of the tree, to have ultimate power, but you still can't get things done when you ask for them. So he revised his strategy: now he works with great detail through every possible problem in advance, and when he actually arrives on the set, his mind, he says, is perfectly empty, and he simply awaits to be delighted. He is rarely disappointed, he says, though one day when he dropped by he confessed that he was having a very bad day—he had cast an actor for his look, and assumed that he could do the very simple acting task involved in the role. But no, he couldn't do it. And Mike was very frustrated because, he said, 'I've forgotten how to direct bad actors.' I once saw him lose his temper, but in the most elegant manner. He was setting up a crane shot—*my* crane shot, the one in which I, as Simon, the tyro English director, try out the crane shot I had set up—oh, it was a Chinese box of a Pirandellian puzzle, this part—and someone from props was placing a chair in the foreground. 'What. Is. That. Chair. Doing. There?' roared Mike through a megaphone as he swooped down on the crane. 'I. Cut. The. Chair. Yesterday!' The man from props roared back 'They said—' Mike snapped. 'Who,' he bellowed, 'Is. They? I. Am. They.'

I noted all this with keen interest, as I tried to make myself ready for my own forthcoming celluloid directorial début. Meanwhile I had simply to act being a stumbling inexperienced director, for which, in fact, very little acting was required. Most of my scenes were with Meryl Streep, whom I as Simon was directing. She was playing an actress on the skids. It is a nice problem, playing someone who has power over the character played by the star of the movie. The shot, of course, will always favour the star, and quite rightly, but knowing that does nothing for one's sense of one's own status. In fact, the movie's Simon was something of a twit, so there was no real difficulty.

I was a little taken aback by the degree to which Meryl had absorbed herself into the role. She is a genuinely private person, and in no way did I feel that I had met *her* (although she had been astonishingly gracious when I first met her at the read-through, remembering my performance in *Amadeus* and telling me that she hadn't come backstage because she 'wasn't famous enough then'). During the frequent gaps in filming, she kept the character's life alive. Often, she would fall into conversation with Carrie, upon whom the role is rather openly modelled, and it was sometimes alarming to see them engaged in a sort of Carrie competition: who was most like Carrie? Carrie? Or Meryl? Of course Meryl won hands down, and I noticed Carrie—who is not without her own small traces of spontaneous eccentricity—becoming more extreme in her behaviour in the presence of this unnerving Doppelgänger, perhaps feeling that her identity was under threat. One would come upon her, lying down on the tarmac on the back lot at Columbia, in her exquisite Azzedine Alaia black dress. 'Psst!' she would say, beckoning one over. 'Is it true that Charles Laughton used to eat *shit*?'

• • • • • • • • • • • • • • • • •

Digression on Hollywood
Simon the Director was essentially a peripheral role, though everybody treated me kindly and respectfully; at the end of my week or so of shooting, the whole 60-strong unit—led by Meryl and Mike—sang 'Happy Journeys' directly at me,

leaving me feeling somehow ashamed that I hadn't contributed more. Hollywood is a curious place, geographically ungraspable, its paradoxes best expressed by the old phrase, 'dream factory.' A place where dreams—the spontaneous expression of the unconscious—are consciously manufactured. Just as Broadway is more Business than Show, so Hollywood is more Factory than Dream. Film-making there is a grasping, thrusting, harsh, ruthless, pitiless way of life, 95 percent finance and deals, 5 percent vision; 98 percent image and 2 percent reality; 99 percent commerce and 1 percent art. I cannot pretend that I feel even remotely at home in Hollywood, torn between feeling that I have nothing to sell and that I wouldn't want to sell it even if I did. People have been nothing but charming to me there, but they are baffled by the sense they experience of my backing away from anything they might possibly be thinking of offering me. My very first visit was in 1982, eight years before I finally worked there, when I found myself teaching and acting for the British American Theatre Institute (later the British American Drama Academy) in San Francisco. At my agent's behest I took a plane to Los Angeles for 24 hours. It was a day of hallucinations. After being smacked in the face by the heat, I watched the so-called city from the window of my cab, bewildered by the temporary feel of everything; nothing seemed built to last. It was like road-side services extended ad infinitum, a frontier town that had been experiencing a rather long boom that would not necessarily last. Even the Hollywood sign, as it loomed up, seemed to have just been nailed up there, like the estate agent's sign that it in fact was, but one that should have been pulled down years ago. I recollected a story told by the late Miklós Rózsa, the composer, among many other things, of the music for *Ben-Hur*. Doing research for the score in Rome, he had secured an audience with the Pope. The Pontiff had enquired where Rózsa was now living. 'Los Angeles,' said the composer. 'A beautiful city,' his Holiness replied. 'It was then,' says Rózsa, 'that I first began to doubt the theory of papal infallibility.'

I was to stay in the Beverly Wilshire Hotel, and once we pulled into Beverly Hills, my heart, I admit, did miss a beat. It was sunset by now, the palms were standing silhouetted

306

against the sky, the flamingos were posing on one leg, and a certain *douceur* filled the air. The idyll soon dispelled. At the time, no bank had yet been rash enough to furnish me with a credit card, so I was unable to check in till my agent had sent round a small bag of money by taxi, and I crept shame-faced into my small and slightly dingy room. That evening, I sat in the famous Polo Lounge, reading a script which my agent had left at the desk for me. A diminutive and rather elderly bell-boy, with wizened features and a high-pitched squeaking voice, walked though the lounge calling out names; it is said that actors would pay him to do this in order to make them familiar. Unaccountably, I couldn't find the part on offer in my script; I went over and over the pages, desperately looking for the character. Eventually I called the agent with my dilemma. 'Never mind,' she said, 'James Mason has just agreed to do it.' Ah yes, I thought, we're always up for the same parts.

The following day I took a total of sixteen cabs and shunted around the various studios. The casting directors in each were as charming as they knew how, which was not necessarily very charming, given that they were being confronted with a 30-year old actor of no obvious physical charms who had just opened in a play in London which no one had heard of with the unpronounceable and incomprehensible title of *Amadeus*. If the New York theatre feels an awfully long way away from Los Angeles (and it does), how much more unreal must the West End be. We made strained small talk, the casting directors and I, and after a brief while parted as I staggered into the next taxi. Finally, hundreds of miles and hundreds of dollars later, I arrived at Warner Brothers, having been in and out of taxis for nearly eight hours, to meet the doyenne of all casting directors, Marion Doherty (she discovered James Dean). 'So tell me about yourself,' she said in her magnificent baritone voice. I launched slightly less vivaciously than I might have liked into an account of my career (all nine years of it). After a few minutes, she sighed and her face filled with compassion. She stretched a hand across the desk and placed it over mine, saying, with infinite tenderness: 'Simon. What are you doing here? *Go. Home.*' 'I think you're right, Miss Doherty,' I said, and did. I've been back many many times, sometimes to direct plays (in downtown Los Angeles, which is almost real), once to make a documentary about Charles Laughton, frequently to do research, occasionally just to see friends, but I still find the Darwinian struggle to succeed which is everywhere in evidence exhausting. Now that the sweetness which was still in the air in the early eighties—the sense of love and peace, man, which pervaded the social scene—has been replaced by ever more ruthless ambition, and ever harder drugs, it has almost no charms for me at all, and the idea, much mooted, that I should go to Los Angeles and just *hang out* for a while—a siren-suggestion which has lured so many British actors into months, sometimes whole years of oblivion—was to me simply an invitation to rot in hell.

●●●●●●●●●●●●●●●●●●●

A Funeral and Four Weddings

Not that there have been many hard offers of any sort, although there was a little flutter of interest after *Four Weddings and a Funeral*, that phenomenon which took Hollywood completely by surprise and caused it to ask tough questions of itself, like how could a film which cost so little make so much? I am invariably asked the question: did you know the film would be so successful when you were making it? To which the answer is: I had no doubt whatever that it would a raging success in Britain and America, but it is still astonishing to me that it was overwhelmingly successful in Paris (I happened to be there the weekend that it opened, when half a million Parisians saw it in its *version originale*), in Tokyo (I was—very courteously, with much bowing and giggling—gently mobbed in the streets there) and in Tahiti, where I saw queues of tattooed men and women in *paréos* winding their way round the block. I can offer no explanation for the universality of the film's appeal, or for the fact that people watch it over and over and over again on video. It derives from an alchemical combination of script, director, cinematographer and cast—and something perhaps more elusive, the time in which it was made. *Casablanca* comes to mind as a similar phenomenon. *Four Weddings and a Funeral* is about finding a partner to whom you publicly commit. In 1993, AIDS had become an ever-present reality in the lives of all young, sexually active people of whatever persuasion. The idea of monogamy, or at least commitment, was suddenly on the agenda again. The brilliance of the screenplay, by Richard Curtis, was not to have placed this fact in the foreground but as an unspoken, underlying ground-note. In an ironic touch, the gay relationship which is held up so radically (and by the film's leading character, no less) as the one example of a real marriage among the group of chums whose friendship we follow is nevertheless one that is only publicly affirmed thanks to the death of one of the partners. The brilliantly conceived funeral scene, in which Matthew (John Hannah) pays tribute to his lover, Gareth, is as close to a public ceremony of affirmation as they ever get.

When I received the screenplay, I took it with me to read on a plane journey to Manchester, where I was directing *My Fair Lady*. I showed the title page to my producer, who was travelling with me. 'I'll bet I'm the funeral,' I said. I knew from the first page—the succession of 'fucks'—that this was a brilliant piece of work. As I reached my own first lines, I found myself speaking them out loud; by the time of my death, I was in tears, and could hardly get through the funeral. Apart from the boldness of bringing a comedy to a juddering halt with the death of one of the leading characters, and the courage and skill involved in recovering from that back into healing comedy—a rather Shakespearean ploy, although, unlike the deaths of Hero in *Much Ado About Nothing* and Hermione in *The Winter's Tale*, Gareth's demise is a real one—it was extraordinary to find a mainstream film which featured without comment a gay man who conforms to none of the usual gay stereotypes, who is happily and deeply involved in a relationship with a beautiful young partner, and who dies of something other than AIDS. Gareth dies from loving life too well, specifically from an excess of Scottish dancing. The scene is in effect a Government Health Warning against the perils of the Highland fling. At the beginning of the twenty-first century we have come a long way from the days when gays were depicted either as shrieking faggots, as scary perverts or as terminally ill, but it is hard to overstate how radical it was in 1994, when the film came out, to show a relationship such as Gareth and Matthew's, and to have celebrated quite so unequivocally such a splendid bugger (as Matthew says in his oration) as the lovable reprobate Gareth. More than one correspondent took the trouble to write to me to say that it had not hitherto occurred to them that gay people had feelings like everyone else.

For once, the part was a direct offer. I had worked happily nearly ten years before, in 1985, with the director Mike Newell on a film which was too sombrely truthful for its own sake, *The Good Father*. It was my third film and one of the last that Anthony Hopkins made before Major Stardom hit. Working with him was a joyful experience, though hazardous, because he is so wickedly funny. In the short gap, maybe five seconds, between the cameraman saying 'Camera rolling' and the director saying 'Action,' he delights to slip into one of the imitations of which he is such a master, suddenly becoming Sir John Gielgud or Sir Laurence Olivier or Marlon Brando, reducing you to incapable hilarity. Particularly lethal is his impersonation of a great, long dead (and scandalously more-or-less forgotten) British actor called Alan Badel, who had a peculiarly distinctive, upwardly rising laugh. Just a note or two of this glissando of merriment, and I was gone. But not for long, and the subsequent scene always had a life and a danger, a freedom, about it which was no doubt part of Tony's reason for becoming Badel or Brando for those few seconds. Most of the reason, of course, was sheer devilment, a welcome quality on a film set, where the great god Time-Is-Money tends to knock a lot of the fun out of the proceedings. In *The Good Father* I played the nastiest young barrister in London, and I was aware that Mike (with whom I had been acquainted socially for some time) had had serious doubts about my aptness for film-acting. He knew and admired, he said—and I believed him—my work on stage, but doubted whether I could adapt to the camera. Fortunately, he had then seen a television film in which I had played Handel, not a notably loquacious or flamboyant character, and had changed his mind. So I felt I had earned his trust. Indeed, one day when Hopkins and I were shooting one of the best scenes in the film—'Does the phrase shit-bum mean anything to you?' he asks, and my character crumbles into the fat little bullied schoolboy that lurks behind his gym-toned exterior—I had seen the way Mike was setting up the shot and had murmured to Tony that I thought that it might be more effective shot from another angle, and Tony had said 'Tell him,' and I did. Well, most directors would have said to this celluloid novice, 'Very interesting, dear' and continued to shoot it they way that had planned. Instead Mike said, 'You bastard. You fucking bastard. You're right,' and then proceeded to re-light and re-stage the scene, which took something over an hour. To say that this is unusual is to understate; it is unheard of.

But it meant that when, nine years later, we came to work on *Four Weddings and a Funeral*, there was trust in the air, and the prospect of pleasure, a very good state in which to embark on any project. I was the first to be cast in the film, but before they got very much further, it ran into money problems, and was postponed for nine months while the investors regrouped. Mike and Richard and the producer, Duncan Kenworthy, used the time they had thus gained to enrich the screenplay even further. By the time they were ready, the rest of the cast were in place; Hugh Grant, with whom I had acted in several things, including *Maurice* for Merchant Ivory and *The Oz Trials* and *Handel* on television, was now playing the lead (I don't know who it had been nine months earlier) opposite Andie MacDowall, fresh from her triumph in *Sex, Lies, and Videotape*. We all assembled—*all* of us, a very unusual event in film-making—for a week in Hampstead before filming began, not so much to rehearse, which is a rather pointless exercise away from the set or locations, not even to read the script (though of course we did that), but mostly to get to know each other—to hear each other's voices, become accustomed to the way each other's minds worked, to test the parameters of what was funny or painful. Day after day we sat and opened ourselves up, and reconsidered the screenplay and our own roles from all sorts of different angles; Richard took notes, made changes, gave clues. The wardrobe department brought photographic references, fabrics, the cameraman came and listened and looked. None of it added up to very much that you could write down on paper, but if people ask me why the film was so good, as opposed to why it was so successful, I point to that week of gentle exploration. By the time we arrived in the studio to take the ebullient photograph—confetti flying, top hats doffed—which became the poster, though not a scene had been shot we knew each other and we knew what we wanted to do. Again, it cannot be said often enough how rare such an experience is. Mike had done exactly the same on *The Good Father*, with equally good results. I'm inclined—it's the romantic in me—to attribute this to his BBC training, in the days when there was a BBC training; when indeed there was a BBC worth the name. When he started out, in relatively unpressured circumstances, he had the opportunity of evolving a script, of casting it carefully, and of rehearsing for weeks before actually shooting the thing. The usual experience of film-making is for a group of strangers to assemble, in the case of the actors—except at the very highest echelons of the cast list—having learned the lines on their own, never having spoken them with the other actors and frequently never having spoken to the director about their characters or the style of the film. It is then in a vacuum filled with panic-stricken bravado that you attempt to give your performance in a space that you have never seen, surrounded by a crew who hasn't the remotest idea who you might be.

Four Weddings and a Funeral was the exact opposite in every particular. Despite the relatively poverty of the budget and the attendant hardships—four or five of us to a car, the first being picked up at 4.30 in the morning, no overnight stays, so you were stuck on the set from the crack of dawn till midnight—the shoot was entirely pleasurable. We would sit around on the steps of each other's caravans, Andie for all her glamour never happier than when hunkering down and sharing a glass of wine at the end of the day, Kristin Scott-Thomas and Charlotte Coleman, polar opposites as people and as characters, becoming fast friends, John Hannah and I talking rather intensely about acting, that wonderful and fiercely intelligent actor David Bauer, himself profoundly deaf, who played Hugh's brother, locked in passionately concentrated conversations, half-signed, half-spoken, all around the set. And when we weren't engaged in this ongoing party, we sat pleasantly occupied in our caravans. For my part, I wrote quite a lot of *The Road to Xanadu*, the first volume of a life of Orson Welles, in full padding and kilt, puffing away at the Café Crème cigars which I had elected to smoke so as not to re-addict myself to cigarettes. In the event, I started smoking twenty-five of the irresistible little cigarillos a day.

Almost every location was either in or next to a field, frequently one growing the treacherous plant rape, which is disastrous for hay fever sufferers like Charlotte, Hugh and me. I proposed that we should wear badges proclaiming us Victims of Rape; instead we mainlined the fierce antihistamine medication Triludan, and were accordingly out of our minds most days. The shooting day I recall more than any other, perhaps unsurprisingly, was the day of my death, or rather Gareth's death, but by the time we came to it, it was hard to tell the difference. That morning I had woken with a terrible sense of foreboding which I could not throw off, and even through all the madness of the Scottish dancing, take after take of it, reeling and leaping and twisting and turning, to the extent that it seemed that no acting would be required for a heart attack, this cloud hovered over me. Not so much so that I wasn't able to ask Richard and Mike a) if I might not change Gareth's opening line on first seeing the kilt-filled Scottish baronial castle in which the reception takes place. 'It's *Macbeth*,' Richard had written, 'It's bloody *Macbeth*.' I volunteered 'It's *Brigadoon*, it's bloody *Brigadoon*' instead, and they bought it; and b) if I could deliver the line, 'No, but I do have his fax number' (in response to the American matron's request for Oscar Wilde's phone number), in a Morningside Edinburgh accent. This Mike had resisted— 'Not funny'—but stubbornly I did it at the rehearsal, and the assembled company fell about, so, 'You win,' said Mike, and it must have succeeded to the extent that when anybody, flatteringly, does an imitation of me in the part, they do the whole thing with a Scottish accent, though in truth, winning was the last thing I or anyone else had in mind, except in the sense of winning through to the best possible film. Anyway, after filming the *Brigadoon* line, on to another orgy of

Scottish dancing. Finally, well-coached by the on-set paramedic, I died, after several takes, to everyone's satisfaction, and suddenly felt reborn, which is just as well since I still had a number of pre-terminal scenes to film. These scenes have, to me, a curious joyful quality which stems from my sense of having been reprieved.

Another scene I remember particularly vividly is the funeral scene. I am frequently congratulated on this, but, needless to say, I wasn't present. I had toyed, as a fully paid-up Method actor, with lying in the coffin, but managed to stay away, feeling very strange. All the actors had reported that they were rather dreading the scene, not in the way that I was, but because they knew they'd have to cry, and they were all so tired that they'd never be able to summon up the feelings, so the make-up department were primed to be on hand with glycerine and eye-drops. In the event, the glycerine was unused, the eye-drops remained in the bottles. John played the speech so beautifully, Richard had placed the Auden poem so artfully, that even the extras who knew nothing of the situation were moved to spontaneous tears. I confess that when I saw the film at the cast-and-crew showing, I wept discreetly when I died, and I wept nakedly during the funeral. This is rare. I have died repeatedly on film and television (clearly producers and directors feel that there's considerable public appetite for seeing the end of me) and never been moved; that I did so here is a further tribute to the excellence of the screenplay and the way Mike directed it. I suppose too, I must admit that the character of Gareth is very close to an aspect of me, the life-and-death of the party side of me, which is not quite as large a component of my nature as people seem to think (though I have been Gareth for whole weeks at a stretch in my own life). The fact that I'm still alive and Gareth isn't is a token of the gap between us. In fact, playing the role required treading a fine line. In a phrase that explains why British journalists regard me with cheerful contempt as the Biggest Luvvie of Them All, I had said to Mike Newell when we were seated round the table in Hampstead, 'I'm going to try to play Gareth like Dionysos, not like Silenus.' Classical scholars will immediately warm to the reference; what I was saying was that

Gareth shouldn't just be a fat, noisy old boozer, but be a god too, magnificent, expansive, generous and filled with divine afflatus, not simply wind. And that was what I tried to do. The script perfectly aided my endeavour: "Tonight these are your orders—go forth and conjugate—find husbands and wives . . . a toast before we go into battle. True love—in whatever shape or form it may come—may we all in our dotage be proud to say 'I was adored once too.' " Gareth spoke in Jove-like, high-flown phrases; he asserted certain eternal verities in florid, funny but finally serious terms. I had tried in *A Room with a View* to find and embody the essential goodness of the Reverend Beebe. Too often the circumstances of filming make any enterprise beyond simply doing one's credible best an impossibly ambitious undertaking; but somewhere in the back of my mind is the belief, confirmed by my study of Charles Laughton's work and career, that film-acting does not simply have to be naturalistic, that it can be archetypal, mythic, iconic. And indeed, the best of film-acting has always been that, whether through the medium of a great star persona, or through a huge creative effort (as in the case of a Laughton or a Brando). The conditions in which *Four Weddings and a Funeral* were made enabled that sort of work to happen.

Hugh Grant's performance is a case in point. Watching this interesting, sardonic, slightly Saturnine individual turn himself into Richard Curtis's alter ego was deeply engrossing. Richard is carrot-topped, freckly, bespectacled and a little clumsy (and also, of course, wildly attractive); Hugh is none of these things, apart from the latter. He refrained from altering his appearance cosmetically; only the spectacles were imposed. But he selected and filtered his own personality in an exceptionally canny way, and he found a pitch for the performance that was perfect. I confess that, on the set, I doubted whether he was doing enough, which only shows how much I know about light comedy, of which Hugh proved himself at a stroke to be one of the supreme masters. It is an enchanting performance, graceful, quick, and with access to some very delicately expressed emotion. It was highly instructive to learn quite how light light comedy can, and indeed, should be. And with this performance, Hugh created an iconic presence which he has since burnished and modified, as his great namesake Cary did, moving very carefully within the parameters of his persona. To a greater or a lesser extent all the actors who made such successes from the film created in it the images which they have since deployed to such remarkable effect: Kristin Scott-Thomas, John Hannah, Anna Chancellor. The astonishingly brilliant Charlotte Coleman, alas, died before she could become what she had every gift for and every chance of being, the Judy Holliday of our times.

For my part, though Gareth gave me an instant recognisability pretty well anywhere in the world, and an affectionate place in people's hearts, it made no serious impact on my career. Once again, I was despatched to Hollywood, and once again, I padded round the sanctified halls of the studios, meeting alarmingly young vice-presidents, all of whom greeted me with the reverence due to someone who has been associated with a Huge Hit, and an unpredicted one at that. They spoke to me with deep deference, and when they adverted to Hugh, or Richard, or Mike, their voices hushed. Like alchemists of yore, they were trying to figure out this deep puzzle, to identify the transforming element that had turned a mere script into pure gold. They shook the film, they turned it upside down, they looked at it through squinting eyes, and in the end they proclaimed the answer: it was Hugh. Hugh! Hugh had made it into a hit. Massive relief ensued, and they proceeded to hurl large sums of money at him, setting him up with his own company, offering him anything he liked. Much as they had enjoyed talking to me—*really*—they knew for sure that I wasn't the answer. And as they sat beaming at me, it was all too clear that they were thinking—because they definitely liked me, and definitely liked my performance—"What do we have for fat bearded men in kilts?" The fact that the man sitting opposite them was neither fat, nor bearded, nor kilted did not suggest to them that I might be good for anything else. They were looking for the sequel to Gareth: Gareth II. But they never found it.

Nature Calls

What did come to me as a result of Gareth was the invitation to be the voice of the Ancient Green Grasshopper in *James and the Giant Peach* (certainly not type-casting) and to play Vincent Cadby, the villain in *Ace Ventura, Pet Detective Two: When Nature Calls*. The former job was pure delight: regular visits to San Francisco over 18 months to voice, re-voice and re-voice the character according to the demands of the ever-evolving animation. Once, when I happened to be in San Antonio, Texas, they called me in my hotel room and asked me to record a stray line. I doubted whether there was a nearby sound studio, but they cheerfully told me that I could do it there and then, down the telephone, and they would clean it up. I had heard of phoning in one's performance, but had never expected to it do quite so literally. The success of this operation made me fear that the visits to San Francisco would cease, but no, the next time they needed a line, I was on the plane, flying over the Golden Gate to that recording studio of believed memory on Russian Hill. *When Nature Calls*, the second windfall from *Four Weddings*, was less of a breeze, but though I had some slight doubts about the script, the possibility of appearing in a potentially great comic movie was irresistible. Who, faced with the prospect of appearing in *A Day at the Races* or *M. Hulot's Holiday*, would turn it down? I had thought Jim Carrey brilliant and original in the first *Ace Ventura*; who knows what the sequel might not bring? At the thought of the residual payments earned by actors in American films, a lump formed in my throat, and my eyes misted over with emotion. I signed with joyful heart.

Arriving on the set, however, one sensed that happiness was not in the air. I had a small personal reversal on bumping into the star. 'Oh,' said Jim, 'you're the guy playing Simon Callow. *Great*.' 'I *am* Simon Callow,' I said. 'Oh, are you?' he said, unfazed. 'Well, *that's* great, too.' I consulted the day's schedule and indeed, there it was. Role: Simon Callow, Artist: Vincent Cadby. Perhaps they thought that my extreme commitment to the works of Konstantin Stanislavsky had led me to become the character in life. The impression of distractedness on Jim's part was not a mistaken one: he was at war both with the director and the producers. I shot for a few days and then returned to England; when I came back, we had a new director, the immensely amiable Steve Oedekerk, screenwriter of both this and the first *Ace Ventura*.

The producers, of course, remained in place, but Jim was on very distant terms with them. He believed, rightly or wrongly, that having paid him a sum of money beyond computation to make this sequel, they were stinting on everything else—props, studio, time. The atmosphere was somewhat strained. Jim was often ill. We shot reaction shots to scenes we had never played. Whenever Jim returned, he was possessed of a manic comic energy many times beyond what you see on the screen. He becomes quite literally possessed by his comic impulses, improvising wildly and brilliantly—sometimes scatalogically, sometimes surreally. These improvisations, only a fraction of which found their way into the movie, were as extraordinary as anything that Lenny Bruce or Woody Allen produced in their days in stand-up. Jim's often-stated ambition is to produce something new in comedy. His idol is Jerry Lewis, but he goes far further than that old-style zany. The rage of which he has so often spoken in interviews is always present, sometimes in the background, sometimes alarmingly in the foreground. To some of us, it seemed he had little to be cross about. A week or two after we started shooting the film, Jim went to Hollywood for the weekend launch of *Batman Forever*, in which he played the villain. We calculated that by the time he returned to the set on the Monday he must have made a million dollars from the weekend's box office returns alone. A day later, it was announced that he had just signed a contract to make a film for which he would be paid $20 million, making him the highest-paid actor in human history. (Sylvester Stallone retaliated by signing a three-picture contract for $7 million a film, which might have done something for his *amour propre* but fooled nobody else. I reflected that I doubted whether Laurence Olivier made as much as $1 million over the course of his entire career.) Jim seemed slightly bewildered by his wealth. "What can I do with it?" he said, lamenting his inability to lead anything remotely resembling a normal life. When his daughter had come to visit him on the film, she expressed a longing to eat a hamburger at McDonald's with him. He accordingly had the make-up department put him in a wig and beard and spectacles for the proposed outing, but his cover was instantly blown by the throng of Jim-watchers on 24-hour patrol outside his hotel. Wherever he went, parents would approach him with their infants in tow. 'He/she does you,' they'd tell him, instructing the offspring to 'Do him now. C'mon, don't be shy. Do him.'

Sometimes, while we were filming, Jim would be unable to do himself. 'I've lost him,' he would say, and try to kick himself back into character. At these and all other times, Steve Oedekerk, his buddy and partner in comic crime, and now his director, would be sympathetic and gentle. He was indeed a most courteous fellow. After one take which involved myself and Ian MacNeice, which he had said was 'good,' I explained to him with straight face that English actors, though both cheap and reliable, required a great deal of praise. The following day, he brought a thesaurus onto the set with him, and after a take would say, 'You were exceptional, egregious, unusual, outstanding,' working his way through the whole lexicon of possible praise. One day he excelled himself: after I had shot a particular scene, he ran over to me crying 'Simon, where are you from? Planet One-take?' Despite his best efforts, however, the atmosphere on the film became increasingly restive and resentful as the stop date receded further and further away; some wit re-named the movie *Ace Ventura Forever*. The considerable charms of Charleston, South Carolina (one of America's oldest settlements, with houses dating from the seventeenth century), started to pall; the ghoulish reminder of the Old Slave Market seemed to have a personal application. At first I was reasonably happy, sitting undisturbed in my caravan, translating *Les Enfants Du Paradis* for the Royal Shakespeare Company, but soon I started to become deeply anxious about getting back to England in time for the opera I was about to direct. We were now some six weeks behind. The production company was deeply sympathetic, and encouraged me to go home whenever there was a reasonable gap in my schedule, so I did, for design and production meetings. The one consolation was financial: the thought of all the overage, eight weeks in all by the time I was finally wrapped, the weekend before rehearsals for *Il Trittico* began.

As it happens, not only was there no overage—the delays in shooting were attributed to Jim's illness and a clause of *force majeure* invoked, relieving the producers of any liability towards the cast and crew—but the cost of every trip that I had taken back to England had been deducted from my rather exiguous salary, leaving me actually in debt to the company. The Screen Actors Guild in America admirably insists that its members must travel everywhere first-class; I had taken six return flights to England. My relief at getting back to England (I had imagined that I might never be allowed to leave Venturaland, forever plodding up the guano hill which was the film's final location) was so great that I shrugged off this financial disaster, directed the opera, then went on holiday to Florence. It was there that I received a call from the delightful Steven Oedekerk. After warm greetings and a reprise of our banter from the set, he spoke seriously. 'Simon, you remember the scene where Jim gets fucked by a gorilla?' I certainly did. 'Well,' said Steve, 'preview audiences don't like it. They don't like to think of Jim being fucked by a gorilla.' 'I see how that might be,' I said. 'But if we just cut it, there'll be a gap in the narrative. So we had a thought.' 'Yes?' I said, dimly. 'Well, we thought how if *you* were to be fucked by the gorilla. Wouldn't that be funny?' 'Um, it might be, Steve, I suppose. But how can that be done? I'm in Italy.' 'Well, Simon,' he said, 'We'd like you to come to Hollywood tomorrow.' I pointed out that I was on holiday. He urged me to take a break from my holiday. I refused. He proposed that we shoot the scene in London. I observed that this would still be breaking my holiday; I was in Italy. Finally, he said that they would come to Rome. I refrained from pointing out that I was in Florence. To a Los Angeleno, the distance between Florence and Rome is a bagatelle, geographically, culturally, every way. Wearily I said to myself that it was a while since I had been in the Eternal City; it could be a pleasant unexpected extension of the holiday. The production company asked me to make all the arrangements—hotels, travel, etc., for which they would of course reimburse me—and a day or two later I found myself in a forest outside of Rome with a non-English-speaking camera crew and half a gorilla suit. The idea was that a crew member would put on the creature's arm, which would then appear in shot apparently lifting me up in the air because I would start the shot with bent knees and would end up on tiptoe. And that, when we all finally managed to stop shrieking with laughter, is what happened, and why, in the midst of a highly polished piece of film-making—technically, at least—there are a few minutes of what appears to be a home movie, at the climax of which Vincent Cadby may be presumed to have been buggered by a primate. I returned to my very expensive hotel, strolled around the Forum and the Campidoglio, had a number of glorious meals and returned to Florence.

The end of this story is so predictable it is hardly worth recording: the producers refused to reimburse my travel or hotel bill because I was still, they insisted, indebted to them. Thus was I rewarded for my ignoble motives in accepting the film in the first place. In addition to the financial distress, I had sustained major physical damage: running out of a burning building for one scene, I had felt a sudden stab of pain and fell down the steps. At first it seemed that someone had inexplicably kicked me in the back, but soon the source of the pain was agonisingly evident—my calf was in extreme distress. The production nurse ran to attend to me, clearly terrified that I was experiencing an embolism or some other life-threatening seizure; then she thought it might be cramp. 'One of the grips,' she said, 'has studied acupressure. He'll help.' This mighty man, with his huge hands and thumbs of steel, plunged the latter into what was pretty obviously a torn muscle. The South Carolina air rang with colourful Anglo-Saxon expressions. Within minutes, my calf was the size of my waist. An anxious assistant director put me on the next plane to England, where my doctor applied sound waves to the tear and a few days later sent me back to Charleston, more or less repaired. The first scene I played in on my return involved me being surprised by a rout of animals bursting through the house, a rogue elephant at its head. Now, I had come to know this charming creature quite well; she was playful and affectionate, but when she suddenly diverged from the rehearsed path and appeared to be making straight for me (her idea of fun no doubt), I didn't wait to share the joke––I leaped nimbly to one side. As I did so, the calf muscle tore again. This time I stayed in Charleston (it was very near the end of the shoot) and limped through the last scenes. My two calves now bear very little resemblance to one another; I look like a piece of furniture that has been wrongly assembled, with legs from two different styles or indeed eras. Ah, well. If I were American I suppose I would have sued somebody––the elephant, perhaps––but it seemed simply one of the hazards of the profession.

The very expensive *Ace Ventura, Pet Detective Two* was held to be less enjoyable than its very cheap predecessor. No doubt lessons have been drawn from that, though not by me. There are few lessons to be learned for actors about this business as a business––though there is much to be learned, of course, about acting in films, which is a deeply interesting skill, though one which in my view can only be acquired by practice. Some actors clearly have a resistance to it, just as some actors have an affinity for it. The irritations of the process have been much described, as have the joys, not least by me. In the end, the crucial difference is the absence of an audience––for some a blessing, for others a curse. But on the absorbing question of why one film, with every advantage of cast and crew, of script and director, is a flop and another, lacking some or all of these elements, is a triumph, there is little to say that is enlightening. Critics, from their lofty eyries, like to point to obvious flaws of conception or execution, but at the time they seemed to the makers of the films in question to be the sensible way to go. It needs to be said again and again that making a film is a huge collective activity, that people not machines are the central element, and that a degree of luck, of a following wind, of a smile from the Gods, is as indispensable as in most human enterprises.

Shakespearean Love

Certainly *Shakespeare in Love* seemed to have had all of the above. The film, as is well-known, was originally slated to be shot with Julia Roberts, who withdrew, it is said, when Daniel Day-Lewis, whom she had been promised as her Shakespeare, declined the role. This may be myth; certainly the sets had been built and much of the film cast when the project collapsed. I myself had been slated to play the role of Henslowe, the lessee of the theatre, and rejoiced at the thought of acting in a screenplay which had been given, so it was intimated, the once-over by Tom Stoppard. Nothing was heard of the project for a couple of years, when it was revived, this time under the direction of John Madden, whereupon my agent immediately called the casting directors to confirm that they would still be wanting me for the part of Henslowe. 'Oh, dear, no,' they said, 'we've got Geoffrey Rush for the part,' and then by way of consolation asked me to play Edmund Tilney, the Master of the Revels, a rather smaller but nonetheless very effective role, which I immediately accepted with a little sigh, thinking, 'O, Fortuna.' Two years earlier, I reflected, had Geoffrey Rush's agent in those pre-*Shine* days put him forward for the role of Henslowe, the casting directors would have cried, 'Oh, dear, no. We've got Simon Callow for the part.'

Tom Stoppard had meanwhile given the script a twice-over, and maybe a thrice-over, and it was now not merely Stoppardised but Stoppard *même*, and a thing of sparky brilliance. The read-through with the entire cast was dazzling and somehow like being present at the first read-through of a play by Congreve or Oscar Wilde—or, indeed, Stoppard. After it, I went away for rather a long time. I was, in effect, a visitor to the set, though I was there for one day more than Judi Dench, who gave her miraculously fresh performance despite four hours in the make-up chair and eight performances a week of *Amy's View*. The acting troupe in the film—Shakespeare's company—had been together since some weeks before the read-through (the director, John

323

Madden, is, like *Four Weddings*'s Mike Newell, a former BBC director who shares Newell's belief in rehearsal) and by the time I arrived on the set they were perhaps a little battle-weary, and rather pleased to welcome occasional visitors like myself. My first scene was a classic instance of the curious conditions of movie-acting. It is the scene in which Tilney denounces the actors, and contains the line I am perhaps more happy to have uttered than any in my screen career: 'That woman is a woman!' The scene starts *fortissimo* and then gets steadily louder as Tilney appears to be on the point of spontaneously combusting. This is quite a tricky feat, technically; add to it that I had had no rehearsal, little discussion of character and no contact with my fellow actors, many of whom I had never met, and that there were about 40 extras and as many crew, all calmly waiting to see what I would do, and you have some idea of the tension incurred. In the event, it went well enough, though Madden wanted it to be louder and faster, words which I have rarely heard coming out of a director's mouth. I happily complied, hoping though that I wouldn't find, when I came to shoot the earlier scenes, that I had stuck myself with a characterisation that would stop me from sounding notes that I wanted to sound. I had discovered something of the real Edmund Tilney, a very distinguished and learned Master of the Revels (soon after the events depicted in the film, he became Sir Edmund Tilney) whose surviving spidery notes on the play *Sir Thomas More*—in which Shakespeare may have had a hand—betray a lively if somewhat caustic wit. For every good dramatic reason, Tom portrayed him as a blundering censor, whereas his function in real life, apart from ensuring that foreign policy was not imperilled by careless insults, was to protect the actors when they went on tour. Local councils, many of whom in that time of rising Puritanism were intent on suppressing the acting profession altogether, were notoriously capricious; if the players had the Queen's imprimatur, they were safe from interference.

Tilney's vanity was monumental, as one can see very clearly from his lengthy and boastful account of his own life on a tablet on the wall of St Leonard's Church in Streatham, now in South London, but then a rural retreat. He was born there; as it happens, so was I, and for a heady couple of days, we were acclaimed by the local press as Streatham's two favourite sons. As before on *Amadeus*, I secretly felt that the film should concern itself not with dreary geniuses like Shakespeare and Queen Elizabeth I, but with the shamefully neglected Sir Edmund, though I fear that the millions and millions of people who saw the film Stoppard actually wrote might not have felt the same way. And, as with *Four Weddings and a Funeral*, I was proud to be associated with the film which, by showing that Shakespeare was a man and not a monument, will have opened so many more people to the idea that the plays grew out of the writer's life and experience of the world, an academically unfashionable notion, but one which both playwrights and actors take for granted. Watching the film, I felt absurdly proud of the extraordinary Joseph Fiennes because I had directed him a couple of years earlier for the RSC in *Les Enfants du Paradis* before he had ever made a film, and was extremely struck by Gwyneth Paltrow, not simply because of her impeccable accent but because of her contained and disciplined use of herself; maybe it was the strain of that which caused it all to come pouring out during her Oscar acceptance speech. She had developed astonishingly from the wild girl whom I had met on the set of *Mr. & Mrs. Bridge*. When I first acted with her a few years earlier, in *Jefferson in Paris*, she was still a crazy tomboyish type, puffing away at her perpetual cigarette and falling about at her own jokes, but now she was a world-ranking beauty, and I felt almost embarrassed to be in such close proximity to her. How had the change come about? It seems to me that stardom brings its own aura, derived from a profound understanding of the camera's ability to detect latent beauty and charisma. Everybody is beautiful at some point in their lives: film stars learn to produce that beauty at will; finally it sticks. With Gwyneth, it had adhered with supreme tenacity.

●●●●●●●●●●●●●●●●●●●●●

A Digression on Disappointment

The film on which we had worked together, *Jefferson in Paris*, was the first fruit of Merchant Ivory's deal with Disney, consequent on their extraordinary run of successes with adaptations of the novels of E. M. Forster, in all of which I had appeared, and *The Remains of the Day* by Kazuo Ishiguro, in which I hadn't. *Jefferson in Paris* was a project that Jim and Ruth had nurtured for some years, a product of their fascination with all things French, with Thomas Jefferson and the rumours concerning his relationship with a young slave girl, and with Jefferson's almost certainly unconsummated love affair with Maria Cosway. The multiplicity of inspirations no doubt resulted in a screenplay which, though characteristically brilliant, was perhaps a little overstuffed with themes and characters. The role I played, that of Maria's husband Richard, was yet another of those parts which research revealed to be unendingly interesting, only a tiny bit of which could possibly be put on screen. Cosway was the outstanding miniaturist of his time (the late eighteenth century) and performed prodigies of physiognomic distillation in the portraits of his great contemporaries which are his claim to historical fame. But he was also one of the great *virtuosi*: though he never travelled outside of England, he assiduously collected artworks from all over the world, devoting each room of his apartment in Albany to a different culture. A tiny, witty and somewhat malevolent man, he was also rather obviously gay, but then surprised the world by marrying the lovely Maria Cosway, whom he placed at the centre of the spectacle that was his London life, inviting his familiars to soirées at which she would play the harp, in clothes specially designed for him—a classic homosexual pattern. How interesting, then, that when Maria gave birth to a child, it was Richard who showed much the greater concern with her welfare, to the degree that when Maria shortly afterwards decided to go to Italy to indulge her religious impulses, Richard took over the care of the child, who presently fell ill and died. Maria remained in Italy, only slowly making her way back to England, while Richard, devastated by grief, took up with a female aristocratic companion with whom he toured England, in a flagrantly sexual liaison. Well, as Lindsay Anderson would have said . . .

Ruth had understandably become fascinated by this relationship, which was essentially peripheral to Jefferson's story. She wrote a number of rich and complex scenes showing on the one hand Cosway's camp and external brittleness, on the other his obsessive tenderness for his wife (played by Greta Scacchi). Emboldened by the texture and the penetration of Ruth's writing, I pushed the public scenes as far as I could go. It was like playing Mozart in Shaffer's play, but with an element of calculation quite alien to Mozart's nature—a deliberate desire to shock. There were remarkable scenes at a party where the slightly sinister aspect of Cosway was manifested—one scene in particular, with a ten-year-old girl, was magnificently warped. Playing all these scenes, I bore in mind the great chance Ruth had offered me, of revealing in the domestic scenes an altogether different aspect to the man, the kindness, awareness and profound sympathy with his wife which amounted to identification. All in all, it was the most complex thing I had yet been asked to play on film.

As I left Paris, having shot all the public scenes, I took my leave of Jim and told him how much I was looking forward to the three private scenes with Greta. 'You will shoot them, won't you?' I asked, conscious that the film had proved much larger than anyone had imagined, and that the sizeable budget was under some stress. He looked at me with horror. 'Of course,' he said. 'They're the heart of the relationship between them.' Reassured, I came back to London. Ten weeks or more elapsed, and I received a call from my agent asking me to make myself available on certain dates to dub my part in the film. Feeling a little sick, I had her check when we were doing the shooting for the missing scenes. 'Never,' came the reply, 'they've been scrapped.' They had had to close down the film, having shot too much material, and now they were editing the results. I immediately wrote to Jim, begging him to find a way of shooting the scenes in question. He wrote back to say that there was no possibility of doing so, but that what they had was wonderful, original, exciting. I knew otherwise. I had played Cosway as I did because I wanted to surprise the audience. Yes, this is how he behaves in public, I wanted to say, but privately he is someone else. I told Jim that it was like cutting the closet scene from *Hamlet*. To have shot the scenes and then to have had them cut would have been upsetting, but this was intolerable. Jim was regretful, but felt that I was overstating. I wasn't. In the finished film, I give an extravagant peacock performance which is simply irritating. I knew exactly what I was doing; Cosway irritated everyone who met him. But if I had known that we would not be shooting the tender domestic scenes, I would have tried to find a way of suggesting that, even at his most showily provocative, there was a vein of humanity running through him.

When I saw the finished film, I had another shock: the whole party sequence had been cut, on account, they said, of the actress who had a prominent part in it. This meant that the scene with the little girl, in which I had been able to show the dangerous ugliness of the man, had also disappeared. So all that remained of the performance were the flashy, slightly hysterical scenes in public, for which I was roundly and rightly denounced by the reviewers. Taken in isolation, it seemed to embody every vice for which I have been attacked as an actor—loud, over-the-top, heavy-handed. I bitterly regret the cutting of the somewhat sinister scenes at the party; but never even to have shot, never to have played the exquisite exchanges between Richard and Maria Cosway, remains a deep sadness. The man deserved better. The film itself was not greatly liked by the critics, and my performance was only one of many things with which they found fault. Again, it is hard to say what lesson to draw from this experience. In the end, the actor is only ever offering up shards from which the film-maker will fashion the final work. Makavejev always urged his actors to be around as much as possible to generate material which might or might not be used in the film. In this way a small role, he argues, could become a major part of the film. This is a frustratingly passive position for an actor who, in the theatre, is accustomed, if necessary, to fight his corner with the director, to prove how brilliant and how contributory his scene can be. In film, the actor's work is history, something which happened in the past, during the shoot. The needs of the film render all other needs secondary.

As a result of my angry outburst, relations between Jim and Ismail and me cooled a little, but only for a while. In the end, we know each other too well and have been through too much together to let a simple thing like my disappointment come between us. If, as Ismail is fond of saying, we are family, then sometimes I am the black sheep, sometimes the favourite son; underneath it all is a bond which is indissoluble. This is uncommon at any level of life, but in film almost unheard-of, and I cherish it, as I cherish them, for the 47 films they have made in 40 years, for their absolute commitment to their own passion for the project in hand, and for their loyalty to their own taste. They make any particular film for one reason only: because they want to make it. Fashion and approval come and go, but they simply do want they want to do. On the set they brawl like cats in an alley, but in the end their shared vision pulls them back to each other: whether Jim or Ismail is directing, there is no such thing as an Ivory movie, or a Merchant movie. They are all Merchant Ivory films. That degree of commitment, to each other and to film, is something of a miracle within the so-called industry, and invigorates anyone who comes into their ambit, though the fur never ceases to fly. Nor should it.

• • • • • • • • • • • • • • • • • • •

More Disappointment

Projects constantly come at one out of the blue, and generally go right back there. If one has any slight success in film, one is inundated with scripts, some of which are brilliant but unfinanced, most of which are simply unspeakable, in the most literal sense. I have described three films that struck me on first reading as superb: *A Room with a View, Four Weddings and a Funeral* and *Shakespeare in Love.* All more than fulfilled my expectations for them. But there were others that slipped away for reasons hard to divine. One whose wackiness was irresistibly enchanting on the page was *Thunderpants.* The director/writer Pete Hewitt, having been toyed with as a potential director of *Thunderpants*, whiled away his waiting time with an alternative film whose hero, Patrick Smash, is afflicted with uncontrollable flatulence. Despite the collapse of his family due to this problem—his father becomes an alcoholic—he is prevented from total despair thanks to his friendship with a fellow-pupil who, as well as being preternaturally gifted intellectually, has no sense of smell. It is this friend who persuades him that he must regard his problem as a talent. Accordingly, when he bumps into Sir John Osgood, the second-greatest tenor in the world, he is initially delighted to discover that he can provide the singer with a note from his bottom that will ensure Osgood's pre-eminence in the musical world. For a while all goes well until Placido P. Placeedo, hitherto the greatest tenor in the world, smells a rat, so to speak, and seeks to unmask Osgood. In doing so, he falls to his death, and Patrick is imprisoned. He is rescued by his friend, who has become an advisor to the American government's space programme. Patrick's productive bottom is harnessed to a rocket and thus he finally earns his self-respect.

The script was wildly funny, and I immediately agreed to play Sir John Osgood as long as I could play him as perfectly circular. Evidently based on Luciano Pavarotti, the character was an exquisitely absurd version of the many tenors I have had occasion to direct in the past. The role was all the more delicious for the obvious fact that the writer/director had no idea whatever what opera was actually like. He had written a three-minute opera for the film which confirmed every mistaken idea that people have conceived about the medium—the hero, a market salesman, has lost his girlfriend ('*La ninfa è morta*') and has decided to go on a crusade to efface her memory, intending on arrival to sing the highest note possible (the one provided by Patrick Smash's nimble sphincter). The opera (*Bartorelli's Unperformable Seventh*, it was called. Duh?) was unalloyed joy to perform, the more so since it was taken so seriously by all involved. I went blissfully over the top both in this sequence but also throughout the film, certain that all the rest of it would be at the same pitch. My amazement on seeing the film was absolute. Pete had treated the whole thing with huge and detailed

330

solemnity: even the opening, where Patrick farts his way out of the womb, was on the brink of tragic, the mother's pain real, the father's despair, as his longed-for infant proves to be an irrepressible petomane, startlingly vivid. I utterly respect Pete's decision to have taken this line. The film becomes a very striking parable about looking for one's talent wherever it might be—a sort of pre-sexual *Boogie Nights*. But funny it isn't. The performance I attended, packed with children already screaming with laughter before the first frame, became very subdued very quickly. They were not bored, but nor were they amused. My own performance leaped off the screen, a unilateral effort at stylisation which could only add grist to the mill of those who believe that the only place for my acting is the stratosphere, or anywhere, really, but this planet, now.

Another screenplay from around the same period was *Bedrooms and Hallways*, a subtle, witty and provocative account of a men's group joined by a gay man who falls for one of the men—hitherto, like everyone else in the group, straight—who then falls for him. The gay man, meanwhile, bumps into his straight lover's girlfriend, whom he knew many years earlier, and has an affair with her. I played the leader of the men's group, presiding calmly and idealistically over the sexual mayhem; Harriet Walter played my wife, leader of a complementary women's group. At first, it seemed that the characters should be American, but Rose, perhaps because she was unhappy with our American accents, pushed it to be English. My performance in rehearsal (yes, we rehearsed) rang horribly false, until I had the notion of playing the character as a recovering alcoholic, measured, clear and absolutely without humour. It fell into place. The screenplay itself was a remarkable feat of writing, balancing satire against a real sense of the complexity of human impulses, and including a fearless celebration of the new-found delights of sodomy by the straight man, ruggedly played by James Purefoy. The feisty American lesbian/feminist director Rose Troche was magnificently unfazed by the British cast, who, as British actors will do, prepare for a take by telling anecdotes. At first, this disturbed her. Why weren't we getting into character, searching for deeper emotional truths?

Soon she found that our anecodtalising was simply a method of keeping ourselves alive mentally, and that our story-telling off-camera was a warm-up for our story-telling on. For our part, we were chastened by her resistance to our occasional attempts to play simply for laughs. Again and again she reminded us of the dignity of the characters, and guided us away from cheap judgements on them. The film was elegantly shot and wittily designed; the end result is highly satisfying. We were all delighted by the finished result; the writer was so taken with the performances that Harriet and I had given that he wrote a proposal for a television series based our characters. When the film was released however, it was dismissed in a phrase or two. So farewell the series; farewell the delight we all believed we would spread around. The reason was simple: for one reason and another its release had been delayed by two years. Between the shooting and the release, the television series *Queer as Folk* had been transmitted to sensational effect. All the taboos gently mocked in *Bedrooms and Hallways* had been shattered forever by the series. The film, which had seemed when we were filming it bold and original, now seemed mild and out of date. It was the same film, excellent as ever, but it had missed its moment.

Recently it was transmitted on British television, and received universally positive reviews, in some cases from the same critics who had dismissed it on its first release. The possibility remains that it is more suited to television than to the big screen; more likely is that even *Queer as Folk* now seems a little passé, and *Bedrooms and Hallways* can be seen for what it is. Timing is all. Fortunately, movies, unlike plays, are always available for reconsideration. I suspect that *B & H* will become a small cult classic with the passage of time; indeed, in America it has already arrived at that position.

● ● ● ● ● ● ● ● ● ● ● ● ● ● ● ● ● ● ●

A Masterpiece

An example of immediate and warranted but no means inevitable acclaim was *No Man's Land*, winner of the 2002 Oscar for Best Foreign Film. Danis Tanovič's mordant parable of war at the end of the twentieth century was a bare, almost laconic screenplay to read. The character I was asked to play, the UN Commander Colonel Soft, was, as his name suggests, something of an emblematic figure, a career soldier who finds himself embroiled in a tedious and incomprehensible war in which his only objective is to escape with his career enhanced. What renders him and all the participants in Tanović's story more to be pitied than to be judged is the tragic absurdity of the central situation: a soldier has fallen on a landmine. If he moves, he will die; nothing anyone—not the bomb disposal unit, nor his friends, nor even his enemies—may do can reprieve him. Finally, he is left to his fate, alone, condemned to die either by moving or by starving. It is a grim metaphor for the lunacy of war. What took it to extraordinary heights was the authenticity of its realisation. Danis, several of the actors and many of the crew had been involved in fighting in the Bosnian war. Here, in the elegant Austro-Hungarian world of Ljubljana in Slovenia, they recreated with urgent, spare passion the situation which was so familiar to them and the source of so much despair. Those of us playing the polyglot forces of the United Nations descended from around Europe—Katrin Cartledge and I from England, others from Belgium, from France, from Germany—to make our contribution, just as the characters we were playing had done. I in particular flew in for a couple of days, exactly as Colonel Soft had done, did as good a job as I could and left with a curious sense of having fulfilled a merely professional commitment while the Bosnians and the Serbs were acting out their lives. This is exactly the effect of the finished film, and I can't be sure whether mine is therefore a good or a bad performance. Certainly I played what was written; Danis had created Colonel Soft from observation and from anger, whereas he had imagined the combatants themselves from his own experience, illuminated by fierce compassion. Even on the set, I approached the Yugoslavian actors with cautious respect; (they are all superb actors, in any case, and I had seen some of them in the theatre in Ljubljana). After seeing their work in the finished film at Cannes, that feeling had turned to something like awe. The showing at the festival provoked a ten-minute standing ovation at which these sinewy tough guys wept, tears so very different from those of the recipients of Academy Awards. They wept not for themselves but for their country and their own blighted youths.

Again, it was a proud thing for me to have been involved, however peripherally, in something which I believe will haunt the imagination of our culture for as long as people watch films. It was the last film Katrin Cartledge made, which ensures that this fine actress will always be remembered, too.

What It's Like

●●●●●●●●●●●●●●●●●●

Getting the Part

It all starts, of course, with the script—or perhaps some of
the script. Especially in the case of Hollywood movies, it is
not uncommon for the script to be kept under lock and key,
a closely guarded secret, so that all that the actor gets is the
scene or scenes in which he might appear. This is almost
useless as a clue to how good a part it might be, or even
how to play it. If you know nothing of the plot or of the
other characters, how can you possibly know what is required or what might be achieved? I am still, after the 20
years of quite the high-level film work described above, being summoned to meetings on basis of scraps of paper.
Sometimes not even that: on the heart-stopping occasion on
which I went to the Dorchester Hotel to meet Woody Allen,
I was sent nothing at all, merely handed a scene of some
three pages on arrival and left to contemplate it in an up-
holstered bedroom for about 40 minutes. The scene was of
course completely incomprehensible to me, though—of
course—there were a number of witty lines in it. On being
released from the bedroom to meet the besneakered and
track-suited Mr Allen, I asked a number of questions about
the scene and the character, but the anguish they caused the
writer-director-star was so intense that I regretted it. His pale
features registered pain and panic in equal measure. We
moved quickly on. With the lovely Soon-Yi located somewhere at the back of the room, I then read the scene, twice,

with the casting director; Woody stood behind me. When I had finished, he said, "You're obviously a very good actor," placed his hand spectrally on mine, and it was all over.

At least I had met the director. This is not always the case. Sometimes one gets to meet the casting director, but it is not uncommon to meet no one at all other than 'someone from the office' who commits one's rendition of the scene to video. Once, many years ago, when I was very young and eager, I was thus summonsed to video-audition for Warren Beatty, who was about to shoot the movie *Reds*, set mostly in Moscow at the time of the Russian Revolution. He had announced that he would only cast genuine Russian-speakers as Russians (the majority of the characters, inevitably). I nobbled a Russophone friend, and learned a poem by Pushkin phonetically. While learning it, I was rather stirred by the sounds I was making, and when the video started to roll, I launched into an impassioned rendition of the poem. Eventually, passion obliterated memory. There being no one to prompt me, I started to improvise Russian gibberish in the manner of an Eisenstein soundtrack. '*Dizhnabri crzhny psyot cruk fleezhabro schnarl!*' I finished triumphantly. 'That was *wonderful!*' cried the casting director, eyes shining. 'Warren will *love* it. Of course, you know he's a fluent Russian speaker himself.' I did not appear in *Reds* (another script which I was never actually allowed to read).

The Hollywood machine subscribes to a very strict and rigidly hierarchical conception of status which would have been recognised by the Duc de Saint-Simon, chronicler of the court of Versailles at the time of Louis XIV. Unlike that of the Sun King, the Hollywood hierarchy is explicitly based on box-office power. The question posed by William Hinton's Maoist cadres in *Fanshen* is the relevant one here: who needs whom? Ninety-eight percent of actors who try to get a part in a film are painfully aware that they need and want the role more than the role needs them. Except for a tiny handful (of whom I am most certainly not one) who are courted by directors, and who have some say in the final result, all actors are chasing the part: in the interview situation, it is the director who makes all the running. So the experience of meeting the director is a rather strained one:

what might he or she be looking for? Whilst plays for the most part live in their language, as I point out in my *Manifesto* diary, the dialogue in a screenplay is only one of many elements, perhaps the least significant, in the overall gesture of the film, so clues as to what might be required are scant. These encounters with directors mostly occur in hotel rooms, bringing to them the ambience of the boudoir, perfumed and prettified, along with a vague feeling that the casting couch might not be far behind. The actor enters in a complete ontological vacuum: who to be? Oneself? Almost impossible. Some semblance of the character? But how do you know what the director feels about the character? Or the screenplay? What's his approach? Sometimes one asks the director these questions, but it always seems impertinent. The boot is on the other foot. He's the one asking the questions. He will probably ask you what you think about the character, but, in the absence of sufficient information, it is very difficult to answer. Otherwise you may be asked simply to talk—about yourself, about your work. It doesn't do to be too smart. I have more than once found myself in affable discourse with a producer and a director, talking about life and art, the books I've written, plays I've directed and so on, everything going swimmingly, and then realised that I have talked myself out of a job: who would want to direct this know-all? The scene in *Tootsie* in which Hoffman screams 'I can be tall! I can be fat!' is the definitive statement of the actor's desperation in the casting situation.

Now, after 20 years at it, there are scripts which are sent to me simply as an offer, especially British films. What is it that makes one say yes or no to an offer? The obvious considerations are the interest of the material, the quality of the writing, and the possibilities of the character. In the case of an actor like myself, who has not played an absolute lead in a film, beyond those considerations the critical question is how central the role is. I once coined a somewhat fanciful distinction between roles that are spinal and those that are peripheral: those connected to the main story, or the main characters, and those which exist at a distance from it. Thus the Reverend Beebe in *A Room with a View*, though not a major character in terms of screen time, intersects with the destinies of the central characters at crucial moments. Simon Asquith in *Postcards from the Edge* does not. There were however, other compelling reasons to play that part, acting with Meryl Streep and being directed by Mike Nichols being among them. In fact Nichols is one of the directors for whom, as I have said, I would play any part in any movie, because for him there are genuinely no small parts, and he refrains from working with small actors. There is little point in playing a very small part if you have achieved a certain note, because you simply draw inappropriate attention to the role. From time to time I have done this for friends; generally I prefer not to take a credit for it, as in the scene in *Howard's End* where I play a lecturer describing Beethoven's Fifth Symphony, a transposition of a purely literary passage from the book. I asked Jim if I could adapt it, too, which I did. There is, sadly, a perception of actors in terms of the sort of level of role that they are suitable for: starring, leading, supporting, cameo, minor. It is very difficult to break out of these bands once one has been placed in them. At an early stage in one's career, one should accept almost anything that is offered. It is vital to have the experience of standing in front of the camera, learning the anthropology of the film set, being at ease in that environment. Ease, relaxation, focus—these are the essential elements of film-acting. And, at that early stage, the smaller the role the better, because it frees you to watch, to absorb, to integrate with the rather strange process unfolding all around you.

Even when the job is an offer, a meeting with the director is generally proposed, largely as a courtesy, though in fact it is essential and indispensable. It can very easily prove to be the case that the director sees the part he's just offered you entirely differently from the way you see it yourself. It is important to discover this early. It is not grounds for turning the part down, but it will awaken your survival instincts. Also, of course, he may persuade you of his view, or you him of yours. The problem is that, except in the rare cases cited above, there will be little or no rehearsal, so there is small opportunity to test out a different view.

Once committed, the best policy is to learn the part so thoroughly that you can be infinitely flexible on the floor.

Live it, breathe it, carry it around with you. But don't work on it too hard; because you may find that your view of the character and the scene needs drastic modification, and if you have become too ingrained in one conception, that may make it hard for you to adapt. Adaptation is all in the situation of filming. If you are aware of all the possibilities of the character and scene, you will be able to contribute from a position of strength, not one of weakness. You are about to be exposed to a large number of elements about which you can know nothing till filming starts. Be prepared for them.

• • • • • • • • • • • • • • • • • • •

Costume

Increasingly, films can be abandoned before they ever start shooting; some are abandoned halfway through. But, in my experience, it is always a good sign when one gets a call from the costume department. The film is really happening, and you are really in it. It is rare for the director to be at a costume fitting; the first he knows about it is on your first day of shooting. So now one has to deal with an additional input into one's already unformed ideas about the character. Here, for the first time, one discovers whether there's a *concept* at work—all the costumes are a variant of green, for example, or that the whole look has been based on the paintings of Hieronymus Bosch. The costume designer if he or she is any good will have thought long and hard about the period, the milieu and of course the character, but, in the latter case, will have been doing so in a vacuum created by the fact that they have had access neither to your body nor to the contents of your mind. Once in possession of this crucial elements, they will adapt and change, while you, the actor, frantically hope that the decisions being made will serve every scene and that you won't want to change your mind when you find how the scene is being shot and being staged. Once filming starts, the wardrobe department will become your closest colleagues. They will see you, after all, more or less naked on a daily basis; no actor is a hero to his or her dresser. Once you get to know each other, they will keep conspiratorially adding this or subtracting that to the costume and making the most of what you've got. They are often experts on how clothes would be worn in the 1820s or the 1930s. More often than not, your garments will either be made by or borrowed from a costume house, of which the greatest is Cosprop in London, where the staff are walking encyclopaedias of sartorial history, deeply imbued with knowledge about underwear through the ages, or the set of cravats before or after the seventeenth century. A fitting at Cosprop is a tutorial and an acting lesson rolled into one; these people—John Bright, the founder of the business, and a multiple Oscar-winner, supreme among them—can tell you more about what it was like to be alive in the eighteenth century, minute by minute, than Simon Schama.

• • • • • • • • • • • • • • • • • •

Make-up

Here you encounter the same problems and the same possibilities as with costume. As described in the *Manifesto* diary, however, for some reason make-up—the reconstruction and reclamation of your face—is an even more intimate area of activity than merely costuming the body. Here, as you stare moodily into the mirror, confronting the absolute inescapable physiognomic truth, all your defences are down. Here tea and sympathy are available in limitless quantities, and here, as in the theatre, a great deal of the work on character transformation is done, as you contemplate the person slowly coming to life in front of you.

Most film make-up artists are brilliantly skilful; in England many of them were trained by the BBC when it had a permanent staff, yet another side-effect of the clandestine dismantlement of the greatest broadcasting organisation in the world. Film make-up, naturally, is a much subtler thing than stage make-up, and these technicians excel at making their own work invisible. Here too, the issues of style and character arise just as they do in costume; period has its rules here, too. In the theatre, on the whole, actors are responsible for their own make-up; in film, we are in the hands of experts. In fact, in the theatre, since the invention of white-light and the (regrettable, some would say) abolition of footlights, actors very rarely use make-up, and are consequently ignorant of its principles, which tends to add to the passivity of the film actor. Stars frequently counter this tendency by importing their own make-up artists, not because they are better, but because they are theirs. The craft of prosthetic make-up has recently become vastly more sophisticated; it is now possible to change an actor's face so completely that it becomes impossible to recognise it, which seems a curious enterprise, especially with a star who is hired for his or her particular individual charisma, and requires levels of calm and patience during the four-and five-hour application sessions comparable to those of Noh actors, for whom the process is a spiritual exercise in a way that it is not in Pinewood. Before long, however, all this skill and industry will no doubt be made redundant by digital technology, able to age you or rejuvenate you, to change the colour of your eyes or the shape of your skull. The actor will simply bequeath his raw material to the film, which will then do with it what it wills.

● ● ● ● ● ● ● ● ● ● ● ● ● ● ● ● ● ●

Limbo

The number of people involved in the smallest movie is quite overwhelming. You may have little contact with most of them, though it is a very sensible idea to talk to as many as possible. The sense of alienation on a set is very strong and the more points of connection you can make, the better. Your first contact will be with the second assistant director, who is essentially a people wrangler: it is he who works out the calls on the schedule, arranges the transport, deals with the caterers. It was no doubt he who gave you your call the day before; he will have co-ordinated the make-up and wardrobe sessions. He is rarely seen on the set itself, but he is your life-line to the production. If there's something wrong with your accommodation, for example, he can fix it. A great deal of your time will be spent in the area of the trailers, which is his kingdom. Generally speaking, everyone goes out of their way to make you comfortable. Sometimes it will feel as if you were in hospital rather than on a film set. People—the third assistant director or the runners—will provide you with breakfast, lunch and supper; they will unendingly bring you cups of tea and coffee and enquire after your well-being with great solicitude. For male actors, the standard form of address is 'sir' ('Simon, sir, wardrobe would like a word with you'); actresses, for reasons I am at a loss to understand, seem not to be treated in the same formal way, although generally great politeness is the norm, much more so than in the theatre. There are, of course, lapses. Lord Snowdon reports that when he was photographing Dame Edith Evans on a film set, the third assistant said: 'Will you come to the set now, please, Edith?' '*Dame* Edith, thank you very much,' the great actress magisterially corrected the hapless young man, observing to Lord Snowdon, 'It'll be Edie next.'

Both here and on the set, there will be tables groaning with tidbits, sweetmeats and snacks and the like, which may make you feel not only that you are in hospital, but that you are in a children's hospital. As you sit in your trailer, waiting, like Rosencrantz and Guildenstern, to be summoned, you are in limbo. You will no doubt seek out your fellow-limbo-dwellers, and you will make merry conversation with them, up to a point, but it is wise to conserve something of yourself, either by reading or writing or meditating or perhaps listening to the radio. Your trailer is your home, your womb, your cell. They vary in size and splendour according to the budget and your status, but most have somewhere where you can sit and a table at which to write plus a power point, and that is enough for me. It is also the absolute minimum, and, regardless of the size of the film, there is always a clause in my contract which formally guarantees this facility. I call it the sanity clause. If there are more facilities, then that is a charming bonus. Some of these trailers have lavatories, showers, ovens, washing machines, CD players, televisions, irons. They are in fact hotel suites on wheels, and in another oddly infantine association, they remind me of holidays of childhood (though considerably more liberally appointed than the caravans of the 1950s).

This strange vacation without sea or sun can be suspended

at a moment's notice, as you are suddenly hustled into the make-up trailer to have the make-up refreshed which was probably applied with high urgency when you arrived, at seven in the morning. (The question of at precisely what unearthly hour you are called to the set is a matter for negotiation with various parties—with your make-up artist, who will generally conspire with you to reduce the time you have to spend in the chair, with your dresser, who will likewise gladly co-operate in discovering short-cuts, with the driver and most importantly with the second assistant director, who, with the best will in the world, will try to call you as early as possible so that, as he will probably tell you, his ass is covered against every possible eventuality). Over the years I have learned not to fight early calls: it is rather lovely time, this pre-dawn period, fresh and clear, and I am more than happy to sit in my trailer, typing or reading, undisturbed by the film, which goes its own sweet way without me. It makes for a long day, but often a productive one. It is a condition of film-making that one has to adopt children's hours, early to bed, early to rise, and I daresay one is all the better for it, though social life more or less disappears.

Once the call for you to come to the set goes out, there is scarcely time to save the document you are working on or to finish the paragraph you are reading. It's all go go go! A mood of febrile urgency prevails and one is swept onto the set where, inexplicably, nothing at all appears to be happening. It may not happen for a long time. Quietly, you may edge back towards the door and back to the trailer, to resume your monastic existence there undisturbed for several happy hours.

• • • • • • • • • • • • • • • • • •

On the Set

If you stay on the set, however, it is wise to come with a book or a newspaper. This is not because you're uninterested in what's going on, but because you may well get in the way, so it's sensible to find a niche and settle down with your reading matter. First, however, you must make yourself known to the first assistant director, the focal figure of the whole activity, even more so, from a purely practical point of view, than the director. He is responsible for actually getting the film shot—persuading the director to be as decisive as possible, ensuring that every department is working at full stretch, keeping the workforce happy, and generating the cheerful energy needed if anything is to happen at all. He or she will know, if anybody does, how much time any particular scene will take, and what the physical demands of each sequence will be. You can work out almost anything to do with the film by studying the first AD's face; you don't even need to talk to him. But it's very sensible to form a relationship with him. You can also very usefully spend your time getting to know your fellow-workers—that army of technicians, the gaffers and the grips, whose skills are deployed with such lightning speed and tight discipline when required, but who have a riotously playful time among themselves at all other times, playing practical jokes, trying to trip each other up, wickedly teasing each other. Other departments conduct themselves with more decorum: props, sound, camera. Obviously, it is vital to say hello to the cameraman. Sometimes hundreds of people a day pass before his lens, most of whom he will not know. Most operators have little lists of the names of the cast above their eye-pieces, to which they constantly and courteously refer, but it's both polite and sensible to identify yourself. For the most part, the director of photography—who may or may not actually operate the camera—is far too busy to have time for any but the briefest of greetings. By definition, they are always involved either in setting up a shot or actually shooting one; like the rest of the crew, and unlike most of the actors, there is no scene in which they are not involved. The sound department often has more leisure than the camera crew, because their work is contingent on the scene itself being rehearsed or performed, and this may not happen immediately—not until the technical aspects of the shot have been determined. As I remark in the *Manifesto* diary, the sound crew is often of a somewhat scholarly disposition; they are generally reading books while waiting for the scene to happen. They are also keeping an ear out for interesting ambient sounds which they sometimes catch, like butterflies, for future use. They will often be able to vouchsafe you very useful information about the way the shoot is going, how quickly or slowly, how many takes, what the mood is. You have to learn to observe from the side and to wait your turn. No one is interested in you or your problems until it's time for your scene, when everyone suddenly will be come very—unnervingly—interested in you: the way you look, your every inflection, your face, your feet, what exactly it is that you think you're doing.

Directors broadly fall into two categories: those who know exactly what they want and those who don't. Those in the latter category may simply not know, or they may have chosen not to make decisions without finding out what the actors' instincts are. You may thus be told precisely where to stand, where to go, and what to do when you get there, or you may be invited to play the scene according to your instincts. Both demands are fairly unsettling in the context of a studio swarming with literally dozens, and, on some productions, hundreds of people who are looking at you with a view to committing your work to celluloid. They cast a trenchantly professional eye over you, wondering what they've got to work with and how to make it look good. If you know your fellow-actors, or the director, or indeed the crew, then of course it is infinitely more relaxed, but it remains a highly exposed experience. Generally, the first assistant will clear the set of all except the director, the actors and the script supervisor (formerly known as the continuity girl) and then you can run the scene for a little while in peace, script in hand if necessary, after which all the significant technicians will be brought in—camera, sound, wardrobe, make-up—and you show what you have to offer. As you get older and more confident, you can throw in your twopenn'orth; for the tyro it is extraordinarily hard to do so. One may sense that the director doesn't like one's work, but doesn't say why; or one may be nervous of one's more famous fellow-actors. The hardest thing is to focus on the truth of the scene, simply to be there, available, centred, listening and reacting. These are the things that grow over weeks of rehearsal in the theatre; they must be instantly present on film.

Shooting

There is a period of grace after your work has been observed by the technicians. They have their tasks to do. If the scene has been worked out from scratch, then there is the whole breakdown of the scene into individual shots to be considered; camera moves have to be facilitated by the laying of tracks; the light has to be arranged. Even if it has all been pre-planned, there are adjustments to be made. You, meanwhile, are sent back to make-up and wardrobe for further repair of face and garments. You then appear on the set and it is all suddenly, horribly real. You will do a sort of walk-through of the scene for cameras and sound. This is valuable, relaxed time: your work is not under scrutiny, simply your features and your body. Are you in the right place at the right time? Are adjustments required? You will be made aware of very specific points where you must stand, lights that you must find, bodily angles you must adopt. Very little of this will feel natural, but it is your job somehow to make it so within minutes, when you actually shoot the scene. You must be exceptionally free, physically, and you must develop the peripheral vision of a dog, taking note of marks on the ground or sandbags that define your path of movement without ever actually looking at them. You must equally forget that there are large pieces of metal, like small tanks, facing you, their Cyclops eyes recording your every twitch and frown, remorselessly seeking out tension; that there are microphones on long booms looming above your head to capture your voice, your very breath; that beyond these are make-up artists scrutinising you for sweat, for stray hairs, for smudges, while their colleagues in wardrobe are desperately concerned about a wrinkle on your collar or the angle of your hat; that the director is poised, unbreathing, over the small screen on which the picture is being transmitted, gauging the impact of the whole frame and you as part of it; and that any one of these people may ask for the shot to be retaken if any deficiencies are too prominent.

The only way to survive the scrutiny is by living in the moment with ease as the actor, regardless of what the character is feeling. There must be a profound relaxation at the core. Excessive preparatory immersion in the character or the character's situation can have a dangerously short-circuiting effect. I have come to believe, indeed, that the best preparation for a scene is to become utterly absorbed in something quite, quite different—the thought of a person whom you love or desire or indeed hate, an intellectual problem not susceptible to easy solution, a childhood memory which has no bearing on the scene in hand. Keep in touch with that thought up to the very moment when the director cries 'Action!' and then play the scene. It will stop you from knowing at the beginning how it is going to end. And it will keep thought alive. The camera above all else records thought. And thought above all emerges from the eyes. The sensation of film-acting is that of becoming a pair of eyes and a pair of ears.

The shot will almost certainly be taken many times. But it will, generally speaking, constitute only one small piece in the mosaic which is the scene. It is a very useful thing to ask the first assistant to let you glimpse the shot list—the way in which the scene has been broken down into single shots, two-, three-, and four-shots, close-ups and wide shots, travelling shots and static ones. Each of these shots requires a different sort of energy, and each has particular demands. In a close-up, for example, especially an extreme close-up, great economy and discipline of action is necessary because your face is filling the screen—an abrupt movement is like cracking a whip, and the sudden raise of an eyebrow can cause physical distress in the viewer; while in a wide shot you can make a particular and bold physical statement about the whole of your character. It is unwise, however, to compose your performance entirely in shards, in the belief that the sum total of them adds up to the character: as has been demonstrated above (see *Jefferson in Paris*), an awful lot of your precious fragments may never be seen in the finished film.

As you acquire more and more ease with the process, you come to see that there are things that you can do in film that you could never do in the theatre, and that the camera's ability to exclude the rest of you while it draws attention to your hands, or your lips, or your feet, effortlessly gives you a range of expressive possibilities that you would have to work very hard for on a stage, where the audience has the whole picture all the time. There are ways, technically and by sheer force of focus, to direct the theatre audience's attention to individual elements of expression, but they are very conscious. What film can do supremely is to reveal the significance of the apparently casual. Sometimes the most powerful thing you can do in a film is to stir your tea. Inevitably, by the end of filming, you will know more about your character. There is every chance that you will have shot the first scene last and the last first, and you will long to reshoot those first days. It is highly unlikely that you will have a chance to do so, but even if you were able to, I suspect that you would prefer your first faltering steps. Innocence is sometimes the best guide.

• • • • • • • • • • • • • • • • • • • •

End of Shoot

Depending on how long you spend on the shoot, you will become attached to the community of the film. There are always unexpected bonuses, encounters with people in which surprising levels of frankness and intimacy can be achieved, but whom you may never see again, or not till the next film. The more you work in the medium, the more familiar faces you will encounter, which breeds more and more ease. It took me many years before I felt on a film set what I always felt in a theatre, namely, that I belonged there, that I understood its rules and its relationships, and that I was confident that I could do the job of work I had been hired to do with freedom and flexibility. It remains a rhythm of work that is somewhat alien to my temperament. I prefer to stick at a task, working on it incessantly till it is right. In film, there are intense bursts of activity followed by languid hours; the relationship with your fellow-artists, particularly the director and the cameraman, the dual monarchs of the shoot, is intermittent unless you're playing the absolute lead.

But emotion nonetheless grows, and parting is sweet sorrow. In America, but now increasingly in England, it is the practice of the first assistant director to call for a round of applause for the actor who has just shot his or her last shot. This is generally a little embarrassing (to the British, at least), but its absence is worse. Unless you happen to be in the very last shot of the movie (and I never have been), you then steal away while everybody else carries on without you. There are hugs and endearments and maybe even little presents, with the usual promises to keep in touch, but you then go and they stay. It feels at some subconscious level as if they are going forward with the journey but you have jumped ship. When the film is finished, there will be a wrap party, and very riotous and necessary they are. If you can't attend, you will feel very distant from things. It is the only time that the whole team will be gathered together on a purely social basis; you can finally talk to the cinematographer or the set designer or the delightful extra with the brown hair who you never quite managed to corner on the set. There is also a release of the emotion which attends any big collective endeavour but particularly an artistic one, perhaps because there is so much vulnerability involved—everyone is offering up their work, actors, costumiers, set painters, grips, in the expectation that it may be found inadequate or inappropriate. It is also the office party, awash with booze and free-floating lust, with the difference that the office itself has just been wound up, which is curiously exhilarating.

● ● ● ● ● ● ● ● ● ● ● ● ● ● ● ● ● ● ●

Dubbing

Probably the next you will know of the film is when you are called to the so-called 'ADR' sessions—Audio Dub and Record. Here the sound so lovingly recorded on the set, and with such anxiety for the possible intrusion of aeroplanes, traffic, voices, the ticking of a clock, is summarily replaced, and you have to re-imagine yourself into the circumstances of filming. Technically speaking, this is a somewhat demanding skill, to the extent that, in Europe, there is a whole sub-division of the profession that does nothing but dub. Matching lip movements exactly while attempting to fill the line with emotion and intelligence is something of a challenge; often an apparently simple line has to be broken down into its component syllables. Any rhythmic quirks in the original have to be closely followed; as an actor of endemic rhythmic quirkiness, I find again and again that I have shot myself through the foot, clinging onto the lips of this wayward lunatic who can't say a single word simply. On the other hand, like all skills, especially those associated with film-making, once you embrace the challenge it becomes exhilarating, even liberating, and it is possible, hunched over a lectern in Wardour Street, to improve on the original shot made a month or two ago in Luxembourg or Fiesole. Here you meet a new team of technicians who have lined up each shot with the oblique bar that runs across the screen to hit the left side at exactly the moment you start speaking. They are astonishingly able to shift what you have said a few frames at a time to make it fit, but they have to be gifted with preternatural levels of patience; for some actors the process of dubbing is a nightmare, a cruel infliction, a dilution and a betrayal of what was perfect, instinctive, filled with truth. This ignores the fact that film, apparently a natural and faithful record of life as it is lived compared with the artificial and stylised theatre, is in fact a contrivance from beginning to end—like a painting, where a combination of pigments and certain archaic principles of composition combine to give the illusion of three-dimensional reality. Film is, in fact, an art, and we should rejoice in its artifices.

The dubbing suite, incidentally, is the first you will have seen of the movie, except for those very rare shoots where the cast is invited to rushes. Your first glimpse of your work may come as a very nasty shock. For a start, the quality of the print is unlikely to be very good, and there will of course be no music attached to it and no sound effects. It is a very bare statement. You will immediately regret the hair style you allowed yourself to be coerced into and wonder why you have developed a strange tic as you speak. You seem to have the eyes of an opium addict and were you really that fat then? You thought you had lost weight specially for the shoot. You may also be rather surprised at the way the scene has been cut together. What happened to that great close-up? And surely there was another bit of dialogue? If the director is present, he may explain, letting you into his difficulties, the length of the film, x's disappointing performance here, a problem with the film stock itself there. It will all be rather vague. However, there is the difficult work in hand to be got on with; you do your best and leave.

• • • • • • • • • • • • • • • • • • •

Cast-and-Crew Showing

This is the moment of truth. It is highly advisable to attend this showing rather than the premiere, because you may be in for some rude shocks. Favourite scenes will have been ruthlessly hacked out, music imposed where you least expected it, the entire film restructured so that your character's journey is, to you at any rate, incomprehensible.

On the other hand, you may find that you have been unexpectedly favoured, that a scene you know never went as you had hoped has somehow, by the miracle of editing, been tightened and tautened, and a look that you were scarcely aware of giving has become pivotal. More importantly, you will know whether the film is any good or not. You won't, of course, know whether it is going to be successful, or whether it will be well reviewed, but you do know by then whether you're glad you did it or not.

Here too, group emotion is very strong, the first reunion of the team since the wrap party. There may be some awkwardness. It will be some time since you were all together; the circumstances in which relationships were formed have disappeared. And some people may be devastated to discover that their work has gone without trace, or with very little to show for months of endeavour. The discovery that the fruit of your labour has been aborted is a bleak one. You have to face your loved ones and your agents. (This has not happened to me yet in film, though it did happen on my very first television job, an episode of *Carry on Laughing* called 'Orgy and Bess': it concerned Queen Elizabeth I, played by Hattie Jacques. I had alerted my entire circle of acquaintances, in those pre-video days, to watch the transmission, from which I was entirely absent, until, that is—bitter blow!—the credits, which said 'A Sailor: Simon Callow.' It was harsh, but represented only five days' work—in movies, one is sometimes talking about five months.)

Of course, the joy of discovering that one is part of a triumph is exhilarating beyond belief. The cast-and-crew showings of *A Room with a View*, *Mr. & Mrs. Bridge*, *Four Weddings and a Funeral* and *Shakespeare in Love* were of this order; but so was that of *Bedrooms and Hallways*. I have described above what I take to be the reason why that triumph was not replicated when the film was released. It seemed to me that Tom Hollander, in that film, gave a performance of absolute stellar brilliance, just as one had instantly recognised Hugh Grant's work in *Four Weddings* and Joanne Woodward's in *Mr. & Mrs. Bridge*. Naturally the audience at these events is somewhat *parti pris*, but I have rarely known a film which was really not working at all to pass the test of the cast-and-crew showing.

• • • • • • • • • • • • • • • • • •

Premiere

Your attendance at this may be dependent on what you felt about the above. Some films slip into the mainstream without it, but generally a premiere adds to the gaiety of nations. It is an astonishing and rather old-fashioned experience to walk past a crowd of maybe a thousand people screaming (not for me, I hasten to add) while the night sky is lit up by the flash of a thousand bulbs. Even someone who is not a star is fodder for the paparazzi, and they demand that you submit to their lens with angry insistence and casual familiarity ('Simon! Over here! Simon! Simon!! Look this way! Look up! Look down! Simon!!! *Over here*!!'). As with most manifestations of celebrity, the attitude is a disturbing combination of exaltation and aggression; and if you fail to satisfy their definition of celebrity, the sense of rejection is overwhelming. This comes from the public as much as it does from the press. A friend of mine, quite a well-known actor, drove up to one premiere, and the moment the car came to a halt, a fan flung open the door, peered inside, then reported back to the crowd: 'Nobody.' He then crawled ignominiously out, entering the cinema to deafening silence.

The actual showing of the film at a premiere is a somewhat unreal event. A large number of the audience will have seen it before—producers, distributors, actors and so on. Most of the rest will have paid a vast sum of money to be in the same room with the stars and possibly a royal personage. At the British premiere of *Postcards from the Edge*, which boasted a staggering number of major American stars, the Gulf War had just commenced, and so they were all banned from flying. Accordingly, the only actor in the film who was in England—indeed, the only person of any sort who had worked on the film in any capacity—was myself, and I was duly seated next to the royal personage, who happened to be Princess Diana. I had met her on a number of occasions, and so was not surprised at how affable and direct she was, though I was a little taken aback by her first question to me: 'You're not going to fall asleep on me, are you?' She was alluding to the fact that most of the big American stars who come over for a British premiere have already seen the film a dozen times. At anything other than a royal event, they would have sneaked out after the first few minutes to have a refreshing beverage or two, but perhaps fearing incarceration in the Tower of London had they done so in the presence of a royal princess, they had sat through the film, swiftly falling into a deep slumber. As it happens, on this occasion I had not seen the film myself, and we laughed merrily through the film; she especially liked the naughty bits, I recollect. At the end, I was a little embarrassed that my contribution had been so modest, but she sweetly squeezed my hand and told me how wonderful I'd been. She always was a champion of the disadvantaged.

ACTING CREDITS

Year	Film (Role)	Director
1984	**Amadeus** (Schikaneder)	Milos Forman
1985	**The Good Father** (Varda)	Mike Newell
1986	**A Room with a View** (Rev. Beebe)	James Ivory
1987	**Maurice** (Mr Ducie)	James Ivory
1988	**Manifesto** (Police Chief Otto Hunt)	Dušan Makavejev
1990	**Mr. & Mrs. Bridge** (Dr. Alex Sauer)	James Ivory
1990	**Postcards from the Edge** (Simon Asquith)	Mike Nichols
1992	**Soft Top Hard Shoulder** (Eddie Cheese)	Stefan Schwartz
1994	**Four Weddings and a Funeral** (Gareth)	Mike Newell
1994	**Le Passager Clandestin** (Major Owens)	Agustín Villaronga
1995	**Jefferson in Paris** (Cosway)	James Ivory
1995	**Victory** (Ziangiacomo)	Mark Peploe
1995	**England, My England** (Charles II)	Tony Palmer
1995	**Ace Ventura II** (Vincent Cadby)	Steven Oedekerk
1996	**James and the Giant Peach** (Grasshopper)	Henry Selick

Year	Film (Role)	Director
1996	**The Scarlet Tunic** (Captain Fairfax)	Stuart St. Paul
1998	**Bedrooms and Hallways** (Keith)	Rose Troche
1998	**Shakespeare in Love** (Tilney)	John Madden
2000	**Christmas Carol** (Scrooge)	Jimmy T. Murakami
2002	**Thunderpants** (Sir John Osgood)	Peter Hewitt
2002	**No Man's Land** (Col. Soft)	Danis Tanovic
2002	**Merci Docteur Rey** (Bob)	Andrew Litvak
2002	**Sex & Violence** (Mr. Wroth)	David Beaird
2003	**George and the Dragon** (King Edgar)	Tom Reeve
2003	**Bright Young Things** (King of Anatolia)	Stephen Fry